# TEACHING AND LEARNING VOCABULARY

# TEACHING AND LEARNING VOCABULARY

**I. S. P. Nation**

*Victoria University of Wellington*

NEWBURY HOUSE PUBLISHERS, New York

A division of Harper & Row, Publishers, Inc.

Grand Rapids, Philadelphia, St. Louis, San Francisco
London, Singapore, Sydney, Tokyo

Director: Laurie E. Likoff
Production Coordinator: Cynthia Funkhouser
Cover Design: 20/20 Services Inc.
Compositor: BookMasters, Inc.
Printer and Binder: McNaughton & Gunn

NEWBURY HOUSE PUBLISHERS
A division of Harper & Row, Publishers, Inc.

Language Science
Language Teaching
Language Learning

Teaching and Learning Vocabulary

Library of Congress Cataloging in Publication Data

Nation, I. S. P.
    Teaching and learning vocabulary / I. S. P. Nation.
        p.    cm.
    Includes bibliographical references.
    ISBN 0–06–632430–0
    1. English language—Study and teaching—Foreign speakers.
  2. Vocabulary—Study and teaching.   I. Title.
PE1128.A2N34   1990
428'.007—dc20                                        89–78541
                                                      CIP


63–24305                              93 92 91 90 9 8 7 6 5 3 2 1

# Contents

# Preface

The idea behind this book is that a systematic, principled approach to vocabulary development results in better learning. The material in the book draws heavily on the large amount of research, experimentation, and classroom experience of teachers and researchers over the last 100 years, which is reflected in the bibliography of over 900 items.

There are two main ideas running through the book. The first is that information about the statistical nature of vocabulary provides valuable guidelines for the teaching and learning of vocabulary. The most important distinction here is between the small number of high-frequency words, which all deserve a lot of attention, and the very large number of low-frequency words, which require the mastery of coping strategies like guessing from context. The second idea is that an analysis of the tasks facing the learner in acquiring vocabulary provides information about how learning can be made more efficient and effective. In particular, this involves looking at the learning burden of words and what it means to know a word.

These two ideas are related to each other. Differences in the distribution of certain words are reflected in the learning task for those words. Thus, although most chapters can be read separately, it is worth following the information on language and learning in the earlier chapters through into the application of this information for teaching and learning in the chapters on the skills of listening, speaking, reading, and writing.

This book is intended for teachers of English as a second or foreign language, and it answers questions about vocabulary teaching and learning that teachers typically ask. Because the majority of such teachers are themselves not native speakers of English I have tried to avoid technical vocabulary and have tried to express myself as directly and clearly as possible. I find vocabulary teaching and learning a fascinating area. I hope you do too.

# Acknowledgments

Parts of Chapters 2 and 4 come from teaching material prepared by Helen Barnard. Parts of Chapter 4 appeared in *English Language Teaching Journal* 32, 3 (1978). Parts of Chapter 8 appeared in *English Language Teaching Journal* 30, 1 (1975), *English Teaching Forum* 16, 3 (1978), the *RELC Journal* 13, 1 (1982) and *Guidelines* 3 (1980). Part of Chapter 10 appeared in *System* 8, 3 (1980) in an article written with David Clarke. The vocabulary levels test in Appendix 8 appeared in *Guidelines* 5, 1 (1983). The university word list in Appendix 2 appeared in *Language Learning and Communication* in an article written with Xue Guoyi.

I am grateful for permission to use this material.

# Chapter *1*

# Introduction

This chapter looks at the following ideas: Should vocabulary be taught? What are the possible approaches to vocabulary learning? Then the following points are considered: What vocabulary do my learners need to know? How will they learn their vocabulary? How can I test to see what my learners need to know and what they now know? The answers to these questions will help teachers plan the vocabulary component of their courses.

## SHOULD VOCABULARY BE TAUGHT?

It is not difficult to find language teachers who think that vocabulary can be left to take care of itself, and there is some experimental evidence to support that position (Elley & Mangubhai, 1981). What this book tries to show, however, is that there are very strong reasons for a systematic and principled approach to vocabulary by both the teacher and the learners. Let us look at these reasons. First, because of the considerable research on vocabulary we have good information about what to do about vocabulary and about what vocabulary to focus on. This means that our vocabulary work can be directed toward useful words and can give learners practice in useful skills. We can thus feel confident that learners will get a good return for the effort that they put in. Second, one of the aims of this book is to show that there is a wide variety of ways for dealing with vocabulary in foreign or second language learning. Some teachers do not feel happy using some of these ways—for example, getting learners to study words out of context, or interrupting learners' reading to get them to guess at an unknown word in context. Dissatisfaction with one approach to vocabulary should not result in ignoring all the other ways of helping learners enrich their vocabulary. It is important that when a teacher chooses or rejects a way to deal with vocabulary this choice or rejection should be based on a good understanding of the way of dealing with vocabulary, the principles behind it, and its theoretical and experimental justification. For example, many teachers too quickly dismiss the approach of getting learners to study lists of words out of context. For a teacher faced with learners with a small vocabulary who wish to go on to academic study in a few months' time, this approach is very effective. Moreover, there is a very large amount of experimental research showing the effectiveness of such an approach and providing useful guidelines on how to go about it (Nation, 1982). Later in this chapter we will look at four broad approaches to vocabulary and at the reasons which would make a teacher choose one over another.

The third reason for having a systematic and principled approach to vocabulary is that both learners and researchers see vocabulary as being a very important, if not the most important, element in language learning. Learners feel that many of their difficulties in both receptive and productive language use result from an inadequate vocabulary.

Simply increasing learners' vocabulary without giving attention to putting this knowledge to use may not be effective, but getting learners to do language tasks when their vocabulary is inadequate for the task is a frustrating experience. Research on readability (Chall, 1958; Klare, 1974–1975) stresses the importance of vocabulary knowledge in reading, as does research on academic achievement (Saville-Troike, 1984).

Finally, giving attention to vocabulary is unavoidable. Even the most formal or communication-directed approaches to language teaching must deal with needed vocabulary in one way or other. Let us now look at the possible ways.

## APPROACHES TO VOCABULARY LEARNING

It is useful to make a distinction between direct and indirect vocabulary learning. In direct vocabulary learning the learners do exercises and activities that focus their attention on vocabulary. Such exercises include word-building exercises, guessing words from context when this is done as a class exercise, learning words in lists, and vocabulary games. In indirect vocabulary learning the learners' attention is focused on some other feature, usually the message that is conveyed by a speaker or writer. If the amount of unknown vocabulary is low in such messages, considerable vocabulary learning can occur even though the learners' attention is not directed toward vocabulary learning. Krashen (1981a) calls this the input theory of language learning. He believes that certain conditions must apply for such learning to occur. First, the learners must be interested in understanding the message. From the point of view of vocabulary learning, this interest creates a need to understand the unknown words in the message. Second, the message should contain some items that are just outside the learners' present level of achievement. These items, however, should be understandable from the context in which they occur. This includes both language and nonlanguage contexts. The chapter on simplification in this book looks at ways of making unknown items understandable. Third, the learners should not feel worried or threatened by their contact with the foreign language.

One of the basic ideas in this book is that there is a place for both direct and indirect vocabulary learning. Opportunities for indirect vocabulary learning should occupy much more time in a language learning course than direct vocabulary learning activities. This is in fact just another way of saying that contact with language in use should be given more time than decontextualized activities. The range of contextualized activities of course covers the range of the uses of language. As long as suitable conditions for language learning apply, such as those described by Krashen (1981a), then indirect vocabulary learning can take place.

Vocabulary teaching can fit into a language learning course in any of four ways. Most courses make use of all four, but the amount of time spent on each of these ways depends on the teacher's judgment in relation to a large number of factors, such as the time available, the age of the learners, the amount of contact with English outside school hours, and the teacher's theory of how language is best learned. The four ways described below are listed from the most indirect to the most direct.

1. Material is prepared with vocabulary learning as a consideration. The most common examples of this are the preparation of simplified material and the careful vocabulary grading of the first lessons of learning English. To an observer of such an English course it might appear as if no attention is being given to vocabulary, but in fact the selection and grading of vocabulary has been given a lot of attention before the course begins.

2. Words are dealt with as they happen to occur. This means that if an unknown word appears in a reading passage, the teacher gives some attention to it at the moment it causes a problem. A lot of vocabulary teaching is done in this way. Although the selection of vocabulary seems unplanned, the way it is treated need not be. Teachers may follow principles when dealing with such words. For example, they draw attention to the underlying concept of the word rather than just giving a contextual definition. They point out regular features of the spelling and grammar so that the learning of this word will help the learning of other words. They focus attention on the learning burden of the word, and they carefully avoid "unteaching." They consider the frequency and usefulness of a word when deciding how much time to spend on it.

3. Vocabulary is taught in connection with other language activities. For example, the vocabulary of a reading passage is dealt with before the learners read the passage. Sarawit (1980) describes the teaching of vocabulary a few days before a type of debate. Through direct teaching and reading the learners become familiar with the topic vocabulary before

they need to use it in the formal speaking activity. Johnson (1980) suggests similar preteaching as a preparation for listening exercises which give further practice in the vocabulary. Another possibility is to have vocabulary exercises following reading or listening texts. "Find the words in the passage which mean. . . " is the most common example of this. In all the activities described in this part, the teaching of vocabulary is directly related to some other language activity.

4. Time is spent either in class or out of school on the study of vocabulary without an immediate connection with some other language activity. For example, time is spent on learning spelling rules or on activities like dictionary use, guessing words, the use of word parts, or list learning. This time can be spent on activities involving the whole class as in learning mnemonic techniques, using pair or group work as in paraphrase activities or combining arrangement exercises, or individually as in the use of vocabulary puzzles or code exercises. Such vocabulary work can have the aim of establishing previous learning or increasing vocabulary so that future language use can go more smoothly.

## POINTS TO CONSIDER IN VOCABULARY LEARNING

To put any of these four ways into practice a teacher needs to answer three questions.

1. What vocabulary do my learners need to know?
2. How will they learn this vocabulary?
3. How can I test to see what they need to know and what they now know?

Let us preview some of the answers to these questions.

### What Vocabulary Do My Learners Need to Know?

Later in this book we divide vocabulary into three groups—high-frequency words, low-frequency words, and specialized vocabulary. Teachers need to decide which of these three groups contains the words that their learners need. This is an important decision because it will affect the way the words are dealt with for learning, it will affect the amount of learning expected, and it will affect the type of learning, receptive or productive, needed. The goals that teachers or learners set for learning English will affect the way vocabulary is selected. If, for example, the goal is to read, then following a word list like that of the Longman Structural Readers, the Newbury House Readers, or Collins

English Library will give access to a large amount of ready-made graded reading material, thus increasing vocabulary knowledge and reading skill at the same time. If the learners aim to cover listening, speaking, reading, and writing, then a multipurpose list like the *General Service List*, or the *Cambridge English Lexicon* will be more suitable. If the learners want to read university texts, then the university word list is a suitable goal. Estimates of vocabulary size, particularly of native speakers of English, can also help in setting goals, particularly in schools where there are both native speakers and second language learners.

As we look at each of the skill areas of listening, speaking, reading, and writing we will give information about vocabulary size.

## How Will They Learn This Vocabulary?

First, we need to consider what kind of learning is required. In the chapter on what is involved in learning a word a distinction is made between receptive and productive learning. Receptive learning involves being able to recognize a word and recall its meaning when it is met. Productive learning involves what is needed for receptive learning plus the ability to speak or write needed vocabulary at the appropriate time. If learners study English in order to be able to read and understand lectures, a receptive knowledge of vocabulary is sufficient. If learners need to cover the whole range of language skills, then a productive vocabulary of around 3000 base words and a larger receptive vocabulary is needed. It is also important to consider previous learning of the mother tongue, other languages, or earlier lessons in English when selecting and teaching vocabulary, and to avoid "unteaching," particularly as a result of organizing and presenting vocabulary. If productive learning is important, then the development of the quality of learning a small vocabulary is important. Intensive practice in using vocabulary in speech and/or writing is therefore a useful activity. If receptive learning is important, then quantity of vocabulary is the main goal. Techniques which give familiarity with a large number of words are needed. As learners read and listen, the quality of knowledge of these words will develop without further attention from the teacher.

Often a teacher may wish to give particular attention to a word. Most of the procedures and techniques for this take words out of context and focus attention on them. These techniques are useful when for a variety of reasons words deserve particular attention. Here are some of these reasons.

1. The word is very frequent and very important for the learners.
2. The word causes particular difficulty.

3. The word is needed for another activity, such as a game, a reading or listening exercise, a talk.
4. The word contains features of regular patterns. Knowledge of these patterns will help learners master other words more easily.

Most vocabulary learning, however, will happen when the learners use the language for other purposes. The aim of techniques which take vocabulary out of context is to speed up the vocabulary learning process. This means that such techniques should occupy only a small part of any language learning program. Later in the book we will look at ways in which simplification can help the learning of words in context by placing them in a meaningful context, a context which can be understood. Activities using simplified material are very important in most language learning programs and deserve a lot of time. The use of simplified reading materials provides learners with an excellent opportunity to continue learning vocabulary through reading outside class time. If learners have access to tape recorders or language laboratories, then there is the opportunity for a lot of vocabulary learning through listening to simplified material. Real vocabulary learning comes through use, both receptive use and productive use. Teachers can help the process along by drawing attention to particular words, by teaching strategies for learning vocabulary, and by providing simplified material, but meeting the words in a variety of contexts and having to use some of them to express new ideas provide the most important opportunities for vocabulary learning.

There are strategies that learners can use to cope with new vocabulary. By far the most important strategy is guessing from context. It is worth spending a lot of class time on this strategy until learners have mastered it. It is the most powerful way of dealing with unknown words. Other strategies like paraphrasing, using word parts, dictionary use, and mnemonic techniques make learners independent of the teacher. They are tools that can be used as a part of usual language activities or can be used outside class time. Guided practice with these strategies encourages learners to use them and gives learners the skill to use the strategies effectively.

It is useful to make a distinction between increasing vocabulary and establishing vocabulary. Increasing vocabulary means introducing learners to new words and thus starting their learning. Establishing vocabulary means building on and strengthening this initial knowledge—that is, encouraging the knowledge of particular words to develop and expand. For example, teachers might increase learners' vocabulary by getting them to learn lists of words. They might establish this knowledge by getting learners to do lots of reading of material that contains those words first learned in lists. Or they might establish this knowledge through puzzles and games involving the vocabulary.

An important teaching principle is that the old material in any lesson is the most important. There are several reasons for this. First, the old material has already had some teaching and learning time invested in it. If the material is not given any further attention, then this material will be forgotten and all the previous investment is wasted. Further attention to the material will bring it closer to the threshold of learning, after which no further attention is needed. Second, the old material is likely to benefit most from further attention because the learners have already had some experience of it and it is at this stage that generalizations about it by the teacher will be meaningful to the learners. Such generalizations at the time the material is first introduced have little significance for the learners because they have no past experience to relate it to. Third, because the learners have already mastered some features of the material, they are able to give their attention to contextual features of the learning rather than the initial decontextualized features.

These reasons apply particularly to vocabulary learning. The effort given to the learning of new words will be wasted if this is not followed up by later meetings with the words. Understanding the concepts behind words and the types of collocations that they have is best done when it builds upon previous experience of the words. Once learners have a basic meaning for a word, they can give attention to what words it collocates with and the patterns it occurs in. Thus, there are good reasons for letting learners meet new vocabulary incidentally and directing attention to it after several meetings.

As you work your way through this book, you should try to answer the following questions.

### Increasing Learners' Vocabulary

1. Do you expect most learning to occur during or outside class?
2. Will you be concentrating on receptive or productive vocabulary learning?
3. Which skills—listening, speaking, reading or writing—will involve most of your vocabulary learning program?
4. Will you be aiming at quality of vocabulary learning or quantity?
5. Will your focus be on particular words or on strategies?
6. How much emphasis will you give to decontextualized vocabulary learning?
7. Will most of your class work involve teacher-directed class activities, group or pair work, or individual work?

When you have answered these questions, go back over them again, listing the techniques, strategies, and procedures you will use. Say where you will get the necessary material.

***Establishing Vocabulary***   What techniques, strategies, and activities will you use only to establish vocabulary that your learners have already met? When you answer the question, consider the questions in the section on increasing learners' vocabulary.

***Individual Needs***   What techniques, strategies, and activities will you use to help learners who know less vocabulary than others in your class?

## How Can I Test to See What My Learners Need to Know and What They Now Know?

Before testing it is important to be clear about why the learners are being tested and what the information will be used for. Here are some of the reasons for testing.

1. To find learners' total vocabulary size.
2. To compare vocabulary knowledge before and after the course.
3. To keep a continuing check on progress.
4. To encourage learning by setting short-term goals.
5. To see the effectiveness of your teaching.
6. To investigate learning.

Testing usually has two effects: (1) It provides information for the teacher and learners, and (2) it influences the teacher's and learners' attitudes. That is, testing can encourage learning and arouse interest in it. It can also be discouraging and give rise to types of learning that do not have useful long-term results. Usually an open discussion between the teacher and learners of goals and the reasons for testing will avoid these problems. Similarly, attention to individual goals and the use of self-motivating records like graphs which are under the learners' control will have good effects.

Before a test is made, it is good to consider how the information gained from the test will be used. Will it be used to make decisions about goals, to guide teaching, to get the learners to keep a record of progress, to form the basis of a discussion with the learners to help them guide their learning, or to help other teachers?

One of the aims of a testing program is to see how the initial learning of particular words is made richer and more secure. Much of this information will come not from vocabulary tests but from thoughtful observation of the learners' speaking and writing and from talking to and studying individual learners. The introspective approach of Cohen and Hosenfield (1981) is especially useful here.

Once the purposes and uses of testing have been decided, the next points to consider are what kind of knowledge is to be tested, and what type of test is most suitable. The chapter on what is involved in learning a word can provide very useful guidelines on what to test, and looking at the learning burden table in that chapter can clarify ideas about what to test.

# Chapter 2

# The Goals of Vocabulary Learning and Vocabulary Size

This chapter answers several questions. How many words does a second language learner need? This is answered by looking at the vocabulary of native speakers and frequency counts of vocabulary in texts. The next question is: How do we choose what vocabulary to teach? This is answered by looking at frequency counts and word lists. The final section looks at setting goals for your learners.

## HOW MANY WORDS DOES A SECOND LANGUAGE LEARNER NEED?

There are two ways of answering this question. One way is to look at the vocabulary of native speakers of English and consider that as a goal for second language learners. The other way is to look at the results of frequency counts and the practical experience of second language teachers and researchers and decide how much vocabulary is needed for particular activities.

### The Vocabulary of Native Speakers

The most notable feature of estimates of the vocabulary size of native speakers of English is that there is enormous variation in the estimates. Fries and Traver (1960) and Lorge and Chall (1963) discuss some of these widely varying estimates. Recent research (Nagy & Anderson, 1984; Goulden et al., in press) suggests that estimates of around 20,000 words for undergraduates are most likely to be correct. This suggests that first language learners add between 1,000 and 2,000 words per year to their vocabulary, or 3 to 7 words per day (Table 2.1).

A study of a young second language learner by Yoshida (1978) found that the learner had about 260 to 300 words in his productive vocabulary after seven months of exposure to English. His main contact with English

**Table 2.1   VOCABULARY SIZE OF NATIVE SPEAKERS**

| Age in years | Vocabulary size | Investigator |
| --- | --- | --- |
| 1.3 | 235 | Kirkpatrick |
| 2.8 | 405 | Kirkpatrick |
| 3.8 | 700 | Kirkpatrick |
| 5.5 | 1,528 | Salisbury |
| 6.5 | 2,500 | Termon and Childs |
| 8.5 | 4,480 | Kirkpatrick |
| 9.6 | 6,620 | Kirkpatrick |
| 10.7 | 7,020 | Kirkpatrick |
| 11.7 | 7,860 | Kirkpatrick |
| 12.8 | 8,700 | Kirkpatrick |
| 13.9 | 10,660 | Kirkpatrick |
| 15.0 | 12,000 | Kirkpatrick |
| 18.0 | 17,600 | Kirkpatrick |

*Source:* Fries and Traver (1960, p. 49); also in Seashore and Eckerson (1940).

was two to three hours a day of nursery school, and his parents did not speak English at home. Tests showed that his receptive vocabulary was about 2.2 times his productive vocabulary, which would give him a receptive vocabulary of about 1000 words in a year.

Tests on learners of English as a foreign language in India and Indonesia (Barnard, 1961; Quinn, 1968) have shown that learners have a 1000- to 2000-word vocabulary after a five-year period of four or five English classes a week.

If second language learners are in the same school system as native speakers of English, they need to match the native speakers' rate of vocabulary learning and make up for the difference in English vocabulary that existed when the second language learners entered the system. So, for example, if a second language learner enters the school system knowing almost no English at the age of 5, he needs to learn, say 2500 words, plus another 1000 words a year.

Jamieson (1976) found that the English vocabulary levels of 5- and 7-year-old Tokelauan children in the New Zealand school system were two years behind their native-speaking classmates. The rate of increase of vocabulary was similar for Tokelauan children and native speakers of English. This suggests that Tokelauan children may continue to be about two years behind native speakers in vocabulary as they progress through the school. So, the difference in size between a native speaker's vocabulary and a second language learner's vocabulary can be quite large, usually several thousand words. Although second language learners may be able to match native speakers' rate of vocabulary learning, they may need special help to overcome the difference in vocabulary size.

## Frequency Counts of Vocabulary in Texts

Let us look at a short text written for young native speakers and see what information it can give us about the vocabulary that a learner would need to read it. The text has been marked to show two kinds of words. The unmarked words are all in the most frequent 2000 head-words of English. These are the high-frequency words of English. Each of these words occurs often in the material we read or listen to. They also have a wide range—that is, they occur in many different kinds of material on many different topics. The underlined words are the low-frequency words of English. Although they may occur several times in a particular text, in our daily use of language most of them are not likely to occur often.

---

### *Finding an Ammonite*   by Graeme Stevens

Two hundred and fifty million years ago, during the age of the dinosaurs, much of what is land today was covered by warm, shallow seas. Most of New Zealand was then under water.

Among the creatures which lived in the seas were ammonites. They had heads and tentacles, like their modern squid and octopus relatives, but were attached to coiled shells. Some were small, some were two metres or more wide. Their food was small fish, shrimps and crayfish, but they too were preyed upon by the giant sharks and sea-lizards which lived then. One ammonite shell has been found which has puncture marks from sixteen bites. A mosasaur—a kind of sea-lizard—had tried to get at the animal inside.

Where the sea has gone back from the land, people find fossils of the shells and bones of the prehistoric sea creatures. There have been fossils or ammonites found in New Zealand, although they have been less common here than in North America and Europe. This is probably because the seas that lapped on to New Zealand in those times were cooler than those of North America and Europe. Until fairly recently, the total number of ammonites found in New Zealand would hardly be enough to fill a large cabin trunk—even though geologists and rock hounds have looked quite thoroughly for them. Most ammonites found here have been quite small. A size close to that of a softball (seven to ten centimetres) is most common.

---

1. About 87 percent of the words in the text are high-frequency words. So with a vocabulary of just 2000 words a learner could read 87 percent of the words in the text. These 2000 high-frequency words of English are clearly very useful and important for a learner of English. Any time spent learning them will be well repaid because they cover a lot of text and will be met often.

2. The remaining words in the text can be divided into two groups. One group is made up of words like *ammonite, fossil, squid, dinosaur.* These words relate closely to the topic of the text and are important for any learner continuing to study in this area. We can call this group "technical words." Within a certain topic or subject area they may occur several times, but they are unlikely to occur in texts outside that subject area.

3. The other group is made up of words like *lapped, cabin, hounds.* They are clearly not technical words in the Ammonite text. It would be easier for second language learners if they were replaced by high-frequency words. It is very unlikely that they will occur again in the book containing this text. These are the low-frequency words of English.

Let us now look at another text. This time it is one from a secondary school textbook for native speakers. This time three groups of words have been marked. The underlined words are in a list of words which commonly occur in all kinds of university texts and which are not in the first 2000 words of English.

---

### Machines

Since earliest times Man has tried to <u>conserve</u> his <u>energy</u> whenever he has to do some work. By a variety of <u>methods</u> (many still in use today) men cut down on the size of the force, or forces, they had to apply to lift objects. Today Man has become more <u>efficient</u> in <u>designing devices</u> which <u>enable</u> him to <u>transfer energy</u> from one place to another extremely quickly, or to do useful jobs more easily. These <u>devices</u> are called machines. A machine is an <u>energy transformer;</u> it can change <u>energy</u> from one form to another (as an electric motor does) or it can hand <u>energy</u> on from one place to another (as a hydraulic press does).

You will have seen many machines around your home—a crowbar, hammers, a bicycle, wheelbarrow; even a sloping piece of board is a machine. Many other and more complicated machines can be seen in factories — pulley systems, presses, fork-lifts and the bewildering complex, <u>automatic</u> machines, sorting and <u>assembling</u> articles at high speed.

However, no matter how complicated the machine is, its parts, or components, are basically one or other of two simple machines—the lever and the inclined plane. The application of these simple devices has been used by Man for many thousands of years—you may have read how giant inclined planes were used during the construction of the Great Pyramid in Egypt.

1. A machine is an _____(two words).

2. A complicated machine is just various combinations of two basic machines—the _____ and the _____(two words).

3. Into what category of basic machine do each of the following fit: a spade; a car screw-jack; a hydraulic lift; a spanner; a winding road up a mountain; a human arm?

**The lever**

The lever (or, as you may have called it when you were younger, the see-saw can be used to multiply forces or to produce turning effects (torques).

A screwdriver opening a paint-tin is a good example of a lever in action. The screwdriver is pivoted on a point (called the fulcrum), and you apply a force called the effort at the handle end, while the blade is pressing against the lid which is to be removed—the force caused by the lid being called the load.

The lever's input energy (E.S1) and its output energy (L.S2) are equal; as a machine it merely hands energy on; it neither creates nor destroys any. This does not prevent a lever from being very useful: it changes the force to a more convenient size (E is smaller than L, if S1 is bigger than S2); it alters the direction of the force; and it can transmit a force to any selected point.

If there is friction at the pivot some of the input energy can be wasted as heat.

1. Once again we can see how useful the high-frequency words are. Those words which are not marked in the text make up 87 percent of the words in the text. These frequent words deserve considerable time and attention from both teachers and learners.

2. The underlined words, which are from the university word list (see Appendix 2), make up 8 percent of the words in the text. These words include *conserve, energy, efficient, design, device*. These words are very useful for learners who study in upper secondary school or at a

university or a technical institute. They differ from technical words in that they are common in most kinds of technical writing. Technical words occur only in a very limited area. For learners in secondary school or at a university, the university word list is a very important goal after the first 2000 high-frequency words are mastered. Adding the first 2000 words to the 800 headwords in the university list gives learners coverage of 95 percent of the text, for a total vocabulary of 2800 words.

3. The words in boxes are the technical and low-frequency words in the text. They account for 5 percent of the words in the text. The technical words include *lever, pivot, fulcrum,* and *torques,* among others. Li (1983) examined the low-frequency words in a first-year university science text. It was found that approximately 16 different words per 400-word page were low-frequency words. Eleven of these 16 words could be classed as technical words—well worth learning by any person specializing in that subject. About 2 of the remaining 5 words per page were not technical words but had useful prefixes. So they would not be difficult to learn. The remaining 3 words per page were nontechnical words that were not repeated in the text and that did not contain useful parts. These included words like *arch, arid, gulp, ramify,* and *turbulent.* If we add the 11 technical words to the 2 with useful parts, then 13 of the 16 low-frequency words per page were worth learning by anyone intending to specialize or do further reading in the subject of a particular text. A study by Becka (1972) supports Li's findings.

Most of the words in boxes in the Machines text are technical words.

4. The low-frequency words in the Machines text include *crowbar, bewildering,* and *see-saw.* These words occur only once in the text and they are unlikely to be met again for a very long time. Most words in English are like this. The large Webster's dictionary contains about 128,000 headwords. The high-frequency words and the words in the university list add up to 2,800 words. Most lists of technical vocabulary contain 1,000 to 2,000 entries. This means that the remaining 123,200 words of English will be low-frequency words for a learner of English (Table 2.2).

So, we can describe low-frequency words as being a very large group of words, covering a very small proportion of any text, with each word occurring very infrequently. It is not worth spending time on such

**Table 2.2   WORD TYPES AND TEXT COVERAGE**

|  | No. of words | Proportion of text |
|---|---|---|
| High-frequency words | 2,000 | 87% |
| University word list | 800 | 8% |
| Technical words | 2,000 | 3% |
| Low-frequency words | 123,200 | 2% |
| Totals | 128,000 | 100% |

words. It is more important to teach learners strategies like guessing from context, or using word parts to deal with these words as they occur.

So far we have looked at short texts. Let us now look at a word-frequency count of much larger pieces of English. We can count the number of words in a book in three ways. (1) If we want to know how long the book is, we can count how many words there are on a typical page and multiply that by the number of pages. So if each page contains around 300 words and the book consists of 200 pages, we can estimate that the book is 60,000 words long. To put it another way, we can say the book contains 60,000 *running words*. (2) If we want to know how many words you need to understand in order to be able to read the book, we must count the words in a different way. First, we have to decide what we mean by the term *word*. Are *mend, mends, mended, mending* one word or four words? Are *branch* (of a tree) and *branch* (of a bank) one word or two? Grouping vocabulary under headwords is an attempt to increase the coverage of high-frequency vocabulary. The implication is that learning a word involves learning its derived and inflected forms as well. Second, we have to go through the book and make a list of all the different words that occur in the book. If the book contains 60,000 running words, we will probably find that it contains approximately 9,000 different words. (3) If we want to do a frequency count of the words in the book, we make a list of all the different words in the book and we count how often each one occurs. The most frequent word will probably be *the*. In 60,000 running words it will occur about 4,200 times. The word *know* will probably occur about 42 times. Many words will occur only once. *The* is a very useful word. If it occurs 4,200 times in 60,000 running words, it accounts for 7 percent of the running words in the book. If we add the frequency of the 10 most frequent words together, we will find that these 10 words account for almost 24 percent of the running words in the text. Table 2.3 gives the typical figures for a collection of texts consisting of 5 million running words.

**Table 2.3    FIGURES BASED ON A COUNT OF
5 MILLION RUNNING WORDS**

| Different words | % of running words |
| --- | --- |
| 86,741 | 100 |
| 43,831 | 99 |
| 5,000 | 89.4 |
| 3,000 | 85.2 |
| 2,000 | 81.3 |
| 100 | 49 |
| 10 | 23.7 |

*Source:* Carroll, Davies, and Richman (1971).

We can see that the figures from the Carroll et al. count, and indeed from all other frequency counts of English, support our findings from short texts. What the table does not show is that 40.4 percent of the different words in the Carroll et al. count occurred only once. That means that if learners read the 5 million running words (the equivalent of about 80 books each 200 pages long), they would meet about 35,000 different words that occurred only once. In the Carroll et al. count, these "one-timers" included words like *malformation, malignancy, maligned, malingering, Malinovski, Popeye, popguns, popinjays, popish,* and *poplin.* Clearly, low-frequency words present a major difficulty for a learner of English.

Before we summarize the features of the various types of words, let us look at their origins. Most low-frequency vocabulary comes to English from Latin and Greek, often through French. Roberts (1965) gives the following proportions: About 44% of the first 1,000 words of English come from French, Latin, or Greek. This rises to a little over 60% in the second 1,000 words, and for the rest of the first 10,000 words of English it stays around 66 percent. Thus, about two-thirds of the low-frequency words of English come from French, Latin, or Greek.

High-frequency vocabulary consists mainly of short words which cannot be broken into meaningful parts. Low-frequency vocabulary, on the other hand, while it consists of many thousands of words, is made from a much smaller number of word parts. The word *impose,* for example, is made of two parts, *im-* and *-pose,* which occur in hundreds of other words—*imply, infer, compose, expose, position.* This has clear implications for teaching and learning vocabulary and we will look at this in more detail in a later chapter. Table 2.4 summarizes the features and their implications for teaching of the different types of vocabulary described in this chapter. These implications will be dealt with in more detail in later chapters of this book.

## HOW DO WE CHOOSE WHAT VOCABULARY TO TEACH?

### Frequency Counts

We can get information about which words will be most useful for learners of English by looking at frequency counts of vocabulary. Usually a vocabulary count is done by making a list of the words in a particular text or group of texts and counting how often and where they occur. Some of the more recent counts have used computers to list the words and count their frequency.

Word-frequency counts can help teachers and course designers in several ways. They can help a teacher develop a feeling about which

**Table 2.4  TYPES OF VOCABULARY, THEIR FEATURES, AND THE IMPLICATIONS FOR TEACHING AND LEARNING**

| Type of vocabulary | Number of words | Frequency | Coverage of text | Origins | Implications for teaching and learning |
|---|---|---|---|---|---|
| High-frequency words | 2,000 | Occur frequently in all kinds of texts | About 87% of the running words in a text | About half are from Latin, French, or Greek | Spend a lot of time on these words. Make sure they are learned. |
| Academic vocabulary | 800 | Occur frequently in most kinds of academic texts | About 8% of the running words in academic texts | | If learners are in upper secondary school or in tertiary education, spend a lot of time on these words. Make sure they are learned. |
| Technical vocabulary | About 1,000 to 2,000 for each subject | Occur, sometimes frequently, in specialized texts | About 3% of the running words in a specialized text | About two-thirds are from Latin, French, or Greek | Learning the subject involves learning the vocabulary. Subject teachers can deal with the vocabulary, but the English teacher can help with learning strategies. |
| Low-frequency words | About 123,000 | Do not occur very frequently | About 2% or more of the words in any text | | Teach strategies for dealing with these words. The words themselves do not deserve teaching time. |

words are useful and should be given attention and which are infrequent. They can provide a principled basis for developing word lists for teaching, for designing graded courses and reading texts, and for preparing vocabulary tests. Where frequency counts give information on range, they are also useful for developing specialized word lists. Several early frequency counts are described in Fries and Traver (1960). *The Teacher's Word Book of 30,000 Words* by Thorndike and Lorge (1944) is the most widely known. It has been used as the basis for vocabulary selection for many English courses and many series of simplified reading books.

The Thorndike and Lorge count tells us how often each word occurs in 1 million running words of text and gives us some indication of its range. The range of a word is a measure of the number of different types of texts in which a word occurs. Words with a wide range occur in many different kinds of texts and fields of study. The most useful words for our learners are high-frequency words which have a wide range. The Thorndike and Lorge count is still used as a source of information about what words to teach, but it is based on work done over 50 years ago. Roberts (1965, pp. 22–23) describes some of its weaknesses.

More recent counts are those done using computers, namely, Kucera and Francis (1967) and Carroll et al. (1971). These counts give information about the frequency and range of words and, unlike the Thorndike and Lorge count, give a list of the words in order of frequency. The Carroll et al. (1971) count gives detailed information about range and could be very useful in making lists of vocabulary for special subject areas.

Frequency counts provide useful information about the frequency and range of words. But they do not give us enough information and there are several problems associated with them.

1. The most serious problem with word-frequency lists is that certain useful and important words do not occur in the first or second 1000 words. They may occur only at the third, fourth, or fifth thousand word level. Often these useful words are concrete nouns. For example, *soap, a bath, (a) chalk,* and *a stomach* are not in the first 2000 words of Thorndike and Lorge's 1944 list. The words *tidy, stupid,* and *behavior* are not in the first 3000 words of that list. *Damage* is not in the first 2000. If we use frequency as our only principle of selection, we cannot include these words in a beginners' vocabulary of 1000 words.

2. Another problem is that some words that are not suitable for a beginners' vocabulary come in the first 1000 words of most frequency lists. Some examples are *bank* (v.), *bill, company, deal, issue, labor, stock,* and *supply.* (All these words are in the first 1000 words of Thorndike and Lorge's 1944 list. *Chicago, thee,* and *thou* are also in the first 1000.) Some of these words would be frequent in business letters. They would not be very frequent in most other kinds of writing.

3. Word-frequency lists often disagree. Sometimes a word has a high frequency in one list and a fairly low frequency in another list. A person who makes a frequency list has to choose what kinds of writing to count. The choice will affect the results.

4. Usually the order of the words in a frequency list is not the best order in which to teach the words. For example, *his* is the 74th word in one list and *hers* is the 4151st word. If we followed this order, we would not teach the word *hers* until senior high school or university level!

5. Word-frequency lists are not reliable above a certain level. Engels (1968) found in his study of *The General Service List* that words above the 1000-word level did not include many of the words in the texts he examined.

When preparing a word list for learners of English, other criteria in addition to frequency and range need to be used. Here is a list of possible criteria (Richards, 1970).

1. frequency
2. range
3. language needs
4. availability and familiarity
5. coverage
6. regularity
7. ease of learning or learning burden

## Word Lists

Some famous word lists have emphasized some of these criteria. Basic English (Richards, 1943) was developed making coverage and ease of learning the main criteria. Coverage is the capacity of a word to take the place of other words (Mackey & Savard, 1967). For example, the word *foot* is a useful word from the point of view of coverage because

1. It can often be used to make a definition of other words, e.g., *Your heel is the back part of your foot.*
2. Its meaning can be extended to replace other words, e.g., *the base of a tree* can be replaced by *the foot of a tree.*
3. It can combine with other words to make new words, e.g., *footpath, football, footstep, foot-and-mouth disease.*

There is one more type of coverage. The word *table* is useful from the point of view of coverage because

4. Its meaning includes the meaning of other words and it can be used instead of them, e.g., *bench, desk, escritoire.*

Mackey and Savard calculated the coverage of French words. They found that words with high coverage were not necessarily the most frequent words. So information about the coverage of words is useful information to add to information about frequency.

West's (1935) definition vocabulary is another good example of a list based on the principle of coverage. The list was made to produce a dictionary where all the definitions were given in the smallest possible vocabulary.

The most famous and most useful list of high-frequency words is West's *General Service List of English Words* (1953). This list is now old (the headwords in the list have not changed since 1936), but it has still not been replaced as a source of useful information about particular words and as a collection of the most important vocabulary for a learner of English. The list contains 2000 headwords. It gives the frequency of the main headword plus the relative frequency of its meanings.

OWN   3244e

own, adj.     *(showing possession)*
              This is my own house; I don't rent it
              Use this pen. Thanks, I'd rather use
              my own

of your own   Why do you use my pen? Haven't you
              got a pen (one) of your own (1.3%)          89%
              [= *for myself*, Cooked my own dinner as the
              servant was ill, 0.2%]

own, v.       He owns a lot of land round here            9%
              [own that, own up to = confess, 1.5%]

owner, n., 314e;    ownership, n., 52e

     —

                                              (*GSL*, p. 347)

Unlike most other frequency counts, the *GSL* includes forms under the same headword. So the entry for *own* includes *own, owns, owned, owning,* and includes *owner* and *ownership*. Other counts would count and list most of these as different words. In the entry, the parts of speech are distinguished (*own* as an adjective and *own* as a verb) and the various meanings are also distinguished. Each of these distinctions is given a percentage so that the user of the list can easily decide which meaning and use is the most important. It is also possible to decide if *own* as a verb is more frequent than *have* with a similar meaning by calculating 9 percent of 3244 and comparing it with the entry for *have*. Each meaning is also accompanied by examples.

The frequency figure (for *own* it is 3244) gives the number of occurrences in 5 million words. The *GSL* is based on a very large corpus of material.

During the making of the list, factors other than frequency and range were considered. These are described with examples in the introduction to the list (pp. ix–x). The list was not designed as a list of unrelated words but was viewed as a "little language" (Salling, 1959). The makers of the list wanted to be sure that most material could be rewritten within the vocabulary of the list and that the list did not contain unnecessary items. Some low-frequency items were included because there seemed to be no other easy way of expressing a particular idea—for example *whistle*, *reproduce*. Some frequent items were omitted because other more useful items could easily replace them. West and others produced enormous quantities of simplifed readers and other language learning texts using the *GSL* vocabulary. The Longman Simplifed English Series and the New Method Supplementary Readers, for example, are based on the *GSL*. The *GSL* is certainly tried and tested and it will not be easily replaced.

Most publishers of simplifed reading books have their own graded vocabulary lists. Some of these, like the Longmans, Macmillan Rangers, and Collins lists, are available in a published form. Some other lists are available only to writers of graded readers. All these word lists arrange the vocabulary into steps.

The *Cambridge English Lexicon* (Hindmarsh, 1980) is a graded word list of about 4500 words with over 8000 meanings. The list is a collation of most of the recent word counts, *The General Service List* (West, 1953), the Kucera and Francis count (1967), the Thorndike and Lorge count (1944), and the Carroll et al. count (1971), in addition to many other lists. The words are graded into five levels (Table 2.5).

The meanings of the words are also graded, from 1 to 7. The principles of grading the words and their meanings are not described in the introduction, and it seems that some of the grading was done by intuition rather than using the figures in the *General Service List* (GSL). In general, however, the gradings do correspond to the *GSL*, and where they do not the grading seems reasonable. For some entries the *GSL* gives a more detailed division of meanings; for other entries the *Cambridge English Lexicon* (CEL) gives a more detailed division. A major advantage of the *CEL* over the *GSL* is that it covers a larger vocabulary—

**Table 2.5**  **WORDS IN THE CAMBRIDGE ENGLISH LEXICON**

| Level | Total | Cumulative total |
|-------|-------|------------------|
| 1 | 598 | 598 |
| 2 | 617 | 1215 |
| 3 | 992 | 2207 |
| 4 | 1034 | 3241 |
| 5 | 1229 | 4470 |

over a thousand words more. A disadvantage is that it does not list derivatives under the headword as the *GSL* does. So, in the *CEL*, *unpaid* is listed under the letter *U*. In the *GSL*, *pay* includes *pay, pay-day, unpaid*, and *payment*.

Other word lists, like the *Longman Lexicon of Contemporary English* (McArthur, 1981), provide detailed information about usage with lots of examples. A review of these word lists and others can be found in Fox and Mahood (1982a, 1982b), and Jeffries and Willis (1982).

In this section we have looked briefly at some of the criteria which can be used to make word lists for the preparation of learning material. Typically these word lists are used to make simplified reading material, to design controlled speaking and writing courses, and to produce dictionaries. Although the information from frequency counts provides an important basis for the development of most of these lists, frequency alone is not sufficient. The purpose of the list affects the choice of criteria. Coverage, for example, is an important criterion if a list is going to be used to define the meanings of other words. Regularity is important when learnability is one of the aims of a list.

The lists described in this section are the result of an enormous amount of work. West's (1935) description of his construction of the definition vocabulary is an excellent example of the thought, care, and effort that go into the making of such lists. Their main aim is to make the learning of English more manageable by providing a tried and principled basis for vocabulary selection.

## SETTING GOALS FOR YOUR LEARNERS

In this chapter we have looked at the vocabulary of native speakers and information from frequency studies of English. The research on native speakers indicates that second language learners in the same school system as native speakers of English may have to increase their vocabulary by around 1000 words a year, besides making up a 2000- to 3000-word gap, in order to match native speakers' vocabulary growth.

The research on frequency counts gives clear guidelines, particularly for learners of English as a foreign language. They may need a productive vocabulary of around 2000 high-frequency words plus the strategies to deal with the low-frequency words they meet. Learners with special goals, such as study at a university, need to acquire a further 1000 high-frequency words. Several lists of high-frequency words are available for teachers and course designers.

Using this information it is now possible for you to apply it to your learners and your language learning course. Table 2.6 will help you.

**Table 2.6  VOCABULARY LEARNING GOALS**

|  | Number of Words |  |
|---|---|---|
| a. My learners' vocabulary at the beginning of the course |  | You can find this information by (1) testing your learners, (2) counting the words in their previous textbooks, (3) checking the vocabulary at the beginning of their coursebook with a frequency count such as West (1953), Thorndike and Lorge (1944), Kucera and Francis (1967), Hindmarsh (1980). This will help you decide the word level of the coursebook, (4) getting this information from the introduction to your textbook or from your syllabus notes. |
| b. Their required vocabulary at the end of the course. |  | You can decide this by (1) counting the words in the coursebook, (2) looking at the uses they must make of English at the end of the year and deciding how many words they need to know in order to do this, (3) setting a goal that you think they could reach, (4) seeing what your syllabus or coursebook sets as a goal, (5) comparing your learners with native speakers of English of the same age. |
| c. The number of words to be learned during the course, $c = b - a$. |  |  |
| d. The number of English lessons, hours, or school weeks in the course. |  |  |
| e. The number of words to be learned in each lesson, hour, or school week, $e = c \div d$. |  |  |

Answer these questions.

What method did you use to answer a? Why?

What method did you use to answer b? Why?

Do you think your learners could master the number of words in c in a year?

Does your coursebook teach too few words?

Do your learners need high-frequency vocabulary, low-frequency vocabulary or specialized vocabulary? Why?

Do you have a list of the words your learners need to master?

If you do not have a coursebook or if your coursebook does not present enough vocabulary, how can you decide what vocabulary is suitable for your learners? Look at the following list of possibilities and decide which one is most suitable for you.

1. Choose a coursebook to follow or to supplement your present coursebook. Which one?
2. Choose a word list and use and adapt material to suit the list. Which list?
   a. The General Service List
   b. The University Word List
   c. The Longman Structural Readers List
   d. The Cambridge English Lexicon
   e. _____
   Make your own word list by studying material or tapes your learners will need to deal with.
   f. _____

## APPLICATION

1. Here are six learners' scores on the Vocabulary Levels Test (Appendix 8). Use the information in Appendix 8 and in this chapter to decide on a vocabulary expansion program for each learner. Learners A and B have been done for you.

| LEARNER | 2,000 | 3,000 | 5,000 | UWL | 10,000 | TOTAL |
|:---:|:---:|:---:|:---:|:---:|:---:|:---:|
| A | 8 | 8 | 0 | 0 | 0 | 16 |
| B | 15 | 10 | 7 | 13 | 2 | 47 |
| C | 12 | 8 | 3 | 3 | 0 | 26 |
| D | 18 | 18 | 15 | 3 | 5 | 59 |
| E | 18 | 18 | 16 | 16 | 8 | 76 |
| F | 18 | 18 | 18 | 17 | 14 | 85 |

| LEARNER | AIM | LEVEL NEEDING ATTENTION | VOCABULARY PROGRAM |
|---------|-----|-------------------------|--------------------|
| A | Continue to secondary school | 2000 | Intensive reading of graded readers. Intensive English classes with work on vocabulary exercises. |
| B | Study at an English medium university | UWL | Independent work on UWL involving rote learning, and intensive reading of textbooks. Work on word parts and guessing from context. |
| C | Continue to upper secondary school | | |
| D | Work in an office using English | | |
| E | Do master's level study at a university | | |
| F | Study at an English medium university | | |

2. Read the passages in Appendix 3. At what level does reading become realistic? How did you compensate for the missing vocabulary?

3. Ask a learner to mark the words that he does not know in a reading text. Decide which of these words are high-frequency, specialized, and low-frequency words. Consider the importance of these unknown words in the text. What kinds of words seem to cause problems for the learner?

4. Sit next to a learner doing a vocabulary test—for example, the levels test in Appendix 8. Get the learner to speak aloud while doing the test and get the learner to comment on what he or she is doing or thinking while doing it. Use this information to write a brief assessment of the test.

# Chapter **3**

# What Is Involved in Learning a Word?

This chapter looks at these questions: What is a word? What is involved in knowing a word? What features make learning a word difficult? The answers to the above questions all have direct implications for teaching and learning vocabulary.

This chapter is written from the point of view of a teacher of English as a foreign language. In many foreign language situations almost all of the English that a learner meets is met in the classroom. Teachers thus can have considerable control over the patterns and vocabulary the learners meet. Teachers of English as a second language do not have the same control, but they can use their knowledge of learning burden to help choose which words to emphasize, to help draw on analogies and patterns to make learning easier, and to help decide what features of a word need attention.

## WHAT IS A WORD?

When we consider vocabulary learning as a whole, criteria for drawing the boundaries between words have an important effect on learning. It is in the learners' and teacher's interest to define words so that the amount of learning is reduced.

Let us look first at the ways in which frequency counts and dictionaries distinguish one word from another. Carroll et al. (1971) distinguish words entirely on the basis of form. Even the presence of a capital letter is sufficient for a form to be counted as a different word. So, *societies, Societies, society, Society,* and *society's* are counted as five different words. Similarly, *soak, soaked, soaking,* and *soaks* are counted as four different words. A reason for this is that the Carroll count was done by a computer, and trying to be consistent with irregular suffixes and spelling changes would have created too many problems for the computer programmer.

Dictionaries try to distinguish several meanings of a word rather than show the common features running through various uses. For example, *root* is given the meanings (1) part of a plant which is normally in the soil . . . , (2) part of a hair, tooth, tongue, etc., which is like a root in position or function, (3) that from which something grows, (4) form of a word . . . , (5) (arith.) quantity which multiplied by itself. . . .

For learning, words can be defined with reference to learners' mother tongue or to English. For example, from the point of view of an Indonesian the word *fork* is several words: *garpu* (the fork we eat with), *pertigaan* or *simpang jalan* (the fork in the road), *cabang* (the fork in a tree. In Indonesian it is the same word as *branch*.).

However from the point of view of the English language, *fork* is one word. It is possible to describe the meaning of *fork* so that this meaning includes most uses of the word. Defining a word by looking for the concept that runs through all its uses reduces the number of words to learn. Instead of having to learn three words represented by the form *fork*, by learning the underlying concept of *fork* the learners have only one item to learn. There are other reasons for approaching vocabulary learning from this point of view. One of the educational values of learning a foreign language is seeing how the foreign language divides up experience in a different way from the mother tongue. From an Indonesian point of view, *fork* is defined mainly by its function—something to push food onto your spoon. From an English point of view, *fork* is defined by its shape. Treating meaning in English as if it was just a mirror of the mother tongue hides this difference. Another reason for drawing attention to the underlying concept is that every occurrence of the word will act as a repetition of what was taught instead of as a different item. That is, each occurrence of the word will contain known features and will build on previous learning.

To decide if you are dealing with one word or more than one word, see if extra learning is required. Can *branch* (of a tree) be taught in such a way that *branch* (of a bank or business) requires no additional learning? If it can, then *branch* (of a tree) and *branch* (of a bank) are the same word. Are *happy* and *happiness* the same word or different words? If the learners are already familiar with *-ness*, and are familiar with the *-y* becomes *-i-* spelling rule, then *happiness* requires no additional learning. It is in the teacher's and learners' interest to make use of the semantic patterns and other regularities in the language to reduce the amount of learning and teaching effort needed. We will look at these patterns and regularities in more detail later in this chapter.

## WHAT IS INVOLVED IN KNOWING A WORD?

What does a learner need to know in order to "know" a word? There are two answers to this question. If the word is to be learned only for receptive use (listening or reading) then there is one set of answers. If the word is to be learned for receptive and productive use (listening, speaking, reading, and writing) then there will be an additional set of answers. Table 3.1 lists the questions we should be able to answer (consciously or unconsciously) if we "know" a word.

Let us look at Table 3.1 in detail. The table is organized using the four general classification criteria (George, 1983). Like all the other subsections, the section headed **Spoken form** is divided into two parts, one dealing with receptive knowledge (**R**), and one dealing with productive knowledge (**P**). Let us look at receptive knowledge first.

### Receptive Knowledge

Knowing a word involves being able to recognize it when it is heard (what does it sound like?) or when it is seen (what does it look like?). This includes being able to distinguish it from words with a similar form and being able to judge if the word form sounds right or looks right. Receptive knowledge of a word also involves having an expectation of

**Table 3.1  KNOWING A WORD**

| | | |
|---|---|---|
| Form | | |
| Spoken form | R | What does the word sound like? |
| | P | How is the word pronounced? |
| Written form | R | What does the word look like? |
| | P | How is the word written and spelled? |
| Position | | |
| Grammatical patterns | R | In what patterns does the word occur? |
| | P | In what patterns must we use the word? |
| Collocations | R | What words or types of words can be expected before or after the word? |
| | P | What words or types of words must we use with this word? |
| Function | | |
| Frequency | R | How common is the word? |
| | P | How often should the word be used? |
| Appropriateness | R | Where would we expect to meet this word? |
| | P | Where can this word be used? |
| Meaning | | |
| Concept | R | What does the word mean? |
| | P | What word should be used to express this meaning? |
| Associations | R | What other words does this word make us think of? |
| | P | What other words could we use instead of this one? |

what grammatical pattern the word will occur in. Knowing the verb *suggest* involves the expectation that this word will be followed by an object sometimes in the form of a clause. Knowing the noun *music* involves the expectation that it will not usually occur in the plural form. Much of this receptive knowledge can be gained only from experience and would not be greatly increased as a result of teaching. However, a teacher can help in some ways and these will be described in a later chapter.

The term *collocation* can be broken into the parts *col-* (from *com-* meaning "together, with"), *-loc-* (meaning "to place or put"), *-ate* (a verb suffix), and *-ion* (a noun suffix). So, *collocations* are words that often occur together. The word *sunny*, for example, collocates with *day* and *disposition*. *Too* frequently collocates with *much* and *late*. The collocations of a word are the company that it keeps. Knowing a word involves having some expectation of the words that it will collocate with.

When we know a word we know whether it is a frequently occurring word or a rare one. For example, we know that *student* is a frequent word but *disciple* is more appropriate in certain contexts. Lado (1956) and Richards (1976) present useful lists of register restraints which affect the appropriateness of a word. These include whether the word is old-fashioned, limited to American rather than British usage, more suitable for spoken English than written English, colloquial or formal rather than neutral, impolite, or blasphemous, limited to children's speech or to speech to children, or considered to be appropriate only to women or to men.

Knowing a word includes being able to recall its meaning when we meet it. It also includes being able to see which shade of meaning is most suitable for the context that it occurs in. In addition, knowing the meaning of a word may include being able to make various associations with other related words.

## Productive Knowledge

Productive knowledge of a word includes receptive knowledge and extends it. It involves knowing how to pronounce the word, how to write and spell it, how to use it in correct grammatical patterns along with the words it usually collocates with. Productive knowledge also involves not using the word too often if it is typically a low-frequency word, and using it in suitable situations. It involves using the word to stand for the meaning it represents and being able to think of suitable substitutes for the word if there are any.

Knowing a word as it is described here probably applies completely to only a small proportion of the total vocabulary of a native speaker. Most native speakers cannot spell or pronounce all the words they are familiar with, and they are uncertain about the meaning and use of many of them. For example, they have difficulty spelling words like *siege* and *principal*, disagree about the pronunciation of words like *controversy*, and do not always call a spade *a spade*.

There are several reasons for this. First, native speakers develop their vocabulary throughout their whole life. They learn new words and expand and reorganize their knowledge of familiar ones. Second, their receptive vocabulary is much larger than their productive vocabulary, and there are many words on the boundary. A large number of items in their receptive vocabulary are words of very low frequency, so they do not need to know much about them because they rarely meet them. Third, they develop their vocabulary knowledge in specialized areas. Many learners of English as a second language have a superior knowledge of vocabulary in specialized areas—for example, in biochemistry, geology, or seed technology—compared with native speakers who are not familiar with those areas.

## WHAT FEATURES MAKE LEARNING A WORD DIFFICULT?

The learning burden of a word is the amount of effort needed to learn and remember it. This depends on three things: (1) the learners' previous experience of English and their mother tongue, (2) the way in which the word is learned or taught, and (3) the intrinsic difficulty of the word. Let us look at each of these three classes and ways of reducing the learning burden.

### Learners' Previous Experience

There is a lot of evidence to show that second language vocabulary learning is influenced by first language vocabulary. In a comprehensive review of studies of compound and coordinate bilinguals, Meara (1980) concludes that "when some kind of cognitive operation other than simple recall of the phonetic form is called for, it does become extremely difficult to keep two languages apart. In this sense, forms in one language clearly evoke the corresponding related forms in the other language, a finding which would be very difficult to explain if the independent lexicons claim were true" (p. 232). Meara adds a caution, however, that it might be unwise to consider the vocabulary of a language as a whole, and it may be more revealing to study small subsets which may differ in organization and storage from one subset to another.

If first and second language vocabulary are stored together in an integrated whole rather than as two separate, independently functioning units, this would encourage borrowing and interference between first and second language vocabulary. There is considerable evidence to show that this occurs.

Yoshida (1978) studied the learning of English vocabulary by a Japanese-speaking child living in the United States. It was found that English loanwords in Japanese helped the child to learn the related English words quickly. Some words were changed to the English sound system by the child and some were not. For example /aisukuriimu / became /ayskriym / but /rendzi / (*orange*) remained unchanged.

The second language learner clearly brings the benefits of knowing vocabulary and of cognitive development in the first language. Dagut (1977) presents some examples of errors by Hebrew-speaking learners of English. These errors can be explained by comparing the vocabulary systems of English and Hebrew.

1. This is a *song* by Wordsworth.
2. Come and sit over here in the *shadow*.
3. I can't *appreciate* anyone that is cruel.
4. It's hard work *growing* children.
5. It isn't *comfortable* to live so far away.
6. The students were examined *by heart*.

According to Dagut, in Hebrew the word *shir* includes both *poem* and *song*. Similarly, *tsel* includes *shade* and *shadow*; *he-erikh* includes *appreciate*, *esteem*, and *estimate*; *gidel* includes *grow, rear*, and *breed*; *noah* includes *convenient* and *comfortable*; and *be'al peh* includes *by heart* and *orally*. Most teachers of English as a second language can make their own list of vocabulary errors resulting from mother-tongue interference. Other examples can be found in Abberton (1963) and Blum and Levenston (1979).

Strick (1980) used rating scales of word meanings to compare first and second language learners' view of words used to refer to people, like *Sir, Ma'am, Prof., Dr., Mrs.*, and *Mary.* Strick's conclusion was that semantic development in a second language is a process of moving from native to second language meanings and meaning structures. That is, the second language learner first classifies second language meanings according to the mother tongue. As the learner discovers more about the second language culture, these meanings change. During the change, importance is first given to features of meaning that are most easily seen, but later importance is given to abstract features that are most suited to the second language culture. Strick sees this move from features which are easily seen to more abstract features as a parallel between first and second language learning.

The effect of first language vocabulary on second language vocabulary learning may result in some meanings becoming "fossilized"; that is, learners always keep a first language meaning for a second language word. However, many learners eventually acquire a second language meaning for the second language word. As we have seen, there are several studies that point at second language learners' incomplete knowledge of second language vocabulary, but there are no studies that follow the development of this incomplete knowledge into a native-speaker-like meaning. One study by Henning (1973), however, investigated the ways in which second language learners at different levels of proficiency store vocabulary. Henning found that learners of English as a second language who were at a low level of proficiency stored vocabulary according to the sounds of words. That is, when such learners remembered English words, they tended to connect similar-sounding words like *horse* and *house*. Learners at higher levels of proficiency stored words according to their meaning. That is, they tended to connect words like *horse* and *cow*. Experiments with native speakers of English agree with this finding. As learners become better at a language, whether they are native speakers or second language learners, the way that they organize and store vocabulary in their memory changes. Storage according to form is replaced by storage according to meaning. This means that words that are very similar in sound or spelling to each other should not be introduced early in second language courses. If they are introduced early, they will be stored together and will interfere with each other.

If many of the features of a word are predictable because the learners already know some English, or because of their mother tongue, the word will be easy to learn. For example, if a learner already knows the word *excite* and knows some words ending in *-ment,* the word *excitement* has a very low learning burden. For an Indonesian learner, the word *communication* has a very low learning burden. First, Indonesian uses Roman script and the learners will already be aware of *c* being pronounced /k / in words like *cup, car,* and *cake.* Second, Indonesian has a word, *komunikasi,* borrowed from Dutch, which has a similar form and meaning to the English word. Third, *komunikasi* collocates with *antara,* often translated as *between,* which collocates with *communication.* Indonesian learners will need to give some attention to the spelling (double *m*) of *communication* and to the pronunciation, but apart from that, *communication* presents very little learning burden. Table 3.2 presents the factors of previous experience which affect learning burden. The general principle is: The more predictable and regular the features of the word, the lighter the learning burden. Let us look briefly at the featues affecting learning burden and look at ways in which the teacher can lighten the learning burden of words.

**Spoken Form** English words which use the same sounds and arrangement of sounds as in the learners' mother tongue will present no learning burden for pronunciation. For example, a Chinese learning En-

**Table 3.2   LEARNING BURDEN**

| | |
|---|---|
| **Form** | |
| Spoken | Does the word contain only familiar sounds or clusters of sounds? Is the stress predictable? |
| Written | Is the script like the mother-tongue script? Is the written form predictable from the spoken form? Does the written form follow regular spelling patterns? |
| **Position** | |
| Grammar | Does the word occur in the same patterns as the corresponding mother-tongue word? Does the word occur in a common pattern or common set of patterns? |
| Collocation | Does the word commonly occur with predictable words or types of words? |
| **Function** | |
| Frequency | Does the mother-tongue word have the same frequency? |
| Appropriateness | Does the degree of politeness, formality, etc., of the word match the corresponding mother-tongue word, or the other English words learned so far? |
| **Meaning** | |
| Concept | Does the English concept correspond to a mother-tongue concept? Are the various meanings of the word obviously related to a central concept? Is the meaning predictable from the form of the word? |
| Associations | Does the mother-tongue word give rise to associated words similar to the English word? |

glish can easily pronounce words like *pen, see,* and *sun.* Words like *rice, regular,* and *eighth* will present considerably more difficulty. It is possible to make a minimum pronunciation difficulty vocabulary for learners of English as a foreign language who share the same mother tongue. If learners begin English with such a list, they can quickly learn a large number of useful words. Learning will be made easier because part of the learning burden—pronunciation—has been reduced.

In the early stages of learning English it is wise to introduce difficult sounds and consonant clusters gradually. In this way new words will contain not too many difficult sounds. Research with native speakers of English shows that even children are aware what combinations of sounds are acceptable and what are not (Messer, 1967). This knowledge can gradually be built up for second language learners and will help their pronunciation and memory of words. Ludwig (1984) looks at some research on this.

**Written Form**   If the learners' mother tongue uses the Roman script like English, learning will be easier. For a native speaker of English, learning a language like Chinese, Arabic, or Thai is difficult because of the unfamiliar script. On the other hand, a native speaker of English learning Maori can read sentences in Maori aloud, without understanding them, after a few minutes' learning. This is because Maori uses the same letters as English, and the relationship of spelling to sound is very regular. There are also regular patterns in English, although most of them seem to have exceptions. Where possible, learners should be made aware of these patterns and exceptions should be avoided wherever possible. Wijk (1966) and Venezky (1970) provide a good description of these patterns.

Most low-frequency words follow regular patterns; high-frequency words are not so regular. Teachers can reduce the learning burden of written forms by choosing words with regular spellings wherever possible, by showing learners patterns which will help them, and by showing learners how the spelling of new words is similar to the spelling of known words. This use of analogy as a way of drawing attention to spelling patterns is the basis for several useful teaching techniques.

**Grammatical Patterns** If a word occurs in grammatical patterns which are similar to the patterns in which its translation occurs in the mother tongue, this part of the learning burden will be light. For example, the translation of *like* in Indonesian is *suka*. *I like ice cream* is translated as *saya suka es krim*. But *I like to sing* is translated as *saya suka menjanji*—there is no equivalent to *to*. So, in the sentence *I like ice cream* the learning burden of the grammatical pattern of *like* is small—it is like the mother tongue. In the second sentence, *I like to sing*, the learning burden of the grammatical pattern is increased. It is not completely predictable from the mother tongue. Predictability also depends on patterns within English. The learning burden of the grammatical pattern of *discuss* is reasonably heavy because it takes a different pattern from words with a similar meaning (Figure 3.1).

It is not surprising to see learners write, *We discussed about it*. Similarly, the grammatical pattern of *suggest* is not predictable by looking at words with a similar meaning (Figure 3.2).

Teachers can reduce the learning burden of grammatical patterns by showing learners where English usage parallels mother-tongue usage, by avoiding vocabulary items which take unpredictable patterns, and by showing learners useful parallel patterns in English.

|     |                                  |       |     |
| --- | -------------------------------- | ----- | --- |
| We  | talked<br>argued<br>joked<br>spoke | about | it. |
| We  | discussed                        |       | it. |

**Figure 3.1** *Discuss* and related verbs.

| He | told<br>asked<br>encouraged | me to write to you. |
|----|-------------------|---------------------|

| He | suggested | that I should write you. |
|----|-----------|--------------------------|

**Figure 3.2** *Suggest* and related verbs.

**Collocation**   If the collocations that a word takes can be predicted from the form of the word, the meaning of the word, or the mother-tongue translation of the word, then the learning burden is light.

Words which begin with a Latin prefix are sometimes followed by a preposition which has a meaning similar to the meaning of the prefix. Here are some examples.

*communicate with*            (*com-* = with)

*adapt to*                    (*ad-* = to)

There are far too many exceptions for it to be a general rule, but it can occasionally be useful. On these occasions the form of the word allows prediction of what collocates with the word.

Collocation is a part of the shadowy area between grammar and meaning. We saw in the previous section how the related meanings of *tell, suggest, ask,* and *encourage* had an effect on the prediction of the grammatical pattern. In a similar way, we expect words of related meaning to be followed by similar words.

Teaching vocabulary in collocations is in some ways a reaction against teaching words in lists and is an attempt to learn words in context while keeping the flexibility of list learning. Taylor (1983) describes the reasons for studying words in collocations: (a) Words which are naturally associated in text are learnt more easily than those not so associated; (b) vocabulary is best learned in context; (c) context alone is insufficient without deliberate association; (d) vocabulary is a distinct feature of language which needs to be developed alongside a developing grammatical competence.

**Frequency**   A learner can get three clues to the frequency of a word, one from the frequency with which it occurs in the English lessons, one from the frequency of its translation equivalent in the mother tongue, and one from its form.

If a teacher spends a lot of time on a word and overuses it, this affects the learners' use of the word. Overusing low-fequency words has a comical effect. If time is given to words according to their usefulness in English then this effect can be avoided.

Eaton (1940) has shown that for European languages there is a high degree of correspondence between words of high frequency in different languages. There are a few occasions, however, where a frequent word in the mother tongue is usually translated to a relatively infrequent word in English, and then this infrequent word is overused. The word *radjin* in Indonesian is usually translated as *diligent*, which, according to Thorndike and Lorge (1944), is not in the most frequent 10,000 words of English. Some Indonesian speakers of English use *diligent* when something like *hardworking* or *a good worker* would be more common.

According to Zipf (1935), the most frequent words in English are usually monosyllabic. That is, they are short because they consist of only one syllable. Thus, if a learner is faced with a choice between words, it is usually better to choose the shortest. The shortest is likely to be the most frequent. This idea of using simple words rather than complex ones is not easy for some learners to accept. Sometimes in their mother tongue complex words are more polite or respectful than simple words.

Frequency adds to the learning burden of a word when learners want to use an infrequent word very often when a more frequent item would be more suitable. Often it is sufficient to tell learners that the particular item is not commonly used.

**Appropriateness** Inappropriate usage occurs when a second language learner uses an old-fashioned word instead of the more usual one, an impolite word instead of a polite one, American usage where British usage would be more appropriate, or formal language when more colloquial usage would be more suitable. The clues for appropriate usage come from the way the word is translated into the mother tongue or from the context in which the word is used. Some of the most difficult words for second language learners in this area are words describing parts of the body and body functions.

When teaching words which might be used inappropriately, the teacher needs to teach the situations for using the words as a part of their meaning. For example, *chuck* (throw), *nick* (steal), *kid* (child) are more appropriate in speech than in writing, and they are very colloquial. *Silver* in New Zealand can mean *coins*; in the United States it refers to the metal. Words like *tummy*, and *potty* are suitable only when speaking to children. Some words also reflect the attitude of the speaker. Here is an example from Bertrand Russell: *I am firm; you are obstinate; he is a pigheaded fool. Slim* is a neutral, possibly positive word. *Skinny* may have a negative meaning. Teaching words like those just described is a good opportunity for the teacher to give some understanding of the values held by some English speakers.

**Meaning** The learning burden of the meaning of a word is light when the meaning of the word is predictable from its form, when its meaning corresponds to the meaning of a mother-tongue word, and when the various uses of the word are all related to an underlying concept. Let us look at each of these three in turn.

The meaning of a word can be predictable from its form for three reasons: because its form and meaning are similar to those of a mother-tongue word, because it is made up of known parts, or because its form sounds like its meaning. Because of borrowing and a common source, European languages like English, French, and Spanish share a lot of vocabulary. The French speaker learning English, for example, will find the learning burden of words such as *table*, *elementary*, and *dentist* very light because the words *table*, *elementaire*, and *dentiste* exist in her own language. Even languages like English and Indonesian share words like these for a variety of reasons. Here are some Indonesian words with their English equivalents. The learning burden of the English words would be very light for Indonesian speakers. Indonesian contains well over a thousand words like these which could be learned very quickly by beginners.

## INDONESIAN-ENGLISH EQUIVALENTS

| | |
|---|---|
| bel-bell | telpon-telephone |
| hotel-hotel | botol-bottle |
| individuil-individual | truk-truck |
| ekonomi-economy | Juli-July |
| Ustria-Austria | garasi-garage |
| lampu-lamp | variasi-variation |

Many English words are derived from other English words. *Ungovernable*, for example, consists of the parts *un-*, *govern*, and *-able*. If these parts are known then the learning burden of *ungovernable* is very light. Here are other words like this which have a light learning burden because their meaning can be predicted from the meaning of their known parts—*centralization*, *certainty*, *precedence*, *procedure*, *unwillingness*, *uphold*. Where possible, teachers should explain the meanings of words by using the meanings of their parts. We will look at this more closely in the chapter on vocabulary strategies.

A few English words sound like their meaning. This is called onomatapoeia! Here are some examples—*buzz*, *hiss*, *burp*, *cluck*, *clap*(?). Unfortunately speakers of other languages do not always agree about these sounds. English hens *cluck*, but Chinese hens *kuku*, and Indonesian hens *ketuk*!

It is unusual for the meaning of a word in one language to correspond exactly to the meaning of its equivalent in another. In the same way words which are similes in one language rarely have exactly the same meaning. However, if there is a large amount of overlap in meaning between an English word and a mother-tongue word, the learning burden will be light. For example, Thais learning the English word *pencil* will find that the meaning of the word corresponds quite closely to the meaning of a word in their mother tongue. Indonesians will find it even easier because it corresponds to their word *pensil*. The English word *remember*, however, has a heavier learning burden because its meaning does not overlap with a single mother-tongue word.

The learning burden associated with the concept of a word depends to a large degree on how it is taught. For example, the word *drag* is divided into four uses in the *General Service List* (West, 1953, p. 137).

| | |
|---|---|
| DRAG, v. 193    1. *(pull a heavy thing along)* | |
|     Dragging a great branch along | |
|     Dragging his foot | 51% |
|   2. *(figurative)* | |
|     There's no need to drag me into | |
|     the quarrel. | |
|     Why must you drag me out to a | |
|     concert on this cold night? | 22% |
|   3. *(intransitive, lag behind, move slowly and* | |
|     *laboriously)* | |
|     He dragged behind the others. | |
|     The meeting dragged on. | |
|     The play dragged a bit in the | |
|     third act. | 10% |
|   4. *(cause to move slowly)* | |
|     Drag out the meeting by long | |
|     speeches | |
|     Drag out his high notes | 6% |
|   [Drag the river, 1%] | |

These four uses, however, are clearly related to each other. In the first use, *drag a branch*, the important features are *pull* and *a heavy object*. In the second use, *drag me into the quarrel*, the idea of *pull* is still there but the heaviness has become *reluctance, unwillingness*. In the third use, *the meeting dragged on*, the idea of *pull* has become *to make longer* and *unwillingness* or *reluctance* remains. The fourth use has a similar meaning but different grammar. By drawing attention to the presence of *all* these features of meaning in whatever use of the word is being taught, the other uses of the word will be more readily learned. So, when teaching *drag a branch*, it is useful to point out how it is pulled and how the branch is heavy and "reluctant" to be moved along easily. If it is not easy to show how the various uses of a word are related to ideas that apply to all uses then the learning burden of the word is heavy. If the various uses can be related to common ideas the learning burden is lighter.

It should be clear from the above discussion of the learning burden of meaning that the teacher and course designer can play an important part in reducing the learning burden. This can be done by making use of lists of loan words, by drawing attention to word parts, and by drawing attention to the underlying concepts of words.

Visser (1989) developed an easily prepared activity for focusing attention on the underlying meaning of a word. Here is an example:

| | | |
|---|---|---|
| If you *release* a person or animal that has been in captivity, you set them free. | *Release* is a feeling that you have of no longer suffering or having to worry about something. | Say what the similar features/ideas are in Columns 1 and 2. |
| Give a reason why a prisoner might be released. | Describe a time when you have had a feeling of release. | |
| If people or things *saturate* a place or object, they fill it so completely that no more can be added. | If someone or something is *saturated*, they are extremely wet. | Say what the similar features/ideas are in Columns 1 and 2. |
| Describe what happens when cheap imported goods saturate the market. | Describe what can happen if you get saturated with sweat. | |

Learners work in small groups taking turns to do each part of the activity. The activity can easily be made by using definitions given in the CO-BUILD dictionary. Research on the technique shows that learners usually succeed in constructing an acceptable underlying meaning, process the information deeply, and are involved and interested in the activity.

**Associations**   The associations attached to a word affect the way that it is stored in the brain, and this will affect the availability of the word when it is needed. Psychologists investigate word association by asking people to suggest other words that a certain word brings to mind. For example, they say the word *table* and see what other words it makes people think of. The most common associate of *table* is *chair*. The most common associate of *boy* is *girl*. This does not mean that these words necessarily are commonly used together. It means that they are commonly associated in people's minds. If an English word shares similar associations with its translation in the mother tongue then these associations can be carried over. The little research that there is in this area, however, suggests that such transfer does not occur readily, and learners may have to develop associations for the English words they learn (Henning, 1973).

The types of associations between words will affect whether it will be helpful or harmful to teach associated words together (Higa, 1963). We will look at this in the following section on interference.

The reduction of the learning burden is dependent on the existence of predictable features from experience of either the mother tongue or English, and on the learners' attention being drawn to these features so that previous knowledge can be used. It is at this point that teaching can have benefits. Teaching, however, can increase the burden instead of reducing it. A "good" teacher can make learning more difficult by successfully teaching items that will upset previous learning or that will interfere with present learning. A good teacher can also be a good "unteacher" (George, 1962). We will look at this in the following section.

## "Unteaching"

The learning burden of a word can be affected by the way it is taught. This means that as a result of bad organization the difficulty of learning a word is increased. Unfortunately, this "unteaching" is common. We shall look at the causes of this difficulty under three headings: repetition and attention, relationship with other words, and exceptions.

*Repetition and Attention* Some psychologists (Craik & Lockhart, 1972; Craik & Tulving, 1975) believe that repetition is not an important factor in vocabulary learning. They believe that it is the type of attention that is given to an item which decides whether it will be remembered or not. Oral repetition of a word form is not an effective way of learning compared with having to recall the form of the word. Seeing the word form and a definition of its meaning is not as effective as having to make an effort to recall its meaning before being shown the definition as feedback. If the teacher does not use challenging ways to draw the learners' attention to a word then learning will be poor. If the learning is poor, the word will need to be repeated for learning to occur. There is evidence to show that there is a relationship between learning and repetition. Kachroo (1962) counted the number of repetitions of words in an English coursebook and tested his Indian learners to see what words were learned. He found that words that occurred seven or more times in the coursebook were known by most of the learners. Over half of the words occurring only once or twice in the books were not known by most of the class.

Salling (1959) found similar results, and he concluded that at least 5 repetitions were needed to ensure learning. Crothers and Suppes (1967), using more controlled experiments, found 6 or 7 repetitions to be necessary. Saragi et al. (1978), using a reading text where learners did not know that they had to learn the new vocabulary, found that 16 or more repetitions were necessary.

A study of the number of repetitions in various coursebooks for teaching English provides considerable cause for alarm (see Table 3.3).

In some courses, half of the different words occur only once and most of the words occur less than five times. In such courses the density index (the ratio of different words to total words, see Appendix 5) comes close to the density index of unsimplified English. Fortunately, there are exceptions.

It is important for teachers in countries where English is not used much outside the classroom to know whether they can rely on a coursebook to provide enough repetition for vocabulary learning to be possible. If the coursebook does not provide enough repetition it will be necessary to add to the number of repetitions provided by the book. Teachers can work together to check the repetition of vocabulary in their textbook and find the density index. The density index of a passage or a lesson or a book is the proportion of different words to the total number of words. If this proportion is high, reading is relatively easy. This is because in order to get a high density index many of the different words must be frequently repeated.

The density index of modern written English is usually of the ratio of 1:2.4. This means that *on an average* each word is repeated between two and three times. In fact, around 40 percent of the words will occur once and will not be repeated at all. Such material is not suited to vocabulary learning. If a word occurs once in a year's schoolwork there will be little chance that it will be learned. A coursebook with a density index of 1:2.4

Table 3.3   VOCABULARY REPETITION IN COURSEBOOKS

| Coursebook no. | Total words | Different words | Density index | Words occurring | | | | | | | | | | |
|---|---|---|---|---|---|---|---|---|---|---|---|---|---|---|
| | | | | 1 | 2 | 3 | 4 | 5 | 6 | 7 | 8 | 9 | 10 | 10+ |
| 1 | 2890 | 249 | 1:12 | 70 | 36 | 24 | 13 | 14 | 9 | 15 | 6 | 8 | 9 | 45 |
| 2 | 3585 | 904 | 1:3.96 | 457 | 174 | 81 | 35 | 29 | 21 | 16 | 13 | 10 | 9 | 59 |
| 3 | 2205 | 483 | 1:4.56 | 263 | 91 | 45 | 18 | 24 | 16 | 1 | 4 | 5 | 2 | 14 |
| 4 | 4307 | 153 | 1:28.15 | 13 | 4 | 10 | 9 | 5 | 4 | 3 | 8 | 4 | 4 | 89 |
| 5 | 1329 | 329 | 1:4.03 | 137 | 60 | 38 | 22 | 19 | 11 | 7 | 5 | 9 | 1 | 20 |
| 6 | 4105 | 200 | 1:20.52 | 15 | 22 | 8 | 17 | 13 | 8 | 7 | 3 | 11 | 7 | 89 |
| 7 | 9640 | 794 | 1:12.14 | 207 | 117 | 75 | 47 | 44 | 28 | 34 | 19 | 20 | 15 | 188 |
| 8 | 3491 | 197 | 1:17.72 | 21 | 13 | 10 | 16 | 10 | 9 | 7 | 10 | 3 | 17 | 81 |
| 9 | 8642 | 399 | 1:21.65 | 59 | 43 | 25 | 17 | 14 | 17 | 9 | 6 | 7 | 6 | 196 |
| 10 | 3523 | 718 | 1:4.90 | 349 | 115 | 60 | 41 | 31 | 18 | 19 | 17 | 4 | 8 | 56 |

or 1:4, which is the density index of spoken English, and with a large number of words occurring less than five or six times cannot be efficient.

If the coursebook does not provide enough repetition it may be necessary for teachers to keep their own word register of useful vocabulary. An efficient coursebook for the first year should have a density index of around 1:20 with a low number of "one-timers." In later years a density index of 1:10 or 1:12 might be enough.

If the teacher or coursebook does not provide opportunity for sufficient repetition or for attention to vocabulary which will result in learning, then the effort spent in dealing with the vocabulary will be wasted. Pimsleur (1967) suggests that repetitions should be spaced with increasing gaps between the repetitions. This means that the first repetitions should occur quite soon after the introduction of a new word. The next repetitions can be a day or more away, and the next a week or more, and so on.

Another important idea is that it is the old material in any lesson which is more important than the new material. The reason for this is that the old material has almost been mastered by the learners. If it is not repeated then it will be forgotten and all the previous work will be wasted. The new material, on the other hand, has not had a lot of time and effort spent on it. If no further attention is given to it, it will be forgotten, but not much previous time and effort will be wasted. It is therefore quite important for a teacher to keep a rough check on the vocabulary that needs to be established so that there are enough repetitions and not a lot of wasted effort and attention.

**Relationship with Other Words**   Similarities between words can make learning easier. Knowing *meaning* and *hopeful* can make the learning of *meaningful* easier. However, similarities between words can also make learning more difficult. Let us look at an example before looking at the general rule behind cases of interference. A common presentation of *long* and *short* is to teach them by contrast. The teacher demonstrates the meaning of *long* and then demonstrates the meaning of *short*. If the learners are Samoan, for example, then what they need to learn is that the association *long* means "umi" and the association *short* means "puupuu." This is shown in Figure 3.3. Experience shows, however, that

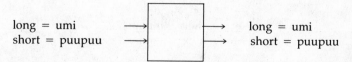

long = umi
short = puupuu

long = umi
short = puupuu

**Figure 3.3**   Output equals input.

this is not what happens. Figure 3.4 is closer to what happens (George, 1978, pp. 9–10).

This means that some learners will make the correct associations and some will cross-associate the word forms and their meanings. That is, some learners will think that *long* means "puupuu" and *short* means "umi." Why does this cross-association occur? The general rule is that when two associated items share similar features but are also different in some way, the similar features will strengthen the association and the differences will interfere with each other. *Long* and *short* share the following similar features: (1) They are presented at the same time; (2) they both describe length (opposites characteristically share a similar feature of meaning); (3) the teacher uses similar actions, pictures, or objects to convey their meaning. These similarities encourage the association of the two words. *Long* and *short* are different in the following ways: (1) *Long* means "umi" and *short* means "puupuu," (2) *long* is spelled and pronounced differently from *short;* that is, they are two different word forms.

By teaching these two words together, the teacher has made the words twice as difficult to learn. The learners have to learn that *long* means "umi" and *short* means "puupuu," and in addition they have to remember that *long* does not mean "puupuu" and *short* does not mean "umi." The difficulty of keeping the two items separate (not cross-associated) has been added to the difficulty of learning the correct associations.

There is experimental evidence to support this. Higa (1963) investigated the effect of various meaning relationships among mother-tongue words on the learning of a list of nonsense syllables. Higa compared six different types of relationships with a control list of unrelated words. Higa found that lists of words that were strongly associated with each other—for example, opposites and free associates—were much more difficult to learn than the list of unrelated words. Lists of loosely or indirectly related words were easier to learn than the control list of unrelated words.

So far we have looked at two sources of evidence for the negative effect of teaching opposites together. The most convincing evidence for a teacher, however, should be what happens in the classroom. It is easy to see cross-association occur by doing the following simple experiment. First, teach five or six pairs of opposites in the usual way. Second, move

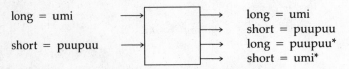

**Figure 3.4**  Cross association.

on to a quite different piece of work like reading or dictation. Third, after 20 minutes of this activity, which has nothing to do with the opposites you have just taught, give the learners a translation test of the opposites you have taught. Say the words—for example, *long, hot, heavy, short,*—and ask the learners to write their meaning in the mother tongue. Finally, collect the answers and look for the examples of cross-association. Usually 25 percent of the words will have been cross-associated.

How can cross-association be avoided? We have seen from the general rule that the more similar the items are, the more likely they are to be closely associated in the mind of the learners. By reducing the similarity between the items, cross-association can be avoided. First, teach opposites and other strongly associated items separately, that is, weeks or months apart. Usually one member of a pair of opposites is an unmarked form, is more frequent, and is easier for the brain to process (George, 1972, pp. 15–18). According to West (1953), *long* occurs 4001 times in 5 million words, *short* occurs 1168 times. There is another argument for teaching members of a pair of opposites separately.

> Teachers should avoid presenting opposites for two reasons: 1 To the effort of learning the two items is added the effort of keeping distinct the two items and their associated meanings. It is much more efficient to teach one of the items alone, and only later, when this first item is established, introduce the second—when necessary. 2 Teaching "opposites" gives a false and undersirable picture of the world. The real opposite of *rich* is *not rich;* the real opposite of *poor* is *not poor.* Obviously, very many people are not rich, and not poor. Similarly, very many places are not hot, and not cold. In the real world, people are not divided into good and bad, right and wrong. It is no business of the English course to teach a propagandist's view of the world and existence in it. (George, 1978, p. 10)

It is best not to teach the second item of a pair until the first item has been learned thoroughly. Second, the similarity between items can be reduced by using different contexts, pictures, or objects for conveying the meaning of the items. Using the same visual aid for teaching several related items is economical for the teacher but not for the learners.

So far we have looked at items which are associated in meaning. Similar problems can occur with formal relationships. By accident when I was learning Indonesian I learned *bintang* (star) and *binatang* (animal) at the same time, and I had great difficulty remembering which was which. Finally, I had to use the mnemonic device of remembering that *binatang* had an extra *a* for *animal* to keep them separate. Imagine learners' (and this includes native speakers') difficulty in keeping separate two words which are related in both form and meaning—for example, *deductive* and *inductive, principle* and *principal,* and *affect* and *effect.* Because they are associated in the teacher's or course designer's brain, they are presented together and are not learned. There would be a greater chance of success if they were learned separately.

**Exceptions**   Most rules have exceptions. Words like *of, yacht,* and *blood* are exceptions to useful spelling rules. Constructions like *going to school* and *road works* are exceptions to useful grammatical rules. The effect of teaching exceptions is to make the learning of the rule more difficult. For example, the words *school* and *town* are most often used as countable nouns. Singular countable nouns are usually preceded by *a, the,* or a similar word like *my, this, John's* or *each.* Every time learners notice a word which is usually countable but which does not have *a, the,* or a similar word in front of its singular form, the learning of the very useful rule is made more difficult. So, teaching sentences like *He is going to town, She is going to school* is upsetting the learning of the rule about singular countable nouns and is encouraging the production of sentences like *\*She is going to house, \*He is going to cinema.* Exceptions are called exceptions because they do not follow the rule. The teacher needs to consider which is more important, the learning of the rule or the learning of the exceptions. Exceptions should not be introduced until the rule has been learned. The early introduction of exceptions is a clear example of unteaching.

## Intrinsic Difficulty

So far we have looked at how the learning burden can be affected by predictability or regularity of patterning, and by the organization of learning. The learning burden of a word can also be affected by features of the word itself. Rodgers (1969) found that the part of speech of a word affected its learning. Nouns were the easiest to learn, and adjectives were next. Verbs and adverbs were the most difficult to learn. This finding partly agrees with experience in guessing words from context. Nouns and verbs are usually easier to guess than adjectives and adverbs. Learners discover the part of speech of a word by looking at the part of speech of its mother-tongue translation.

Whether words are learned to be recognized (receptively) or to be produced (productively) affects their difficulty. It is easier to learn to recognize a word form and recall its meaning than it is to learn to produce the word at suitable times. Rough estimates indicate that learning a word productively is 50 to 100 percent more difficult than learning it receptively. An experiment by Stoddard (1929) found that if words were tested receptively, the results were better if the pairs had been learned receptively rather than productively. That is to say, the extra effort involved in learning words productively did not result in better receptive learning. Words which are needed only for listening and reading are best not learned productively.

Higa (1965), in his excellent discussion of vocabulary learning difficulty, includes *simple versus complex* and *codability* as features of intrinsic difficulty. In our survey these have been included under the learners' previous experience because they are both affected by correspondences between English and the mother tongue. The features listed under intrinsic difficulty are not readily affected by teacher and learner behavior.

Let us summarize the factors affecting the learning burden and bring together the ways of reducing it.

1. Learners' previous experience of English and their mother tongue affects the amount of transfer that they can make from this to their present learning. The more regular and predictable the relationship between past and present learning, the greater the opportunity for transfer to occur. Similarly, the more the teacher or the course designer draws attention to the similarities and patterns, the greater the opportunity for transfer. For this reason, knowledge of the learners' mother tongue and a knowledge of the linguistic features of English are of benefit to a teacher.

2. Teaching can have three effects, positive, neutral, and negative. When its effect is positive, the learners move one step closer to a mastery of English. When the effect of teaching is neutral, nothing is learned. When the effect of teaching is negative, learning occurs, but this learning will upset what has been taught before, what is being taught at the same time, or what will be taught in the future. Teaching which has a negative effect is far worse than teaching which has a neutral effect. Negative teaching (unteaching) can be reduced by careful consideration of the effect one item will have on another. More specifically, opposites and other items which have a close form or meaning similarity should not be taught together. One should be well learned before the related item is introduced. In addition, careful thought should be given to the introduction of exceptions. Each exception unteaches the rule.

3. A teacher cannot do a great deal about intrinsic difficulty caused by the part of speech and the need for receptive or productive learning, except to be aware of these sources of difficulty and to recognize their effect.

## APPLICATION

1. Describe the learning burden of the following words: *suggest, kid* (child), *extradite, blackboard, yacht, mirror, tick* (✔), *radio*. Here is an example for you.

*person*   The spelling and pronunciation of this word follows regular patterns. It is a countable noun, but this may be predictable. There are no unusual collocates. Frequency and appropriateness are not a problem. The meaning of the word is not predictable from its form, so this will need the most attention.

2. Look at these collocations. Decide on the predictability of each collocation on a scale of 1 to 3. Use mother-tongue collocations and collocations with semantically related words (substitutes and opposites) as a check.

| | |
|---|---|
| live coverage | spend time |
| widely differing | a poor response |
| a hazardous mission | give advice |
| his membership lapsed | break a promise |
| make a suggestion | deadly dull |
| your full name | |

3. Think of some vocabulary errors that your learners make. Analyze the learning burden of the word involved to see if you can see the reasons for the errors. Here are two examples for you.

It is difficult to remember every *vocabulary*.

I enjoy walking through the garden and *watching* the surroundings.

# Chapter 4

# Communicating Meaning

This chapter looks at meaning from the viewpoint of communication theory and concept formation. It makes the point that learning the meaning of a word involves knowing the features of meaning that are present in all uses of the word. It describes ways of defining the meaning of a word, and shows how learners can be encouraged to give effort and attention to learning word meanings.

## THE TEACHING OF MEANING

The meanings of words can be communicated or taught in many different ways. The following list includes most of the possibilities.

By demonstration or pictures

1. using an object
2. using a cut-out figure
3. using gesture
4. performing an action
5. photographs
6. blackboard drawings or diagrams
7. pictures from books

By verbal explanation

8. analytical definition
9. putting the new word in a defining context
10. translating into another language

These techniques are only ways of teaching the meaning of words. This is apparent if we look at the teaching of meaning from the viewpoint of communication theory (see Figure 4.1).

In vocabulary teaching the information source may be the teacher's brain. The transmitter can be many things—for example, the teacher's voice (if giving a verbal explanation), the teacher's hands (if drawing or pointing to a picture), the teacher's body (if giving a demonstration), a

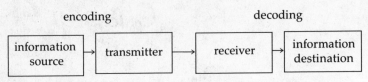

**Figure 4.1**  The communication process.

real object (if the teacher shows it to the class). Unless the teacher changes the meaning that is in his or her brain (the information source) into something that can be perceived (via the transmitter), no communication (and thus no learning) can take place. This changing, or encoding, is usually an unsatisfactory process. Indeed, it is one of the weaknesses of all communication. We know what we want to say, but we cannot say it exactly and clearly. It is difficult to find an exact correspondence between the idea in our head and a way of expressing it. Direct communication from brain to brain (from information source to information destination) is ideal but does not normally occur. Instead, we must be satisfied with indirect communication through the intermediaries of the transmitter and receiver, and the processes of encoding and decoding.

Thus, the meaning of a word exists only at the information source and the information destination. This meaning can be perceived by someone else only if it is encoded. The encoding usually results in something not exactly the same as the meaning. Our idea of a chair and a real chair are not the same. A particular example of a chair—for example, the one I am sitting on now—is brown. It is made of wood. It has two arms. These features are irrelevant for the idea of a chair. Chairs need not be made of wood, be brown, and have two arms. A real chair is probably a bad example of the idea (or meaning) of a chair for teaching purposes because the real chair has so many distracting features that are not essential to the idea of a chair. For the teacher, a real chair is an encoding of the idea of a chair.

If we wish, we can use the word *translation* instead of *encoding*. A real chair is a *translation* of the idea of a chair into something that can be seen. If the teacher describes a chair, that description is a translation of the idea of a chair into something that can be heard or read. We can translate the idea of a chair in many ways. We can translate it into a real chair, gestures with our hands, a drawing, a photograph, a description in English, or a description or word in the learner's mother tongue. A translation into the mother tongue represents the same processes as translation into a picture, a description in English, and so on.

Some people criticize translation into the mother tongue as a way of communicating or teaching meaning. Their objections are generally like this (see, for example, the introduction to Hill, 1965):

1. There is usually no exact correspondence between one language and another.
2. Translation into the mother tongue is indirect.
3. The use of the mother tongue takes time which could better be spent in using English.

All of these criticisms are true. But they can also be applied to the use of pictures, drawings, demonstration, and the use of real objects. For example, a picture for one group of learners does not always have the same meaning as it does for the teacher. The use of a picture to convey meaning is indirect because it requires decoding. Time spent using pictures could be better spent in using English. So, if translation in the narrow sense of translation into the mother tongue has no place in the classroom, then translation in the broad sense of encoding also has no place in the classroom, and this is clearly absurd.

At the beginning of this chapter there is a list of the many ways of communicating meaning. Is any one better than the others? Let us take an example. *Fork* is a useful English word. Its meaning can be communicated by showing a real fork, showing a picture of a fork, drawing a fork, explaining what a fork is, putting the word in a context, or translating the word into the mother tongue. For the word *fork*, translation into the mother tongue is unsatisfactory because in most Asian languages the mother-tongue word will refer only to a fork used for eating, and perhaps to the fork of a bicycle. A picture of a fork and a real fork are just as limiting. They will not include a fork in the road or a fork in a branch. Perhaps the most suitable translation for *fork* is a drawing like this ─C . This most closely approximates the idea of a fork that native speakers of English have. Certainly it fits most of the uses of *fork* in English.

It is apparent that other ways of communicating the meaning will be more suitable for other words. There is no rule that one type of encoding is better than another. Each has to be considered on its merits. How well does it translate the idea in the information source?

## CONCEPTS

Let us now look at the teaching of meaning from a slightly different point of view. We can distinguish the concept of a word from particular uses of the word. For example, our concept of the words *a person* is not the same as particular persons. Our concept of *person* is a generalization and abstraction from our experience of many persons. Color of skin, color of hair, and age are not criterial features of *person*. So if we want learners to understand the concept of *person* we should help them ignore these features. In the case of *person* this is easily done by presenting the learners with several examples of persons and helping them to see what is the same in all these examples. There are several conditions which help the establishment of concepts (Carroll, 1964). First, there need to be positive examples of the concept. Second, there need to be negative examples. That is, the learners are shown things that are not persons and they are told that these are not persons. Third, these positive and negative examples need to be arranged in the best way for learning. We can test to see if a concept is learned in the following ways.

1. We can present the learners with several examples, and we can see if they can tell which are examples of the concept (positive examples) and which are not (negative examples).
2. We can ask the learners to describe the important features that make up the concept. For example, we can see if they tell us that a person is human, male or female . . .
3. We can ask learners to translate the English word into the mother tongue. This is not a useful way of testing knowledge of a concept if the English concept is not like a mother-tongue concept.

The learn-and-test exercises described at the end of this chapter provide useful ways of checking.

Let us look at an example of teaching the concept of *produce*. It is taken from Barnard (1980, p. 78).

---

Farms *produce* grain and vegetables, milk and eggs, butter and cheese. Some farmers only produce grain. Canada pr_____es large quantities of grain. The earth p_____s many different kinds of plants. Factories p_____ce various things; some factories p_____ machines, others p_____ automobiles, others p_____ soap, others p_____ shoes. Poets p_____ poems.

The cows on Mr. Green's farm p_____ce 200 gallons of milk a day; his hens produce 400 eggs a day. The new factory produces 30,000 bicycles a year.

Nowadays furniture is mainly p_____ed by machinery; fifty years ago it was mainly p_____ed by hand.

When a farm, or a field, or a country, or a factory, or a cow, or a man produces something, it (or he) brings that thing into existence or causes it to exist—either by making it or growing it.

We use the verb produce when we think of the thing resulting from our work or actions, or even from natural causes.

---

The previous example used an inductive approach (*in-* = in, *-duct-* = to lead). This means that the examples of particular meanings were given first and then the concept was described. The process is called inductive because the examples *lead* the learner *in* to the concept. The following example, also from Barnard (1980, p. 70), uses a deductive approach to teach *solve*. The learners are given the concept and they are *led away* from the concept to the examples.

---

We *solve* a problem when we find the answer to it.

*Examples:* The problem of determining the speed of light was not s_____ed until the twentieth century. There are some mathematical problems which have never been s_____d. To s_____e this problem, special measuring instruments will be needed. His teacher gave him ten problems to do, and he s_____d all of them in twenty minutes.

---

The choice between inductive and deductive approaches to teaching meaning depends on which approach will suit a particular word and where the teacher wants to direct the learners' attention. Some words are difficult to define satisfactorily, so an inductive approach is the most suitable. The word *ticket* is like this. An inductive approach to teaching allows the teacher to repeat the form of the word many times while the learners give it their close attention. In the *What is it?* technique for example, the teacher says sentences containing the new word. The learners listen to the sentences and try to find a mother-tongue translation of the word. The teacher carefully chooses the examples so that the learners have to listen to several sentences and hear the new word many times before they are able to guess the meaning. So, an inductive approach allows repetition of the word and encourages the learners to make an effort to get the meaning.

A deductive approach communicates the meaning quickly and allows the teacher to arrange controlled practice for collocations of the word. In addition, the learners can have an opportunity to test their knowledge by suggesting their own examples.

The important points to get from the previous examples are these:

1. An example of the meaning of a word is different from the concept of a word. To find the concept we must see several examples.
2. In order to know the boundary of a concept we should see several positive examples and some negative examples. It is useful to have both positive and negative examples, but it is best to have more positive examples than negative examples (Carroll, 1964, p. 190).
3. We can test the understanding of a concept in several ways. Good vocabulary teaching techniques should include an opportunity for testing so that the teacher and the learner can get information about the progress of the learning.
4. Concepts can be learned inductively or deductively.


## DEFINITIONS

To define a word is to show or explain its meaning. An adequate definition of a word shows its meaning (as distinct from the meanings of other words), its whole meaning (insofar as this is possible for a first presentation), and nothing but its meaning. In other words, it names or points to the features which belong to this concept as distinct from others, it gives some indication of the range of situations to which the symbol can refer, and it makes the boundaries of a concept clear.

An adequate definition indicates (1) the grammatical function of the word, a noun, a verb, an adjective, etc.; (2) the typical sentence patterns in which the word enters; (3) other formal aspects of the word—e.g., countable, uncountable, irregular past forms, irregular plurals.

Some words have a considerable range of meaning, which any good dictionary will illustrate, e.g., the word *hard:*

He works hard.

Yesterday it rained hard.

This road does not have a hard surface.

He is a hard taskmaster.

He is a hard worker.

The problem is too hard for me.

It is a hard winter.

She is hard of hearing.

Why are you so hard on him?

She is a hardheaded business woman.

When a single word has various meanings, a teacher must decide where to draw the line—i.e., which meaning or set of meanings is so different from the others that it needs to be taught as a separate word. Of course, the teacher may decide that the meanings of a word are not sufficiently distinct to need such separation. Not all teachers will make the same decision.

Suppose the teacher decides that *hard* is basically three different words (one adverb and two adjectives: i.e., "difficult", and "hard" as opposed to "soft"). The next decision is which word to teach and define first. Both tasks require careful inspection of the range of meanings associated with the word form. The following considerations are relevant.

**Grammatical Function**   Different parts of speech should usually be taught separately because they occur in differing sentence patterns, but they need not be widely separated in a course if their meanings are very similar.

**Links Between Areas of Meaning**   (or overlapping features between two different areas of meaning) The teacher should decide which features of the conceptual range give greatest opportunity for extension into other meanings and should probably teach these basic or central features first.

**Possible Interference Between Areas of Meaning**   A *hard worker* should not be taught along with *a hard surface,* because learners may infer that a hard worker (like a strong surface) is strong. Misunderstanding cannot so easily arise with *a hard problem* if it is taught soon after *a hard surface;* the association helps, because the teacher can explain that a hard surface is difficult to break and a hard problem is difficult to solve.

**Usefulness**   The teacher must decide which meanings out of the range the learners need most, and which meanings are needed as defining vocabulary.

**Frequency**   Other things being equal, the meanings in the range which occur most frequently should be taught first. The *General Service List* (West, 1953) gives this information.

We usually speak of *a* definition of a word, not *the* definition. We do this because there are several possible definitions to most words. Also there are various kinds of definitions; some words are best defined in one way, and some words in another.

## Definition by Demonstration

This kind of definition is associated with what is often called the "direct method." When we define words by demonstration we try to show their meaning without using other words; we point to things:

Draw on the blackboard
Use simple pictures
Do simple actions

This kind of definition is useful especially as a beginning for

Objects in the classroom
Objects which can easily be brought into the classroom
Colors (when using the guessing method to teach colors, they are also being demonstrated)
Certain actions which are easy to identify (e.g., catch, throw)
Certain adverbs (slowly, quickly, loudly, softly)

For many words this kind of definition is quite unsuitable (e.g., *expect, a purpose*), and some words which can be demonstrated cannot be defined by demonstration alone, while in many other cases definition by demonstration is likely to cause misunderstanding. We cannot be sure that our learners interpret the things we are pointing to or the actions we are demonstrating in the way that we want them to. For example, we may demonstrate *suddenly* by a series of actions which the learners will interpret merely as *quickly* performed.

We can help our learners to grasp the concept by varying the situation in which it is demonstrated, and by giving a verbal definition as well as the nonverbal one.

## Definition by Abstraction (Analytical Definition)

In this sort of definition we try to find the most important ideas which the word contains. We examine the different parts or elements of the meaning of the word. When we look at the elements of meaning of the word, we say that we analyze the word—that is, take it to pieces to find out what it is made of. So this kind of definition is called an analytical definition. We can also say we analyze the concept by abstracting (separating out) and stating its basic features, so we can also call these definitions "definitions by abstraction." For example, a thing is *simple* if it is unmixed, or not divided into parts, or has very few parts, or is not highly developed, or is very easy to learn to do.

Each word in a language has one or two main ideas which are accepted by everybody, and we try to mention these ideas when giving a definition by abstraction.

Even when a definition of this kind is accurate, clear, and complete, learners will not understand, let alone remember it, unless there are examples as well. As a teaching technique it is often better to guide the learners through a number of examples (see Contextual Definitions) until they can make a "definition by abstraction" for themselves. Until our learners have grasped the abstraction—i.e., what the examples have in common—they have not really grasped the concept.

A teacher must be sure of the concept before helping a learner to grasp it. This sort of definition is a good example of the theory that "you can only teach someone something when they know it already." It is impossible to define or describe something which is *totally* strange to the learners.

Can you choose the two most important elements of meaning in the word *to attract?*

| | | |
|---|---|---|
| need | to pull | notice |
| to push | pleasure | to imagine |

The answers required are *to pull* and *notice*. Then we are given two sentences. To attract something to something is to pull or draw it toward you; for example, a light *attracts* moths. If you *attract* attention, people will notice you.

or

Give the two words from the following list which are included in the meaning of *balance*.

| | | | |
|---|---|---|---|
| ready | heavy | steady | round |
| thin | nervous | normal | equal |

The words *steady* and *equal* are the basic elements of meaning. Things which are held in *balance* remain *steady* or unmoving because they are equal in weight or force.

This sort of little test is useful when your learners nearly know the meaning of the word. The list of alternatives is hard to make up, but doing so is good practice for the teacher!

Never try to define by starting:

The meaning of _____ is _____ or _____
means _____ .

These are hopeless beginnings and usually produce very poor sentences which are incorrect. A definition of a verb can begin with a "when" clause—for example:

When we expect something to happen, we believe it will happen, we think it will probably happen.

Note that definitions of verbs about thinking, feeling, believing and other mental concepts always need to be supported by contextual definitions.

A definition of an adverb can begin with an adverb and must show a typical position of the adverb in a sentence—for example:

When something happens that we do not expect, and it happens so quickly that it surprises us, it happens *suddenly;* when people do something we do not expect and when they do it so quickly that it surprises us, they do it *suddenly.*

Note that this is a definition in limited vocabulary. It can be given only after the words *expect, surprise*, and *quickly* have been established. It should be combined with contextual definitions.

A definition of an adjective can take the form of "A _____ person is a person who _____" or "An _____ book is a book which _____." The noun used should be typical of the class of nouns to which the adjective applies.

Definition by abstraction should always take the form of complete sentences. When the typical position of the word in sentences needs to be learned, the definition of the word should be quickly followed by a substitution table or some form of exercise which will assist this learning. Scholfield (1980) describes a set of practical principles for explaining meaning by paraphrase. The COBUILD dictionary (Sinclair, 1987) is an exciting attempt to use analytical definitions in a sentence context.

## Contextual Definitions

These are very useful for teaching purposes. They are more natural than any other kind of definition because it is through the contexts of words that we learn most about their meanings. Remember that some linguists claim that meaning is use. We also know that the meaning of a word is spread over that word and the neighboring words.

The word *context* comes from a Latin word *texture*—to weave, and the prefix *con-* —with. This sort of definition is particularly useful because people can acquire meaning for a formerly meaningless sound from other words that they see and hear at or about the same time as the new word.

A contextual definition does not directly explain the meaning of a word but encourages learners to make an effort and find out the meaning by seeing how the word is used (its grammar) and with what other words it is associated. It is important to find contexts where the word occurs naturally.

*Advanced English Vocabulary,* by Helen Barnard (1972), makes a lot of use of contextual definitions. Here is an example.

---

*a factor*—a countable noun

The quality of the soil is one *factor* which helps people decide whether to use a piece of land for agricultural purposes.

The rapid rise in the world's population is the result of various *factors*.

An important *factor* in his decision to take the job was the large salary offered.

The economic development of a country depends mainly on these *factors:* its natural resources, its human resources, and its industrial resources.

---

After the learners look at the sentences, you can ask them to select a definition from several alternatives. Do not ask them to give the definition themselves right away. It would be too soon after meeting the word in the sentences. Do not ask your learners, "What does _____mean?" until you are sure they know.

Teachers should vary the contexts in which their learners see and hear new words and should make sure that they meet them often enough to grasp the meaning themselves. You cannot rely on the textbook. Contextual definitions can be added to, where necessary, by definitions abstracting the basic features of the concept.

Mentioning typical examples is another type of contextual definition. It is similar to definition by demonstration, except that we mention examples instead of pointing to them or acting them. The learners have to work as well because they have to try to find out what the examples given have in common. For example:

*A dog, an elephant, a bird, and a snake are animals.*
*Wellington, Tokyo, and London are cities.*

Any definition will not often be understood without examples, but it is also true that examples are seldom sufficient to define a concept. Except in very obvious cases, something else must be done to show or to elicit from the learners what it is that is common to the examples given.

## Definition by Translation

This kind of definition may be used to save time, if the concepts in English and the learners' mother tongue are the same. If it is used very much it will reduce the learners' experience of English in the class, and it will encourage them to make false equations between concepts in English and in their mother tongue.

Translation into the mother tongue, however, has certain features that can be used by the teacher to the learners' advantage.

1. Translation can be done quickly. This is a disadvantage if the teacher wants to spend time on a word so that the learners will be sure to remember it. The speed of translation is an advantage, however, if the teacher wants to pass quickly over an unimportant word in a reading text. By giving the meaning quickly, using translation, the teacher has satisfied the learners and has avoided spending too much time on an unimportant word.

2. Translation is not limited, as are pictures and objects, to nouns, adjectives, and verbs. It can be used to explain many different types of words.

3. The teacher can ask the learners to respond by using translation to see if they have understood something which was presented in another way. Except where the teacher provides a multiple-choice list of definitions or pictures, there is not really any other way in which the learners can respond freely, quickly, and easily to show they have understood something.

It is true that the use of translation as a way of teaching meaning has its drawbacks. It is usually too quick, it takes away time that could have been used to expose the learners to English, and often there are not exact equivalents of English words in the mother tongue.

However, translation shares these drawbacks with other ways of conveying meaning. It is necessary to look at translation as just one of many similar ways of presenting meaning. By careful use of translation in suitable teaching techniques many of these drawbacks can be avoided.

The exclusion of the mother tongue from the classroom as a way of communicating meaning robs the teacher of one useful technique of encoding. It also leaves the learners to make their own uncontrolled and often incorrect translations. It is worth mentioning two other possible effects. Exclusion of the mother tongue is often seen by the learners as a criticism of the mother tongue as a language, thus making it seem like a "second-class" language. The effects of this degrading of the mother tongue are not beneficial to the mother tongue nor to the people who use it. Second, learning a foreign or second language provides an opportunity for learning about the nature of language, how a language works, how different languages organize the world and experience in different ways. Comparison between the mother tongue and the foreign language is a good way of doing this.

The type of definition given by a teacher should depend on:

1. the word being defined and what is involved in defining it adequately.
2. the importance of the word, and the extent to which the learners need it in their vocabulary.
3. the words that are available to define it.
4. the learners' age, interest, and sophistication.
5. the need for variety in presentation.

It is usually best to combine two or more types of definition—for example:

A definition by abstraction combined with contextual examples.

A contextual definition followed by a definition by abstraction.

A definition by demonstration combined with contextual examples or (where possible) definition by abstraction.

A contextual definition followed by translation.

## COMMUNICATING MEANING AND REMEMBERING THE MEANING

So far we have looked at ways of communicating the meaning of a word quickly and clearly. However, in order for learning to last, the learner must make an effort. The best way to make sure a learner forgets a word is for the teacher to present a short, clear explanation of the meaning and then pass on to the next piece of work. If the teacher's aim is to get the learners to remember the word form and its meaning, then it is useful to find ways of holding the learners' attention and encouraging them to make an effort. The following groups of techniques use different ways to challenge the learners and to encourage them to make an effort.

1. Teach-and-test exercises make the learners think about new words. The new words are taught using pictures, definitions, and similar aids. Then, soon after the teaching, they are tested by a different method. So, if the words were taught using pictures, then they are tested using opposites or definitions. If they were taught using definitions, they can be tested by asking the learners to put them in sentences that have a word missing, and so on. For example, the teacher does an action to show the meaning of a word that has been written on the blackboard or is in the learners' books. The teacher then checks by asking the learners to use translation, pictures, or description to show the meaning. This can also be used as review. When the teacher does the action, the learners must guess the right word. Learners often enjoy taking the teacher's place for this exercise.

Here is another type of teach-and-test technique. The teacher explains the meaning of the new word and then asks questions which use the new word. The learners answer the questions. This makes them think about the meaning of the new word, and their answers show if they understand or not. So, if the new word is the noun *patient*, the teacher can ask,

"Who does a patient go to see?"

"Is a patient a well person?"

"Have you ever been a patient? What happened to you?"

Other kinds of tests can be used too. They can also be used for review at a later time. Here are true/false statements testing *a carpenter*.

A carpenter takes care of people's teeth.

A carpenter often works with wood.

A carpenter uses many tools.

Here are some multiple-choice items.

go head first into water     a. conquer

b. urge

c. dive

d. refer

dive         a. go to a person for information
                 b. move backward and forward
                 c. go head first into water
                 d. make a small hole

He walked out on the board to _____ into the water.

**a.** conquer
**b.** urge
**c.** dive
**d.** refer

2. Some techniques hold the learners' attention because they have to use various clues to try to get the meaning which is partly hidden from them. The most useful of these techniques is the *What is it?* technique (Nation, 1978). In this technique the learners use information from a context to find the meaning. In other similar techniques the information may come from seeing, hearing, or touching. In all these techniques part of the information is hidden. Here are some examples. Some will be good only for young learners.

(a) A real object is covered or wrapped in cloth or paper or is in your pocket. While you repeat the new word, the learners must try to guess, by touching or looking, what the object is. When the exercise is used for review, you do not say the name of the object.

(b) Some learners have their eyes covered with a piece of cloth. They are given objects to hold in their hands and to feel. While they do this you tell them the name of each object. You repeat the names as often as possible while the learners are touching the objects. Then the objects are put on the table, and the learners' eyes are uncovered. You say the names of the objects, and the learners must point to the correct objects. This checks that the learners guessed the objects correctly when their eyes were covered. You can get more repetitions by saying the words again very quickly while the learners point. Then you can ask other learners to come out and point while you say the names.

(c) Instead of showing an object to the class or describing it, you ask the learners to close their eyes. You make a noise with the object by hitting it or rubbing it. You also say the name of the object in English. This name is a new word for the learners. The learners have to guess what it is by listening to the sound it makes. You check by asking the learners to translate, to point to a picture, or to choose the object from a group of objects.

**Figure 4.2**                    **Figure 4.3**

When this is used for review, the learners listen and say the English name. A tape recorder can be used to bring some sounds into the classroom. The learners listen and guess.

(d) The learners' eyes are covered and you give cut-out shapes to the learners and say the English word. The learners try to guess the meaning of the word by feeling the cut-out shape. You check by asking the learners to translate, point to a picture, etc.

Words like *apple, ball,* the names of fruit, and the names of animals, all can be taught in this way. Their shapes can be cut out of cardboard or thin sheets of wood.

(e) When teaching a new word that can be taught by using a picture, you do not draw the picture. You draw some dots that give a rough guide to the picture. Then you say the new words while the learners try to connect the dots correctly to draw the picture and thus get the meaning. If a learner draws an incorrect line, you say, "No." If the line is correct, you say, "Good."

The dots for *a heart* are shown in Figure 4.2. The real picture is shown in Figure 4.3.

This exercise is easier and can be done as individual work if the dots are numbered in order and the name of the picture is written underneath, as in Figure 4.4.

(f) The *What is it?* technique (Nation, 1978) can be used to introduce new vocabulary. Let's imagine that you want to introduce the word *stirrup.* You may describe it as follows:

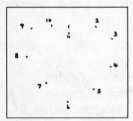

a heart
**Figure 4.4**

A stirrup is silver.

A stirrup is strong.

A stirrup is made of iron.

A stirrup has a flat bottom.

We can find a stirrup on a horse.

A stirrup is used to put your foot into when you ride a horse.

When you finish your description you tell the students to try to translate the word into their mother tongue. (If there is no roughly equivalent word in the mother tongue, they can draw a picture or point to one of several pictures that you may make available.)

While describing a stirrup, you repeat each sentence once or twice before going on to the next one. You also go back and repeat the previous sentences several times before you reach the end of the description. In this way the students will have heard the new word *stirrup* many times by the end of the description. They will also have listened with close attention because they want to discover what the new word means. Some teachers make the mistake of giving the meaning of new vocabulary too quickly. Once the students have been given the meaning of the word, they have no reason to pay attention any longer. Experiments on remembering (Jenkins, 1974) have shown that recalling the *form* of a word (its spelling or sound) is more difficult than recalling its *meaning*. For this reason, techniques that give the student an opportunity for repeated attention to a new word *before* discovering its meaning are important for vocabulary learning. If the learners are asked to translate *stirrup* after listening to the description, this is in some ways the same as a direct translation where the teacher says, "*Stirrup* in your mother tongue is _____." But the differences are important: Direct translation is quick; the *What is it?* technique, involving the describing of the object before the learners are asked to translate, wastes some *teaching time*, but it makes valuable use of *learning time*. By listening to the description, the learners have heard the new word several times, they have had to make an effort to get the meaning, and they have been active in telling the teacher what they think the translation should be.

The order of the sentences in the *What is it?* technique is important if the teacher wants to keep the meaning of the new word away from the learners for as long as possible. The following example shows how this may be done. This time the new word is a technical word used in botany. As the learners read the description, they make a note of the point at which they felt that they knew the common name for the technical word.

Brassicas are green.

Brassicas are made of leaves.

Brassicas have big leaves.

One costs about sixty cents.

We can find brassicas in most vegetable gardens.

Brassicas are round.

Brassicas are used for eating.

Many people cook brassicas before they eat them.

The students should not have been able to guess that the new word, *brassica*, referred to cabbages, cauliflowers, and similar vegetables until after they had read almost all of the sentences. So in constructing a *What is it?* exercise you should make sure that the first sentences do not provide too much information. In this way you can give the students an opportunity to meet the new word several times.

When the exercise is used for review, the teacher does not say the new word, but says "it" or just "mmm." For example:

It is usually in the town.

It is a big building.

The learners give the answer by telling the teacher what it is. Verbs, adjectives, adverbs, prepositions, and other parts of speech can all be taught in this way.

3. The following technique uses guessing among possible choices as its motivation. It is great fun.

You draw about 12 pictures on the blackboard. The learners do not know the English names for the pictures. A learner comes to the blackboard. While you repeat one of the new words, the learner tries to guess, by pointing, which picture is the right one. If the learner points to the wrong picture, you just repeat the word. When the learner points to the right picture, you say, "Yes." Then you say another word and the learner tries to point to the right picture. This continues until you have said all the words and the learner (or several learners) has correctly pointed to the right pictures. When some words have been guessed correctly, you should repeat them many times while the learner points. Each time, before you say a word that the learners have not tried to guess before, all the known words should be said again for review while the learner points.

It is good it if takes the learner a long time to point to the right picture, because then the teacher can repeat the new word many times (George, 1972). Instead of pictures, definitions can be written on the blackboard. Objects may also be used.

4. If the word contains a known prefix or stem, the teacher should explain the meaning of the word through an analytical definition using

the meaning of the prefix or stem. So, for example, if you explain *decay*, you should show the learners how it can be broken into *de-* and *-cay*, ask them for the meaning of *de-* (down), and then give a definition including the meaning of *de-* ("When a plant decays, its parts break *down*."). Teachers can easily develop this skill of explaining a word by including the meanings of its parts. It helps learning because the meaning of the new word is related to previously met items (the prefixes or stems). Chapter 10 has more information about this technique.

The idea behind the techniques in this section is that communication and learning are not the same. A teacher can communicate something clearly to the learners, but this does not mean that it will be learned. For learning to occur the learners must give their attention to the new material and make an effort to learn it.

## INVESTIGATING LEARNING

It is worthwhile making questioning strategies to investigate vocabulary learning. Feifel and Lorge (1950), for example, classified children's oral responses to questions about vocabulary.

> To illustrate some of the differences found in the qualitative responses given to the words of the Vocabulary Test by the younger and older children, a few typical definitions are listed below to the following words of the Test, i.e., "puddle," "tap," and "gown." To the word "puddle" the younger children responded with answers like the following: "a puddle of water," "mud," "what you step in," etc. The older children responded to the same word with definitions of the following kind: "a small pool of water," "water that gathers after a rain," etc. To the word "tap" the younger children gave replies of the following variety: "tap your foot," "tap on a door," demonstrated the action with their fingers or foot, etc. The older children gave definitions of the following kind to the same word: "a faucet," "a light knock," "kind of a rap," etc. To the word "gown" the younger children responded with definitions of the following type: "you wear it," "nightgown," "what you sleep in," etc. The older children responded with answers of the following kind: "an evening dress," "a long dress the women wear," "a beautiful dress you put on going to dances," etc.
>
> It should be cautioned, however, that no particular type of definition response is the exclusive possession of any specific age group, or, for that matter, any group. (Feifel & Lorge, 1950, p. 15)

Feifel and Lorge (pp. 4–5) used the following set of categories to classify the responses.

1. Synonym category

   |   |   |
   |---|---|
   | a. Synonym unmodified | Orange = a fruit |
   | b. Synonym modified by use | Straw = hay that cattle eat |
   | c. Synonym modified by description | Gown = long dress |
   | d. Synonym modified by use and description | Eyelash = hair over the eye that protects you |
   | e. Synonym qualified as to degree | Tap = touch lightly |

2. Use, description, and use and description category

   |   |   |
   |---|---|
   | a. Use | Orange = you eat it |
   | b. Description | Straw = it's yellow |
   | c. Use and description | Orange = you eat it and it's round |

3. Explanation category

   |   |   |
   |---|---|
   | a. Explanation | Priceless = it's worth a lot of money |
   |   | Skill = being able to do something well |

4. Demonstration, repetition, illustration, and inferior explanation category

   |   |   |
   |---|---|
   | a. Demonstration | For words like tap, eyelash |
   | b. Repetition | Puddle = a puddle of water |
   | c. Illustration | Priceless = a gem |
   | d. Inferior explanation | Scorch = hot |

5. Error category
   (Incorrect demonstration, misinterpretation, wrong definition, clang association, repetition without explanation, omits)

   |   |   |
   |---|---|
   | a. Incorrect demonstration | Eyelash = point to eyebrow |
   | b. Misinterpretation | Regard = protects something |
   | c. Wrong definition | Orange = a vegetable |
   | d. Clang association | Roar = raw; Skill = skillet |
   | e. Repetition without explanation | Puddle = puddle |
   | f. Omits | When the word is left out |

Feifel and Lorge (1950) found significant differences in the types of responses given by younger children as against those used by older children. The approach used by Feifel and Lorge could easily be adapted to provide us with information about how second language learners' knowledge of English develops. In such a study it would be useful to use several questions for each word tested to try to get as broad a picture as possible for the learners' knowledge of the word. These questions could include asking the meaning of the word, checking on related meanings and homonyms, asking about collocations and sociolinguistic implications, and asking about related word forms. Cohen and Hosenfield (1981) describe the application of similar types of investigation in other areas.

Russell and Saadeh (1962) investigated word meaning by using a multiple-choice technique. Each word tested had four choices. One choice gave a concrete definition, another a functional definition, another an abstract definition, and the fourth an incorrect definition. Here is an example based on the word *count*. The definitions in this example follow the order functional, concrete, abstract, incorrect.

> *count*    a. to find the number of things in a group
>               b. to find how many pennies are in your pocket
>               c. to say the numbers in order—upward or downward
>               d. to tell the numbers one after another

Their results were similar to those found by Feifel and Lorge (1950). A preference for abstract definitions was found with an increase in age.

Corson (1983) describes a test for measuring the breadth of knowledge that learners have of particular words. The learners are presented with the word to be tested plus another word which helps to limit the field of use of the word. Here are some examples. The underlined words are the ones being tested.

| | |
|---|---|
| approach | animal |
| branch | business |
| tap | wall |
| approach | problem |
| tap | knowledge |
| branch | medicine |

The learners have to make a sentence using the two words. The second word in each set is there to limit the meaning of the tested word. Corson used the test orally. This seems to be a very promising test for measuring quality of vocabulary knowledge. It would be wise to pretest the items to make sure that the second word in each set does its job properly.

With younger children, teachers can find out a great deal about how learners understand words by using pictures and objects. Learners can be asked to group pictures into sets ("put all the cups together"), to name pictures in a group, to describe the important features of a set of pictures, and to choose the best example of a particular item. Interesting work on this has been done with native speakers of English by Rosch et al. (1976) and Andersen (1975). By using the techniques described here, teachers can see how learners classify objects and distinguish various classes of objects.

Finally, careful observation of the results of learning in the classroom can provide valuable information for a teacher. Teachers of English as a foreign language particularly may be able to see the effect of teaching on learning if the English classroom is the only source of English for learners. Miller (1977) describes an interesting incomplete experiment with native-speaking children when a newly created word was deliberately introduced incidentally to see what learning would occur. Because Miller and his associates created the word themselves and kept a record of when they used it with the children, they were in a special position to see the effect on the children. Teachers of English as a foreign language should also try to see the effect of their teaching on learning and thus improve learning by changing what they do. Questions such as "What is the effect of teaching opposites together?" and "Can learners understand the meaning of derived words like *incapability* if they already know the meaning of the parts through having met them in different words?" can be answered by teachers giving careful and thoughtful attention to the effects of their teaching.

## APPLICATION

1. Your learners asked you to explain the following words. Three possible responses are given for each word. Choose the response you think is best (or make your own response if you do not like those given). The response you give would be supported by examples, so think what examples you would provide.

| GSL | *basin* | 1. a bowl for holding water, etc. |
| | | 2. a shape like this→ ⌣ |
| | | *3. a hollow place where water collects |
| | *run* | *1. move with quick steps |
| | | 2. go quickly, smoothly, or continuously |
| | | *3. hurry, rush |

*Oxford Advanced Learner's Dictionary of Current English.*

UWL             *transfer*         [+]1. move from one place to another

                                   2. carry goods, information, people, etc., across from one place to another

                                   [*]3. change position

                *exhaust*          [+]1. make very tired

                                   2. take everything out of something

                                   [*]3. use up completely

Low frequency   *punctilious*      [+]1. giving great attention to delicate point of form

                                   2. fussy

                                   [*]3. very careful to carry out correctly details of conduct and ceremony

                *kindle*           [+]1. make on fire

                                   2. start

                                   [*]3. rouse to a state of strong feeling

2. Find the concepts of the following words and decide on the best ways of communicating their meanings: *neck, wait, transport, corner, vegetable, agree.* Use your dictionaries.

3. Practice making simple definitions for some words that will be useful for your learners. Give more than one kind of definition for each word.

4. How would you test learners' understanding of the concepts of the following words: *complaint, dish, flesh, slip, weak?*

## Explaining Unknown Words

### Answers

*basin*   2 is the best choice because it comes nearest to the underlying concept of *basin* and includes most of the uses of the word, such as *a wash basin, a river basin, a pudding basin.*

*run*     2 is the best choice because it covers most of the frequent uses of *run*, such as *the girl ran, the road runs up a hill, run a business.*

[+] *General Basic English Dictionary.*

The meanings chosen for *basin* and *run* are based on the principle that we should explain the meaning of a word so that we reduce the number of different words in the language. That is, *run* in *the girl runs* and *run a business* is treated as one word, not two words.

transfer    2 is the best choice because the definition contains the meaning of the prefix *trans-*, i.e., across.

exhaust    2 is the best choice because the meaning of the prefix *ex-* (out, away) occurs in the definition "take everything out of something."

The meanings chosen for *transfer* and *exhaust* follow the principle that it is easier to remember the meaning of a word if its meaning or part of its meaning is related to the form or part of the form of the word.

punctilious    2 is the best choice if the learners know *fussy* because it is short and probably fits the context in which the word occurred. If the teacher wanted the learners to relate the word to *punctual*, *punctuate*, and *puncture*, then 1 is the best choice because it contains the meaning of *punct-* (point).

kindle    2 is the best choice because it is short and covers most uses of *kindle*, such as *kindle a flame*, *kindle a desire*.

The meanings chosen for *punctilious* and *kindle* follow the principle that low-frequency words should be dealt with as quickly as possible unless the teacher is focusing the learners' attention on a strategy for dealing with such words.

# Chapter 5

# Assessing Vocabulary Size

We ended the last chapter by looking at ways of investigating the quality of vocabulary knowledge. In the following chapters of this book we will look at vocabulary knowledge in relation to listening, speaking, reading, and writing, and it is useful to know how much vocabulary learners can draw on for each of these skills. At the beginning of the following chapters, vocabulary size goals are described. This chapter on assessing vocabulary size describes the various kinds of tests teachers can use to see what learners now know or what they have learned during a course. Applications of these tests are described in later chapters.

## MEASURING TOTAL VOCABULARY SIZE

The two most commonly used ways of investigating vocabulary size involve the use of a dictionary or a frequency count. In the dictionary method, the investigator randomly chooses words from the dictionary. One method would be to choose the second word on every tenth page of the dictionary, depending, of course, on how many words were needed for the test. The learners are tested on these words. Various types of tests could be used with second language learners—for example:

Multiple choice tests, all in English

*a tome*       1. a rough split
              2. a pain in the back
              3. a large, heavy book
              4. a type of horse

Multiple-choice tests using the mother tongue

*a tome*       1. sakit perut
              2. alat masak
              3. buku besar
              4. semacam kuda

Translation tests

*a tome* _____

Instead of the tested word appearing alone, it could be put into a simple, nondefining context:

*It is a tome.* _____

The vocabulary size is estimated by using the following simple formula:

$$\frac{N \text{ correct answers} \times \text{total } N \text{ words in dictionary}}{N \text{ items in test}} = \text{vocabulary size}$$

In such a test it is important to use the biggest dictionary possible. Lorge and Chall (1963) have shown that there are many problems in making such a test, particularly in choosing the words from the dictionary, and these problems have led to some of the wide variation in estimates of vocabulary size.

If a teacher wants to gain a very rough and probably very unreliable estimate of a learner's vocabulary, the teacher can open a dictionary at random and ask learners to explain the meanings of the more uncommon words on one page. Any rough approximation to the meaning should be accepted. The proportion of words known on the page can be converted to the proportion of words in the whole dictionary. So if the dictionary contains 20,000 words and the class seems to know about two-thirds of the words on a page, then a rough positive estimate of vocabulary size would be about 14,000 words. It must be stressed that this is a very unreliable method and should be used with caution. It should be used positively to show how much someone knows rather than how little.

The frequency count method of estimating vocabulary size involves the use of a list like the Thorndike and Lorge list (1944). The same number of words are randomly selected from different frequency levels—for example, 10 words from the first 1000 words, 10 from the second, and so on. These words are tested using items like those described above. Lorge and Chall (1963, p. 147) describe the method of calculating vocabulary size: "Thus, if a person knows all the words sampled from the commonest thousand words, one-half of the words sampled from the 2nd thousand, one-fourth of the words from the 3rd thousand, and none from the 4th or subsequent thousands, he is credited with a knowledge of 1750 words—the entire first 1000, 500 of the 2nd thousand, and 250 from the 3rd thousand."

The most serious problem with the frequency count method is that the results are limited by the size of the frequency count. The Thorndike and Lorge (1944) count is the most suitable for such tests because of the criteria used for distinguishing different words, but it is limited to 30,000 words. So even a person who got every answer correct on a vocabulary size test could not be credited with a vocabulary larger than 30,000 words. This problem may not be so serious if such a test is used with learners of English as a second language who are not at a very advanced level of proficiency. Ellegard (1960) reports on such a test with Swedish learners of English. In his test learners could answer by translating the tested word into Swedish or by giving an English synonym. The results showed a very clear relationship between frequency level and amount of words known. However, it was clear from the results that the more advanced groups of learners knew many words that were not included in the frequency count. Ellegard suggested using a hypothetical extension of the graph of the learners' results to account for this.

Another problem with frequency counts is that there is not likely to be a direct relationship between the frequency of an item in a particular count and the likelihood of its being known. The frequency of a word depends on the type of material counted. This is particularly true for low-frequency words. Studies of the vocabulary of university textbooks have shown that there is a large group of words that occur relatively more frequently within those books than they do in the language as a whole. Thus, it is not surprising for a word to occur in the 15- to 20-thousand-word level in one frequency count and in the 5- to 10-thousand-word level in a different count. However, for learners of English who are not very advanced, a test using words selected from the various vocabulary ranges can provide a very rough estimate of how many hundred or thousand words the learners know. Campion and Elley (1971, pp. 11–12) found that just getting learners to indicate which words in a list they knew or not gave similar results to a matching test. To encourage honesty the learners did not have to put their names on the test papers. Graves, Ryder, and Slater (1983) suggest that for native speakers, looking at frequency groups may result in a closer correspondence between frequency and knowledge.

## MEASURING KNOWLEDGE OF A PARTICULAR GROUP OF WORDS

We have looked at the many difficulties involved in measuring total vocabulary size. While knowledge about total vocabulary size is interesting and useful, it is more important for a teacher to know whether learners have enough vocabulary to do particular tasks. For example, if learners know the 500-word vocabulary of level 2 of the Longman Structural Readers, they will be able to read all the books at that level and at lower levels. If learners know the vocabulary of the *General Service List*

(West, 1953), then they can read the enormous amount of material written using that vocabulary. They are also ready to study the words in the University Word List (see Appendix 2), which builds on the *General Service List* for learners who want to do university study. If they know the words in the university list they are able to read university texts and need only guess or look up less than 1 unknown word in every 18 words.

As we have seen when looking at tests of total vocabulary size, there are two important steps to consider. The first is the selection of the words to be tested and the second is the testing of the words. Let us look at these in turn.

## Selecting

Usually it is not possible to test all the words within a particular group. A vocabulary test with 100 items is a long test. When we make a test we have to be very careful in selecting the items for the test so that the items we choose are good representatives of our total list of words. For example, if we wish to make a test of the words in the *General Service List*, we have to choose between 60 and 100 words which will be used to represent the 2000 headwords in the list. First, we must exclude all the words that we cannot easily test—for example *a, the, of, be*. In fact, the test will be easier to make if we test only nouns, verbs, adjectives, and adverbs. Decisions like this will depend on the type of test item we will use. If the learners translate the tested words, we may be able to test words that we could not test with a multiple-choice test. If we are using pictures instead of synonyms or definitions, then the words we can test will be an even smaller group. If we used only pictures, our list of test items would not be a good representation of the total list because it would consist mainly of concrete nouns. Thus, our test would not be a good one.

Second, after we have excluded the words we cannot test, we must find a good way of choosing the test items from the words left. The best way is to number the words and then to choose every tenth word if this will give us enough words for the test.

One test of the *General Service List* (Barnard, 1961) included almost every testable word in the list. The only exclusions were a few words which were needed to make simple contexts for the tested words. The following items are taken from the test. The learners had to translate the underlined word into their mother tongue.

I cannot say much about his *character*.    _____

Her *idea* is a very good one.    _____

I want to hear only the *facts*.    _____

The test was divided into several parts and different learners took different parts. The aim of the test was to find which words in the *General Service List* were known and which were not known. The test was used in India (Barnard, 1961) and Indonesia (Quinn, 1968). Barnard found that university entrants knew 1500 of the words in the *General Service List*. Quinn found that a similar Indonesian group knew 1000. Appendix 1 contains the poorly known words.

The vocabulary test in Appendix 8 was designed to decide where learners should be given help with vocabulary learning. The test is divided into five levels. The 2,000- and 3,000-word levels contain high-frequency words. Because all the words at these levels occur frequently, it is worth spending class time on them. The university word level represents one type of specialized vocabulary. The 5,000-word level is on the boundary of high- and low-frequency words. The 10,000-word level contains low-frequency words. A matching type of item was used with six words and three meanings in each section.

| | | |
|---|---|---|
| 1. acquiesce | _____ | to work at something without serious intentions |
| 2. contaminate | | |
| 3. crease | _____ | to accept without protest |
| 4. dabble | _____ | to make a fold on cloth or paper |
| 5. rape | | |
| 6. squint | | |

It was found that having more words and meanings in a section put too much memory load on those taking the test. Appendix 8 describes how to use and interpret the test.

## Testing

The first question to ask when testing vocabulary is: Do we want to test recognition or recall of vocabulary? That is, do we want to test if learners can remember the meaning of a word when they see or hear that word, or do we want to test if they can say or write the word when they see some representation of its meaning?

In recall tests, we are interested in the learners' producing the word. In such tests the learners hear or see a mother-tongue word or a simple English synonym or definition, or they see a picture and then they write or say the English word.

In recognition tests, we want to see if the learners know the meaning of a word after they hear or see it. In such tests the learners hear or see an English word and then (a) write or say a mother-tongue word, or

English synonym or definition, (b) check or underline the word to show that they think they know it, or (c) choose one from a set of pictures, mother-tongue words, or English synonyms or definitions. There are variations on this type of item. In one type it can be reversed. That is, the learners see just one picture, mother-tongue word, or synonym and then choose an English word from a set of four or more. In this way more English words are tested. Figure 5.1 gives an example.

a. vaccination
b. gauntlet
c. pestle
d. slingshot

**Figure 5.1**

In another variation, instead of having four or five choices for each word, a list of English words is given and these have to be matched with a set of pictures or a list of translations or English synonyms. The list of pictures, etc., should contain three or four more items than the list of English words. This variation makes it easier for the test-maker to produce test items because it is not necessary to find three or more distractors for each correct answer.

Campion and Elley (1971) tried a list of 10 English words and 13 definitions. Here is an example.

1. alternative
2. mode
3. category
4. emphasis
5. fragment
6. hypothesis
7. instinct
8. analogy
9. doctrine
10. heresy

a. idea put forward as a starting point for reasoning
b. partial likeness or agreement between two things
c. the body of teaching or beliefs of a church, etc.
d. a belief which is against what is generally accepted
e. a person or thing that succeeds another
f. choice between two or more things
g. force or stress laid on words
h. speed, quickness
i. separate or incomplete part
j. natural tendency to behave in a certain way
k. a division or class in a complete system

l.  way in which something is done
m.  a list of names, subjects, etc.

Anderson and Freebody (1983) devised a checklist test where the learners are given a list of words and have to indicate if they know them or not by marking the words they know. To control for learners' overestimating their vocabulary, the list contains a mixture of words and nonwords. The nonwords were made by changing one or two letters in real words (e.g., *flirt* became *flort*, *perfume* became *porfame*) and by forming unconventional base-plus-affix combinations (e.g., *observement, adjustion*). The learners' score can be calculated using the following formula.

$$\text{words known} = \frac{\text{real words marked} - \text{nonwords marked}}{1 - \text{nonwords marked}}$$

In a later use of this test (Nagy, Herman, & Anderson, 1985) words unlike existing English words (e.g., *felinder, shumet, sprale*) but with Englishlike spellings were used in addition to the other types of nonwords. In the experiments done by Anderson et al. a large proportion of the test words, more than 30 percent, were nonwords. Anderson and Freebody (1983) were pleased with the validity of the checklist test and saw its advantages as (a) taking away irrelevant tasks from the learners, like making choices or writing translations or definitions, and (b) being able to test twice as many words as a multiple-choice test would in the same time. The disadvantages of the test are that it cannot be used as a pre- and posttest, or to assess direct vocabulary instruction. It is also unsuitable for testing multiple meanings of words.

Let us now look at the three main types of recognition items again to see their advantages and disadvantages.

1. Items which require the learners to provide a mother-tongue equivalent are the best type of recognition item. Their advantages are that they are very easy to make, and they ask the learners to perform a task which is very similar to what they ordinarily do when reading or listening. Their disadvantages are that marking can be complicated, and markers need to know the mother tongue of the learners.

Asking the learners to respond with English synonyms or definitions requires the learners to have a reasonable proficiency in English. It can be used successfully with advanced learners.

2. Checklist tests using some nonwords have a great deal of promise. Further research on the types and proportions of nonwords needs to be done, as does research on the formula used to calculate the final score. The research on checklist tests without nonwords suggests caution in using this approach. Bear and Odbert (1941) checked this method against multiple-choice tests with native speakers of English. They found

that learners' indications of whether they knew a word or not were a poor guide to their knowledge of vocabulary. Using texts and lists gave roughly similar results. There was a tendency for learners with a small vocabulary to overestimate their vocabulary knowledge. Campion and Elley (1971) also tested this method with native speakers. First, they compared this method with the matching method. They found that "the mean percentage of words whose meaning was known . . . was very similar by each method" (p. 11). The amount of agreement over particular words, however, was by no means perfect. Second, Campion and Elley tried the "rating" method with similar groups of learners. Very high correlations were found, showing that different learners approached the task in a similar way. Brutten (1981) found that teachers' and learners' choices using the rating method corresponded quite closely. The weaknesses of the rating method are that it requires the cooperation of the learners, and it would be unreliable with learners who are poor at spelling and with words with multiple meanings. Some of these weaknesses could be overcome by putting the words in a simple sentence. Advantages of the method are that it is easy to prepare and score, and learners can deal with a large number of words in a short time. When nonwords are added to control overestimating, it is a very efficient and useful test.

3. Multiple-choice items are difficult to make and require careful pretesting and analysis. When they are well made they do a very good job. They are very easy to mark. The use of matching items is one way of reducing the difficulty in making multiple-choice items. However, the item writer should take great care in deciding which words to place in the same matching group. All the items in a group should be the same part of speech so that the learners cannot use clues other than meaning to make their choice. But the words in the group should not be closely related to each other in meaning. Campion and Elley (1971) found that changing the group a word was placed in often resulted in a big change in the number of correct answers for that word. This problem is of course present in ordinary multiple-choice items too. Its effect can be reduced by careful checking of test items.

It should be clear from the examples given above that there is a very wide range of types of items for checking and encouraging vocabulary learning. The choice of a particular type of item should depend upon the following criteria.

1. Is the knowledge required to answer the item correctly similar to the knowledge required by the course? That is, the type of item should reflect the type of teaching and learning done in the course. Thus, word-building items would not be suitable if the course has not focused on word building at all. Similarly, asking learners to make sentences using words is not suitable if the aim of the course is to develop a reading vocabulary.

2. Is it easy to make enough items to test all the vocabulary you want to test? If the teacher is spending hours on a test that the learners will complete in a short time, something is wrong. For this reason traditional multiple-choice items are often unsuitable.

3. Will the items be easy to mark? If the teacher plans the layout of the test carefully with marking in mind, a great deal of time can be saved. For example, if a matching lexical cloze test is used, typing it double-spaced will make it easy to make a marking key with holes cut in it to fit over the answer sheets. Similarly, if the place for the learners to write their answers is clearly indicated, marking becomes easier.

4. Will answering the item provide a useful repetition of the vocabulary and perhaps even extend learners' knowledge? It is not usually a good idea for a test item to be an exact repetition of what occurred in the course. Using language is a creative activity which involves understanding and using words in new contexts. Unless learners can do this we cannot be sure if useful learning has occurred. When testing knowledge of prefixes, for example, it is a good idea to test the prefixes in unknown words which are made of known parts. Then the learners cannot rely solely on memory but have to use their analysis skills. When getting the learners to do a matching lexical cloze, the passage should be one the learners have not seen before, even though it is made up of known vocabulary and constructions.

Items for achievement tests should be suggested by the nature of the course. If teachers use such tests skillfully and often, they can have a significant effect on vocabulary learning.

## APPLICATION

1. You would like to give short vocabulary tests each week to encourage your learners to work on their vocabulary. You had the idea of getting a different group of learners in the class to make a test each week. What item types are the most suitable? Make a model test.

2. Look carefully at the vocabulary test in Appendix 8. What are the weaknesses of the test? What type of vocabulary knowledge is measured in the test? What could you use the test for?

3. A teacher wants to make a vocabulary test based on a reading text to see if learners will be able to cope with most of the vocabulary in the text. The teacher has decided to use a simple translation test just listing the difficult words in the text and asking learners to translate them. Use the questions at the end of this chapter to help you decide if this is a suitable test. If it is not, suggest another kind of item type.

# Chapter 6

# Vocabulary and Listening

This chapter looks at the following questions: What vocabulary is needed to understand spoken English? How can you test the size of a learner's listening vocabulary? What should you do when your learners do not have enough vocabulary to understand spoken English?

## WHAT VOCABULARY IS NEEDED TO UNDERSTAND SPOKEN ENGLISH?

From the small amount of evidence available, it seems that about half the words needed to understand written English are needed to understand spoken English. This figure comes from a comparison of the Schonell, Meddleton, and Shaw (1956) count of spoken English and the Kucera and Francis (1967) count of written English (see Table 6.1).

Part of this difference could come from differences in the degree of formality of the material in the two counts. In spite of the small number of headwords in the count of spoken English, well over half of these occurred only once or a small number of times. About once in every 100 running words a word occurred which was not likely to occur again in that conversation or for several days.

The Schonell et al. count was based on colloquial English. A count of more formal spoken English, such as the English of university lectures, might give a larger proportion of low-frequency words.

**Table 6.1  COMPARISON OF COUNTS OF SPOKEN AND WRITTEN ENGLISH**

|  | Headwords | Word types | Tokens |
|---|---|---|---|
| Schonell | 4,539 | 12,611 | 512,647 |
| Kucera | — | 25,203 | 500,000 |

## HOW CAN YOU TEST THE SIZE OF A LEARNER'S LISTENING VOCABULARY?

Vocabulary is rarely tested through listening. However, a dictation test of vocabulary was devised by H. V. George and refined by Fountain (1974) based on frequency levels. Here is an example of the test.

INTRODUCTORY PARAGRAPH:

Every year/a large number of young people/leave school and begin work./

PARAGRAPH 1:

Some obtain jobs on farms or in industry./ Others accept positions/in the government service./ Many seek posts in business or a trade./ A few with skills in art or music/apply for work in these fields./

PARAGRAPH 2:

Their level of education frequently affects/the range of possible openings./ Many firms, for instance,/only select excellent candidates/for training as future executives./ They will not consider applications from people/with only average records of achievement at school./

PARAGRAPH 3:

What factors influence the choice of a career?/ The information available on this is uncertain/but it is probable that finance,/working conditions and prospects of improvement/ are the most significant considerations./ It seems apparent/that organizations which retain their employees/give them satisfaction in these respects./

PARAGRAPH 4:

A thorough investigation of the motives/which operate in the selection of employment/would prove a profitable topic for research./ Employers who would appreciate the assistance of the findings/to enlist and maintain stable staff/might be induced to invest in the project./

The test consists of five paragraphs. In the example the tested words are underlined. All the tested words in the first paragraph are from the first 500 words of the Thorndike and Lorge (1944) word list. The tested words in the second paragraph are all in the second 500 words. Table 6.2 contains all the data.

The learners hear the test *only once*. There is a pause at the end of each group of words to let them write what they have heard. Each paragraph is read a little faster than the preceding paragraph. When the test is marked, marks are given only for the underlined words. All other words and errors are ignored. The test has been used for several years and has proved to be a useful and reliable method for assigning learners to groups for studying English.

**Table 6.2    DESIGN OF THE DICTATION TESTS**

| Paragraph | N key words in each paragraph | Frequency level for tested words | Average words (not key) per chunk |
|---|---|---|---|
| Introductory | 10 | 1st 500 | 4.5 |
| 1 | 20 | 2nd 500 | 5.0 |
| 2 | 20 | 2nd 1000 | 5.5 |
| 3 | 20 | 3rd 1000 | 6.0 |
| 4 | 20 | 4th–6th 1000 | 7.0 |

By applying the controls listed in Table 6.2 it has been possible to make several equivalent forms which correlate above 0.9. Learners' scores on the dictation test correlated 0.78 with their scores on the Vocabulary Levels Test in Appendix 8. It was also found that the same word occurring in several different graded dictation tests showed quite different difficulty indexes, usually as a result of its context. So, although vocabulary knowledge plays a significant role in this kind of test, it cannot be considered simply as a vocabulary test.

Other possible tests include drawing or annotation tests where learners listen to a description and respond using a minimum of language.

## WHAT SHOULD YOU DO WHEN YOUR LEARNERS DO NOT HAVE ENOUGH VOCABULARY TO UNDERSTAND SPOKEN ENGLISH?

Some learners have a large reading vocabulary and read well but have great difficulty in following spoken English. Others may not have enough vocabulary to understand spoken English. Let us look at each of these reasons separately.

*Activities to Turn a Reading Vocabulary into a Listening Vocabulary*   Typically, learners of English from countries where English is rarely used outside the school may read well but have had little experience in listening to English. These learners need to have the chance to transfer their reading vocabulary to listening. Quantity of listening experience is important, along with some help to see the written-spoken connection.

1. A very effective technique is to choose an interesting simplified reading text like *In the Beginning* (Christopher, 1972), *Of Mice and Men* (Winks, 1975), *Animal Farm* (Orwell, 1945) which is at a vocabulary level well below the learners' reading level. The teacher then reads the story aloud to the learners for 10 or 15 minutes each day trying to keep the learners interested in the story. Wherever a word occurs which the teacher feels the learners might not recognize, the teacher writes it on the blackboard while repeating the sentence containing it. This is done

without interrupting the flow of the story. If the word occurs again, the teacher simply points to it on the blackboard. If an irregular verb form appears, the teacher says its stem form immediately after it. In this way a list of 20 or so words is written on the board as an aid to understanding the story. Gradually, as the story progresses, there is less need to write words and the telling can speed up. The interest of the story keeps the learners' attention and the story line helps with the interpretation of the vocabulary. It becomes almost as addictive as the daily radio serial or soap opera on television.

2. Dictation and predictation exercises (Brown & Barnard, 1975) provide a useful bridge between writing and listening. One variation is to put a fairly simple text on tape and get the learners to transcribe it. The text has no special pauses like ordinary dictation so the learners need to use the pause and replay buttons often.

3. At the word level, exercises like the following make use of learners' knowledge of written English to support listening:

> The teacher writes the letters of a new word on the blackboard in the wrong order. *Correct*, for example, is written as *r c c t e o r*. Then the teacher says the word many times. By listening to the sound and looking at the letters, the learners must try to spell the word correctly. Learners can be asked to write the word on the blackboard when they think they know how to spell it.

**Activities to Increase Vocabulary Through Listening**   If learners have a very limited vocabulary, then vocabulary needs to be taught through listening. The first requirement is that the teacher must be able to simplify and control. Krashen's (1981a) input theory of language learning says that a foreign language is learned by understanding messages that the learner is interested in understanding, that the learner does not feel worried or threatened by, and that contain some unknown language items which are understandable from the context. In such a theory of language learning, simplification becomes very important because it is the way in which messages are made understandable. According to this theory, vocabulary is learned by meeting it in context where the context makes it understandable. This theory of language learning comes under several different names—the input theory, the comprehension approach, the natural approach, the listening approach—but all agree on the importance of making the language understandable by various processes of simplification.

Vocabulary control while speaking is an important skill for a teacher to master. This can be set as a goal for learners and can also be used by teachers as a base for introducing new vocabulary. Some courses for teachers of English as a foreign language train course members to be able to speak within a limited vocabulary. Vocabulary control is a way of making sure that teachers repeat words. Teachers who know the members of their class well and are sensitive to them do not have great difficulty in suiting their spoken language to their learners' understanding. There are, however, several other ways of simplifying spoken language in addition to structure and vocabulary control. Among these are the use of a slower rate of speaking with clear pronunciation and plenty of pauses, stressing and pausing before important words, increasing the redundancy of the message by repetition using the same words or different words, providing definitions, using writing, gestures, pictures, or real objects to explain unknown items, giving opportunity for feedback between the speaker and the listener, and giving possible answers within questions, such as alternative questions and yes/no questions (Chaudron, 1982; Long, 1983; Terrell, 1982, p. 123).

In his excellent description of teachers' vocabulary elaboration techniques, Chaudron (1982) suggests that some types of elaboration, particularly those involving parallelism,

*Vaudreil was a native. He was born there.*

may cause difficulty because the nonnative listener may not be sure "whether the same information has been provided redundantly or whether new information has been supplied" (p. 170).

1. Just as learning vocabulary by guessing from context is important in reading, so is it important in listening. An advantage that occurs in guessing from context in listening is that a skilled and sensitive speaker can easily provide extra information if necessary to help with guessing of an unknown word. As we have just seen in the discussion of simplification above, this information can be repetition or increased redundancy in the spoken material, or extralinguistic help like the use of gestures, pictures, or demonstration. Elley (1989) carried out research on vocabulary learning in oral contexts. He found that if the speaker happens to give a little extra decontextualized attention to a word when telling a story, that word has a much greater chance of being learned. Thus, in order for a teacher to help learning from context in spoken material, it is useful for the teacher to be able to gloss quickly and demonstrate or illustrate new vocabulary when it occurs in the story. Teachers' intuitions about what words will not be known by their learners are usually reliable (Brutten, 1981), and so it is not difficult for a teacher to prepare for this before reading a story to a class or before explaining something. The chapter on communicating meaning describes a range of ways of explaining vocabulary.

2. Teachers can control and help with vocabulary input. So can learners. A useful strategy is to help and encourage learners to control

the teachers' spoken language. Here is a technique for doing this. First, the teacher writes several sentences on the blackboard. They include the following.

Please speak more slowly.

What was the word before _____ ?

How do you spell it?

Could you please say that again.

What does _____ mean?

The teacher then tells the learners that he or she is going to read them a short text. When the teacher reaches the end of the text, the learners will be expected to have understood it well and be ready to be tested on their understanding of it. The learners' job is to stop the teacher reaching the end by requesting things such as those listed above. When the learners feel that they understand the text well, they can then stop telling the teacher what to do. After this has been explained to the learners, the teacher then starts to read the text, but deliberately reads it too fast, or mumbles some important words. The learners are then forced to tell the teacher to repeat, explain, spell, slow down, etc. This can be a very amusing activity and is one way of getting a shy class to participate. The teacher can deliberately introduce difficulty into those parts of the text where learners should give their attention.

3. There are many controlled listening exercises that can be used to teach new vocabulary. In the *What is it?* exercise the teacher explains a new word by turning the explanation into a kind of puzzle (Nation, 1978). This and other techniques are described in Chapter 4. Information transfer exercises also provide a useful context for the introduction of new vocabulary (Palmer, 1982). In these exercises the learners listen to a monologue, conversation, or description and complete a diagram or table while listening. For example, the learners listen to a conversation between a young person and a bicycle repair man. While the learners listen they each have a picture of a bicycle in front of them. They circle the parts of the bicycle which need to be repaired. The introduction of new vocabulary is helped by the use of a picture and by the redundancy in the recorded conversation. In addition, most learners of English will bring previous knowledge of bicycles and the kinds of things that go wrong with them.

## APPLICATION

1. List at least six activities that could be used with a tape recorder or in a language laboratory to help turn knowledge of written vocabulary into listening vocabulary.

2. For each of the following situations, suggest how the speaker could make the listed vocabulary clear to the learners without interrupting the message too much.

**a.** The words *paw, insurance,* and *to limp* occur in a story the teacher is telling the class.
**b.** The words *frequency, random,* and *calculate* occur during a lecture.
**c.** The words *whistled, thumped,* and *withered* (adj.) occur in a poem the teacher is telling the class.
**d.** The words *evaporate, moisture,* and *vapor* occur during a description of the water cycle.
**e.** Choose a piece of material you use in class and show how you would deal with the vocabulary.

## Answer

| | |
|---|---|
| *paw* | give a brief definition—"an animal's foot" |
| *to limp* | demonstrate—these are low-frequency words and should be dealt with quickly |
| *insurance* | give a brief contextual definition as if it were a part of the story—"A few days later the family received $1000 from their son's insurance. *He had paid money to insure his life so that if he died his family would get a large amount of money."* *Insure* and *insurance* are high-frequency words and deserve special attention. It is probably worth writing the word on the blackboard. |

# Chapter 7

# Vocabulary and Speaking

This chapter looks at these questions: What vocabulary is needed to speak English? What should you do when your learners do not have enough vocabulary to speak? The vocabulary development activities looked at include controlled activities, form-focused activities, grids, clines, clusters, and collocation activities, pair activities, repetitive activities, and paraphrase activities.

## WHAT VOCABULARY IS NEEDED TO SPEAK ENGLISH?

West (1960) developed a minimum adequate speech vocabulary of 1200 headwords that would be sufficient for learners of English to say most of the things they would need to say. This seems a very small number of words, but evidence from the few frequency counts of spoken English indicates that in spoken English a small number of words accounts for a very large proportion of spoken language. Schonell et al. (1956), in their investigation of the spoken vocabulary of the Australian worker, found that far fewer different words were used in spoken English than in any comparable study of written English. Moreover, the 1000 most frequent words in the Schonell et al. count covered 94 percent of the material. The first 2000 words covered almost 99 percent of the material. About 5 percent of these very frequent words in spoken English were not among the most frequent words in written English. Clearly, to speak English it is not necessary to have a large vocabulary. In developing learners' spoken English vocabulary it is best to give learners practice in being able to say a lot using a small number of words. The 2000 words of the *General Service List* (West, 1953) is a reasonable goal.

Using the Vocabulary Levels Test (Appendix 8) will give an indication of learners' receptive vocabulary. Their spoken productive vocabulary can be checked by doing the pair exercise with pictures based on the *General Service List* in the section on pages 103–104 of this chapter. Learners with a good speaking vocabulary should be able to do this quite easily.

## WHAT SHOULD YOU DO WHEN LEARNERS DO NOT HAVE ENOUGH VOCABULARY TO SPEAK?

From the point of view of vocabulary, there are two reasons why learners may not be able to say what they want to say. First, they may not know enough vocabulary. If this is the case, then the teacher can work on ways of increasing their vocabulary, like using controlled activities and techniques for the receptive learning of vocabulary. There are several teachers who suggest that spoken production should not be encouraged until learners have had a lot of opportunity to listen to the language and develop their own hypotheses about it. When the learners feel ready to speak, they can then draw on this previous learning (Gary & Gary, 1981; Nord, 1980; Terrell, 1982). So when learners have enough receptive vocabulary, they can be helped to use some of it productively. Second, the learners may know enough vocabulary, but they are unable to put this vocabulary to productive use. It is not unusual to meet learners of English who can read quite well but who have great difficulty producing spoken language. In teaching, a distinction is often made between active vocabulary, which is to be used by the learner in speaking or writing, and passive vocabulary, which is needed for listening and reading. At most stages of language learning, learners' passive vocabulary is much larger than their active vocabulary.

Corson (1983, pp. 5–6) also distinguishes between productive (active) and receptive (passive) vocabulary in the following way: He calls the active vocabulary a "motivated" vocabulary. It consists of all the words we need to use and feel no reluctance in using in our everyday life. A passive vocabulary includes the active vocabulary and it also includes the learners' "unmotivated" vocabulary. The unmotivated vocabulary can be divided into two groups: (1) words which are only partly understood and are not well known enough to use actively, and (2) words which are not needed in daily communication. (1) and (2) may overlap with each other. When a person's daily communication needs change, then the words in (2) may become a part of the "motivated" active vocabulary.

Learning a word for productive use requires more learning than for receptive use (Crothers & Suppes, 1967; Stoddard, 1929). The difference between these two types of learning was examined in more detail in Chapter 3. If learners have a reasonably large receptive vocabulary but are unable to put enough of this to productive use, then the teacher needs to concentrate on activities which enrich the learning of known words and improve access to them (Horowitz & Gordon, 1972).

### Controlled Activities

Such activities give learners little choice in what to say. The most controlled are repetition and substitution drills and dialogue memorization. In these activities the relevant vocabulary is usually explained briefly before the drill or is demonstrated during it through the use of pictures or objects. The new vocabulary goes straight into the learners' productive vocabulary without spending time in their receptive vocabulary. This can have the disadvantage of getting the learners to make use of words before they really understand them. Other techniques just ask for the recall of known vocabulary, perhaps in a sentence context. These activities are like games and can be used quite often for a short time.

1. The teacher shows the learners about 12 or more objects or pictures. The learners already know the names in English. The learners are allowed to look at them for one minute and then the objects are taken away or covered with a cloth. Then, using their memory, the learners must write or say all the things that they saw. When they become better at this, the teacher can ask them about the color and position of each object.

Another way of doing this is to show the learners about 12 or more objects. These are then put in a box so that the learners cannot see them. The teacher puts a hand in the box and holds one object, keeping that hand in the box so that the learners cannot see which object is being held. The learners try to guess which one it is. When they have guessed correctly, the teacher takes his or her hand out and shows them the object.

2. About 10 or 12 cards with pictures on them are put in a row so that the whole class can see them. The teacher points to the cards and says the names. Then the teacher turns some cards around so that the learners can see only the backs of them. When the teacher points to a card the learners must say the name by remembering the position in the row. When all the cards are turned around, the teacher changes the position of two of the cards. The learners watch while this is done. Then the teacher points and the learners say the names. Then the position of two more cards is changed, and so on. This can be made into a game. Learners answer individually. When anyone makes a mistake, that learner is "out" and must watch. The game continues until only one learner is not "out."

Another way of doing this is to show the cards one by one in a fixed order. The teacher shows the cards and says the names of the items on each card. When the learners are beginning to be able to associate the words and their meanings, one or two cards are turned around so that the learners see only the backs. By remembering the order of the cards, the learners should be able to say the names even when they are shown the back of a card. This continues until all the cards are turned around. The teacher should write the name of each picture on the back of the card and then, when using the cards, move the back card to the front. In this way the teacher will always know what picture is being shown without having to move the card to look at the picture.

If the teacher has often used a chart or a big picture with the learners, one day the chart can be turned around so that the learners can see only the back. Then the teacher says the names of things on the chart, and, by using their memory, the learners must point to the correct place on the back of the chart. This is not as easy as it seems because when the chart is turned around, right becomes left and left becomes right.

## Activities to Help Recall the Form of a Word

If teachers want the learners to recall and say a word that they have already learned, they can say a context for the word and ask the learners to provide the missing word.

I got up and went into the bathroom to clean my _____.

If the learners cannot guess the word, the teachers can give another context or

1. Say the first sound(s) of the word.
2. Say the word without making any noise so that the learners must read lips.
3. Write short lines on the blackboard, with one short line for each letter of the word.

Then the teachers write in the last letter: _____ h

then the second to last letter:_____ th

and so on until the learners guess.

If it is clear that the learners cannot guess the word, teachers can pretend that one of the learners at the back of the class has said it. "What did you say? Teeth? Yes, good." Then they can move quickly on to the next part of the lesson.

While doing any of these techniques, teachers should keep repeating the context many times. The context should not be too clear but should allow a few possibilities so that there is a challenge for the learners to guess. All these techniques can be used for verbs, adjectives, and adverbs as well as nouns. Teachers should make sure that the learners do not call out the answers.

## Activities to Improve Access to Vocabulary

The techniques in this section aim at increasing the associations that learners make with a word. They do this by being encouraged to think of words of related meaning (paradigmatic associations) and words that they typically occur with (syntagmatic associations).

**Grids, Clines, and Clusters**    Grids, clines, and clusters can be used to help learners expand and establish the meanings of words that they are already familiar with.

1. Grids consist of a list of words down one side of the page with another list, usually of meanings or some other way of classifying the words, across the top of the page. The example in Figure 7.1 comes from Channell (1981). Stieglitz (1983) has other examples.

The learners are shown the grid without the asterisks, and through group discussion they mark the features which are a part of the meaning of each word. This exercise makes learners aware of differences in meanings between words and the features of meaning of individual words. It helps learners expand the concepts of words that they are already familiar with because the words in a group help to define each other.

2. Clines are usually shown by sloping lines (in-clin-ation). Words are arranged on them to show variations of degree. Figures 7.2 and 7.3 are from Brown (1980).

Where will these words be placed: *immediately, right away, in a little while, before too long?*

Usually the teacher shows some of the points on the cline and then gives the learners a list of words that have to be put in the most suitable place in relation to the given words and to each other.

3. Clusters are words grouped around a central point. Figure 7.4 is from Brown (1980).

Being Surprised

| | affect with wonder | because unexpected | because difficult to believe | so as to cause confusion | so as to leave one helpless to act or think |
|---|---|---|---|---|---|
| surprise | + | + | | | |
| astonish | + | | + | | |
| amaze | + | | | + | |
| astound | + | | | | + |
| flabbergast | + | | | | + |

**Figure 7.1**    A vocabulary grid.

I will do it _____

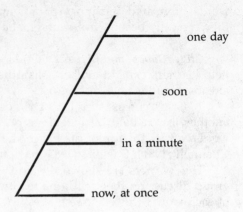

one day

soon

in a minute

now, at once

**Figure 7.2**  A vocabulary cline.

When new words are met, they can be fitted into the most suitable place in the cluster, and this always provides a good opportunity for revising related words. Harvey (1983) uses grids in a similar way. Figure 7.5 should make this clear. The learners are shown an incomplete grid and they work together to complete it.

There are several dangers involved in using grids, clines, and clusters. Presenting unfamiliar words with related meanings together can cause interference and make learning much more difficult. However, if these exercises are used with words that are already familiar to the learn-

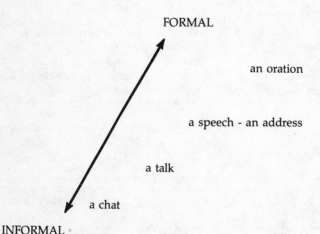

FORMAL

an oration

a speech - an address

a talk

a chat

INFORMAL

**Figure 7.3**  A cline based on talks.

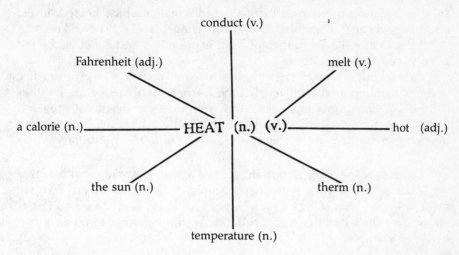

**Figure 7.4**   A vocabulary cluster.

ers, this difficulty is avoided. Second, the use of charts that have to be completed can lead to a mixture of frequent and very infrequent items, with all being given equal attention. Words deserve attention from learners because of their usefulness. Completing grids can lead to absurdities

| | | | | *Categories* | | |
|---|---|---|---|---|---|---|
| *sports* | *location* | *teams* | *equipment* | *scoring* | *in charge* |
| soccer | ground<br>pitch<br>stadium | 11 players | ball<br>boots<br>strip<br>goal posts | goals<br>draw<br>1–0 (one nil)<br>2–2 (two all) | referee<br>2 linesmen |
| tennis | court | singles<br>doubles<br>mixed doubles | racket<br>balls<br>net | 15–0 (fifteen-love)<br>30–30 (thirty all)<br>40–40 (deuce)<br>points<br>game/set | umpire<br>line-judges |
| boxing | ring<br>arena | by weights<br>(flyweight,<br>heavyweight,<br>etc.) | gloves<br>boots | rounds<br>points<br>K.O. (knock-out) | referee<br>judges |
| basketball | court | 5 players | ball<br>baskets | points<br>baskets | 2 referees |

**Figure 7.5**   The language of sport.

such as learning the names for male and female rabbits, horses, foxes, and other groups. This misuse is easily avoided if the teacher keeps in mind the idea of the usefulness of what is presented and is not led by the need to complete a pattern.

Grids, clines, and clusters are best used as activities to give practice and organization to vocabulary that the learners have met before in other contexts. By looking at this vocabulary from the new viewpoint provided by the organizing nature of grids, clines, and clusters, the learners can deepen their understanding and improve access to the vocabulary.

**Collocation**    A very important part of learning a new word is learning what words it goes with. For example, to know the word *save* we need to know what things we can save. This list is likely to be quite different from the list of items that collocate with the mother-tongue equivalent. For example:

|  |  |
|---|---|
|  | money. |
|  | time. |
| We can save | souls. |
|  | people or animals. |
|  | energy. |
|  | face. |

Brown (1974) discusses collocation and describes several exercises to practice collocation. These exercises consist mainly of matching lists of words. Here is an example.

> For each adjective choose the 2 or 3 (not more) nouns from this list that you think would collocate (go together) most usefully. Write these out, e.g., *a narrow bridge*. Check your answers with those given, and discuss any others that you have with your teacher. Be careful with articles.

### ADJECTIVES

1. intense
2. narrow
3. sealed
4. political
5. limited
6. related
7. various

### NOUNS

feelings          a bridge
a road            a letter

| | |
|---|---|
| an envelope | geography |
| a situation | money |
| a number | by marriage |
| an idea | ways |
| reasons | a tube |
| heat | knowledge |

## ANSWERS GIVEN

1. intense feelings, intense heat
2. a narrow road, a narrow bridge
3. a sealed envelope, a sealed letter, a sealed tube
4. a political situation, political geography
5. a limited number, limited money, limited knowledge
6. a related idea, related by marriage
7. various reasons, various ways, various ideas

(Brown, 1974, p. 4)

Here are some other techniques to give practice in collocation.

1. The teacher suggests a word and learners work together in small groups to make a list of collocations. Each group tells their list to the teacher, who builds up a big list on the blackboard.

2. The learners have a passage which has nouns and associated adjectives or verbs and associated subjects and objects removed from it. These words are put in two lists under the passage in random order. The learners fill in the blanks with suitable collocations.

3. The learners are given a word and four of its collocations. They write four sentences for each pair.

4. The teacher suggests a word and the learners find collocates by looking at the dictionary or other word lists and by finding examples of the word in context. The learners can also try to guess what collocations might occur.

Grids can also be used to practice collocation (Channell, 1981). These grids can consist of a list of words down one side of a page and a list of words across the top. The learners draw on their previous experience and discussion to decide which collocations are acceptable. They can use a cross to mark the acceptable collocations. Figure 7.6 is from Rudzka, Channell, Putseys, and Ostyn (1981).

Such exercises can help learners expand their knowledge of words that are already familiar to them. Channell (1981) reports that her learners averaged only 3 wrong collocations when doing such an exercise; they actually missed an average of 14 possible collocations. Thus, collocation exercises can be very useful in encouraging learners to make wider use of the vocabulary they know.

| | sb's car | a painting | the environment | one's health | sb's reputation | children | one's legs | sb's feelings | sb's pride | sb's speech | sb's enjoyment | sb's happiness |
|---|---|---|---|---|---|---|---|---|---|---|---|---|
| **damage** | + | + | + | + | + | | | | | | | |
| **harm** | | (+) | + | + | + | + | | | | | | |
| **impair** | | | | + | + | | | | | + | + | |
| **hurt** | | | | | + | + | + | + | | | | |
| **injure** | | | | | + | + | + | | | | | |
| **mar** | | | | (+) | + | | | | | | + | + |
| **spoil** | | (+) | + | (+) | | + | | | | | + | |

**Figure 7.6**   A collocation grid.

## Pair Activities Which Give Help with Vocabulary

Combining arrangement activities (Nation, 1979) can be used as vocabulary learning exercises. When combining arrangement activities are used in pairs, one learner has one piece of information and the other has a different piece of information. They must combine these pieces of information to reach some conclusions. They can do this only by talking to each other. They must not show their sheets of information to each other. The combining exercises on the following pages can be used to revise vocabulary or can be used to introduce new vocabulary.

1. In the first example, the same or different, each learner has a set of pictures (Figures 7.7 and 7.8). By describing their pictures to each other, the two learners in the pair try to decide if their pictures are the same or different. Note that one learner (the one who speaks first, which is indicated by the X next to the number) has an annotated picture. So this learner can use these words in the description of the picture. These annotations help the learning of vocabulary. Notice that each word appears twice in the exercise. For example *a bucket* occurs in items 1 and 28. Notice also that the annotations are shared between the learners—1 is annotated for learner A and 28 is annotated for learner B.

2. The next example of the combining arrangement, on pages 106–109, which is at the 1000-word level, is mainly for vocabulary revision.

**Figure 7.7** The same or different? (A)

GEORGE.

**Figure 7.8** The same or different? (B)

There are many possible variations of the combining arrangement—A has a picture, B has words; A can be more advanced than B. Nation (1979) outlines many of the possibilities.

3. Feeny (1976) did a simple informal experiment with his class of learners of Spanish. He made the learners work in pairs. The learners in a pair, A and B, had 10 pictures each. Each picture was labeled and illustrated with an unknown word in the label. Learner A had to teach learner B the unknown word without showing his picture. After learner A had taught his words, learner B taught A her words. Before the teaching, the words were unknown to both learners. After the 20 words had been taught (10 from A, 10 from B), Feeny tested the class. He was interested in seeing if the people *teaching* the words learned them too. The results were very encouraging. When he checked the learners again 12 days later, he found that they still remembered most of the words. During the learning the learners were encouraged to ask questions about the words, and they were given a list of useful questions, like *What color is it? What is it used for? Where can we find it?*

4. When native speakers are available to work with second language learners, the native speakers have a list of words and the second language learners have a set of pictures arranged in a different order. The native speaker in each pair says a word from the list and explains its meaning. By listening to the explanation of the unknown word, the second language learner tries to find the corresponding picture.

## Repetitive Activities to Improve Fluency

When learners first speak about a topic they may have to struggle to find the right words and may realize after they have said something that they already knew a better way to say it. There are some techniques to practice speaking that give the learners the chance to improve on the same topic.

1. The 5/4/3 technique (Maurice, 1983) uses a change in audience to provide the opportunity for repetition. It works like this. The learners work in pairs. Each learner has a few minutes to mentally prepare a short talk on a given topic. Learner A then takes five minutes to present her talk to learner B. Learner B then takes five minutes to present his talk to learner A. Then they change partners. They now have one minute less, four minutes, to present the same talk to their new partners. After this is done, partners change again. They each have three minutes to present the same talk. Because the audience changes each time, the repeated communication remains real. The decreasing time adds a challenge to the activity.

### 1000-Word Level    A

You have part of a sentence on your sheet.
Your partner has the other part of the sentence.
If you have X by your sentence, read it to your partner.
Your partner will finish the sentence.
You must decide if the complete sentence is a sensible one.
If the sentence is sensible, write the missing part on your sheet.
The first sentence is done for you.

| | |
|---|---|
| XI | A door <u>is made of wood.</u> |
| 2 | _____ live in houses. |
| X3 | A boat_____ |
| 4 | _____ are very good for us. |
| X5 | Gold_____ |
| 6 | _____ catches thieves. |
| X7 | Water_____ |
| 8 | _____ is a season. |
| X9 | Bottles_____ |
| 10 | _____ is green. |
| X11 | Eggs _____ |
| 12 | _____ in a bed. |
| X13 | Sugar_____ |
| 14 | _____ shines at night. |
| X15 | A bicycle_____ |
| 16 | _____ paints pictures. |
| X17 | An island_____ |
| 18 | _____ live on the moon. |
| X19 | Flowers_____ |
| 20 | _____ tells the time. |
| X21 | A banana_____ |

22    _____ at night.

X23    We hear_____

24    _____ shine at night.

X25    A girl_____

26    _____ are for sick people.

X27    We have ten_____

28    _____ grows on your head.

X29    The Prime Minister_____

30    _____ is Sunday.

X31    A fire_____

32    _____ with a spoon.

X33    Winter_____

34    _____ is an animal.

X35    We read_____

36    _____ hurts people.

X37    A wheel_____

38    _____ the race.

X39    A wise person_____

40    _____ my sister.

---

### 1000-Word Level    B

You have part of a sentence on your sheet.

Your partner has the other part of the sentence.

If you have X by your sentence, read it to your partner.

Your partner will finish the sentence.

You must decide if the complete sentence is a sensible one.

If the sentence is sensible, write the missing part on your sheet.

The first sentence is done for you.

1    <u>A door</u>            is made of wood.

X2    Tigers_____

3    _____ flies in the air.

X4    Cigarettes_____

5    _____ is very expensive.

X6    A policeman_____

7    _____ is wet.

X8    Monday_____

9    _____ are made of glass.

X10    Blood_____

11    _____ come from cows.

X12    We sleep_____

13    _____ is sweet.

X14    The sun_____

15    _____ has two wheels.

X16    A writer_____

17    _____ has sea on all sides.

X18    People_____

19    _____ are very ugly.

X20    A clock_____

21    _____ is red and round.

X22    We dream_____

23    _____ with our ears.

X24    Stars_____

25    _____ is a young man.

X26    Hospitals_____

27    _____ fingers.

X28    Hair_____

29    _____ is the leader of New Zealand.

X30    The date_____

 31    _____ is cold.

X32    We cut things_____

 33    _____ is a hot season.

X34    A dog_____

 35    _____ books.

X36    A doctor_____

 37    _____ is square.

X38    The fastest person wins_____

 39    _____ is very stupid.

X40    He is_____

2. Ordering activities use the same set of items over and over to provide the opportunity for repetition. The learners work in pairs or small groups. Each learner has the same set of pictures, preferably about 6 to 10 pictures, which are only slightly different from each other. The learner who is going to speak secretly arranges her pictures in a certain order. She then describes her pictures in order, and by listening to the description the other learners have to arrange theirs in the same order. They check that they have done it correctly. Then the speaker rearranges her pictures and does the exercise again.

## Paraphrase Activities to Make the Fullest Use of Known Words

An important vocabulary strategy when speaking is being able to cope with gaps in vocabulary or with the temporary inability to recall a word that is needed. Several teachers (Baxter, 1980; Brown, 1979; Woodeson, 1982) describe their learners' failure to be able to use a paraphrase, definition, or some other substitute to make up for a word they do not know. For example, when faced with the need to use the word *toothpick*, which is not in their English vocabulary, they cannot make up for this gap by saying "a thin piece of wood for cleaning your teeth" or "something used like this" accompanied by a demonstration. This skill is particularly useful in speaking because there is no time to refer to a dictionary and there is the chance of getting feedback from the listener to show if the paraphrase has been successful or unsuccessful.

When learners have mastered this strategy, they have several advantages. They are able to operate effectively with a small productive vocabulary. They have independence from the need to ask for translation. Their speaking can remain fluent, thus making it easier to maintain a conversation. Baxter (1980, p. 329) sees the development of the paraphrasing strategy as a result of a dynamic view of vocabulary:

> Vocabulary cannot be construed only in terms of an accumulation of items, but also must be seen as including the dynamics of use. Pedagogically, this means that simply predicting items which may be needed by students then teaching these items, is inadequate. We must assume that in many instances the items supposedly learned will be unavailable for use; yet students must nevertheless be able to express their meaning in an appropriate manner.

> The basic principle in developing the strategy is that it is not necessary to be exact. Because speaking allows interaction between the speaker and the listener, there can be continual checking to make sure that the meaning gets through.

Baxter (1980, p. 330) believes that a major cause of the failure to develop the paraphrasing strategy is the continual use of bilingual dictionaries.

> The user of this type of dictionary must therefore continually refer to matchings of lexical items. What is cumulatively learned is that meaning is always expressed through use of a lexical item. Long-term use of a bilingual dictionary will produce in students the tendency always to seek a given lexical item. If it should be unavailable, there will be no recourse, in speech, to conversational definition.

Bialystock and Frohlich (1980) studied the strategies second language learners used to make up for gaps in vocabulary. They classified the strategies into those that were based on the mother tongue (L1 strategies), those based on the second language (L2 strategies), and those not based on language. Their list was as follows:

L1-based strategies

1. Language switch—putting a mother-tongue word in place of the unknown word.

*I have a horloge.*

2. Foreignizing L1 words—creating a new L2 word by applying L2 morphology and/or phonology to an L1 word.

*Have you makaned yet?* (*makan* = "eat" in Malay)

3. Transliteration—using L2 words and grammar to create a literal translation of an L1 item or phrase.

*I want some soft cheese.* (the Thai translation for *butter*)

L2-based strategies

1. Using an approximate synonym—using a single L2 word of related meaning to do the job of the unknown word.

*The boat is sick.* for *The boat is broken.*

2. Description—describing the object by
   a. referring to physical properties

*It is round.*

   b. referring to specific features

*It has four legs.*

   c. referring to functional characteristics

*We sit on it.*

3. Creating a word—making an L2 word based on another L2 word and using the L2 morphological system.

*Where is the timer?* ( = clock)

Nonlanguage

Using gestures or sounds

They found that the number of L2-based strategies increased with increasing proficiency in the second language. They also tried to measure the comparative effectiveness of the strategies. There were several problems involved in doing this, although it was generally found that L1-based strategies were not as effective as L2-based strategies.

The following techniques can be used to develop the paraphrasing strategy.

1. Make a class rule that learners are not allowed to say sentences like "How do you say *malu* in English?" Instead they have to say, "What's the English for when you feel you have done something wrong?" (Woodeson, 1982).

2. Teach learners a range of substitutes for giving a word. A list of these can be found at the beginning of Chapter 4. These include showing objects, gestures, and demonstration. These substitutes can be practiced by describing pictures and recorded sounds (Brown, 1979).

3. Teach language items like *-ish* as in *greenish, girlish; sort of, kind of,* as in *kind of round, sort of ran; you know;* and the use of simile as in *tastes like lemons, looks like a ball with a stick through it* (Brown, 1979). These get a lot of practice in combining arrangement exercises (Nation, 1979) using abstract pictures. Without showing their pictures to each other, the learners work in pairs and describe their pictures. They decide if they are the same or different.

4. Encourage the use of a monolingual dictionary. This has two effects. It helps the learners master a definition vocabulary, particularly the use of general class words, and it makes learners familiar with the possibility of defining and paraphrasing words (Baxter, 1980).

5. The *What is it?* technique described in Chapter 4 and the game *Twenty Questions* give a lot of practice in defining and describing.

6. Woodeson (1982) describes an excellent technique for practicing paraphrase and definition. Learners work in pairs. Each has a crossword puzzle. Figure 7.9 is an example. The puzzle has no clues, but learner A has half of the words written in, and learner B has the other half. They ask each other for the words missing from their version. They are not allowed to say the words themselves or show their puzzles to each other, but they must give paraphrases of the words. So if A asks, "What is 5 down?" B has to say something like "The part of your body where your food goes just after you eat it." Suitable graded puzzles can be found in Hill and Popkin (1968).

## APPLICATION

1. Some of your learners have a very good reading vocabulary but have difficulty listening to and speaking English.

   a. What and how would you check to help you decide what to do?
   b. What solutions seem the most suitable for you and your learners? Why?

2. Give a learner a picture and then get him or her to describe it to someone who tries to draw it from the description. What vocabulary problems did the learner have? What could you do about them?

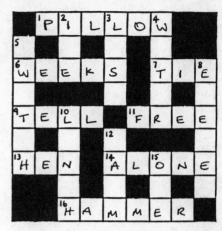

**Figure 7.9**

3. Choose one of the techniques mentioned in this chapter.

a. Decide what the vocabulary aims for this technique are, and what features of the technique help meet these aims.
b. Observe the technique being used.
c. Participate in using the technique.
d. Report on your evaluation of the technique, citing evidence from your analysis, observation, and experience of the technique. How would you use the technique for best effect?

4. Two techniques using repetitive activities are suggested in this chapter. One uses a change of audience to get repetition and the other uses reorganization of the same material. Think of other applications of these two principles. Can you think of other ways of getting learners to repeat material while still staying interested in it? Other principles might include gradual removal of cues, chain activities, and so on.

5. Choose some useful words and prepare a grid, cline, or collocation activity around them. Check carefully that you are not causing interference problems (see the "unteaching" section of Chapter 3.).

# Chapter 8

# Vocabulary and Reading

This chapter looks at the following questions. What vocabulary is needed to read English? How do you test a learner's reading vocabulary? What should you do when learners do not have enough vocabulary to read their set texts? What should you do when there are some unknown words in the text? What should you do when there are unknown words in an English for Special Purposes text? A wide range of procedures, strategies, and techniques is described.

## WHAT VOCABULARY IS NEEDED TO READ ENGLISH?

Learners of English as a foreign language usually begin their reading with specially simplified texts. The vocabulary and often the sentence structure guidelines which are followed in these simplified texts are very explicitly described for writers. Typically, the vocabulary levels go in steps of around 300 words. This means that with a vocabulary of only 300 to 400 words learners have enough vocabulary to read several simplified books. Most series of simplified texts aim at taking learners to the 2000-word level, although some aim higher. The *Newbury House Writers' Guide* lists six levels.

| | |
|---|---|
| Stage 1 | 300 words |
| Stage 2 | 600 words |
| Stage 3 | 1000 words |
| Stage 4 | 1500 words |
| Stage 5 | 2000 words |
| Stage 6 | 2600 words |

The article on simplified reading texts by Bamford (1984) is an excellent introduction to such texts and gives an indication of the hundreds of titles available at the various levels. The chapter on simplification in this book also gives more information.

When learners are faced with unsimplified texts, the vocabulary load can be very heavy. It is clear from the statistical information we looked at in the first chapter of this book that a vocabulary of at least 3000 head-words is needed to read unsimplified texts with any ease. Even with 3000 headwords, around 5 or 6 percent of the words on each page (about 15–18 words) will be unknown. Guessing is possible at this density, but the vocabulary load is still high. Developing a large reading vocabulary as quickly as possible is a very important priority for learners who wish to pursue academic study in English.

## HOW DO YOU TEST A LEARNER'S READING VOCABULARY?

The types of tests described in the chapter on assessing vocabulary size are used to test reading vocabulary. These include isolated words tested with multiple-choice meanings or translations, words in simple nondefining contexts, and checklist tests. The Vocabulary Levels Test (Appendix 8) can be used as a test to see if learners have enough vocabulary to read, but it is important not to confuse having an adequate reading vocabulary with skill in reading. Vocabulary is clearly an important factor in reading, as readability studies show, but it is only one of a range of factors (Nation & Coady, 1988).

As well as checking to see if a learner's vocabulary is sufficient for a certain task, tests can do other jobs. Achievement tests are based very closely on a particular course. They can have two aims, to check if learning has taken place, and to help this learning take place. They can help learning take place by providing motivation to study ("Learn these words because they will be in the test") and by giving another meaningful repetition of the words. It is important that such achievement tests require the learners to use vocabulary in ways which relate closely to the aims of the course. *Advanced English Vocabulary* by Helen Barnard (1980) has short blank-filling tests at the end of each unit which provide one more chance to repeat the vocabulary taught in the unit. Because the course aims at understanding words in written and spoken material, the words are tested in a passage rather than in isolated phrases. Here is an example.

---

To test yourself on the vocabulary of this section, fill in the missing letters in the incomplete words.

To make a cake, it is best to use a good b_____c recipe.* If you want to make a bigger cake than the one in the recipe, you must

*A recipe tells us how to prepare and cook something.

m_____ly the qu_____s in the recipe, and if you want a smaller one you must d_____e the qu_____s.

The qu_____s of flour, butter, and sugar must be measured ac_____y. The sugar and butter are u_____y mixed together first, and the flour and eggs a_____d afterwards. But in some recipes the butter and flour are mixed first, i_____d _____ the butter and sugar. N_____s many people use an electric mixer for this part of the work, which needs s_____l care.
When you put the mixture into the cake pan, it is n_____y to a_____w enough space for the cake to rise, because the mixture will e_____d when it is h_____d. St_____d s_____s of cake pans can be bought which have the correct w_____h and d_____h for one pound, two pound, and three pound cakes.

When you are s_____ that the t_____e of the oven is right for this kind of cake, put the pan in the oven. When you take it out of the oven, you must a_____w the cake to c_____l before taking it out of the pan. If you follow the recipe carefully, your cake may not be p_____t but it will pr_____y be eatable.

----

Achievement tests which also try to teach should be easy to mark, like the example given above. If the tests are easy to mark the teacher can give them often. The matching lexical cloze is a similar type of test. Some nouns, verbs, adjectives, and adverbs are removed from a passage that the learners have not seen before and a blank is left in their place. The words are listed below the passage and three or four distractors are added. The learners have to write the appropriate words in the correct place in the passage. In the true matching lexical cloze the words are omitted according to a system. In an achievement test, the words will be chosen because they are ones that occurred in the course. Here is an example.

----

Choose appropriate words from the list below to complete the passage. You may need to change the forms of some of the words.

Money has no meaning apart from what it _____. Its meaning is provided by the _____ and services of which it is a _____ and for which it can be _____.

Money we earn at home and spend abroad becomes part of our national _____ to another country and can be _____ by exports to that country. Similarly, money spent on _____ represents goods and services which our country must _____ to repay in some form, not to the individual who _____ or produced the imports but to the country of their _____.

|               |          |
|---------------|----------|
| symbol        | origin   |
| manufacture   | debt     |
| represent     | goods    |
| exchange      | imports  |
| balance       | attempt  |

---

Heaton (1975) provides examples and guidelines for writing multiple-choice items. Among his examples of items which could be used in achievement tests are the following.

1. Multiple-choice in context

    Later I _____ to them for my bad behavior.

    (a) apologized   (b) applauded   (c) enquired   (d) entertained

2. Sets

    Three of the four words in each line are similar in meaning or share some common features. Draw a circle around the word that does not fit.

    1. conference, congress, meeting, ethics
    2. collapse, dissipate, speculate, decay
    3. fallacy, controversy, argument, debate
    4. assemble, convene, orbit, gather

3. Matching words and meanings

4. true/false

    The words to be tested are put in sentences. If the tested word is not known the learners will find it difficult to answer correctly.

See the section on definitions in Chapter 4 for help in making suitable sentences.

If your food is deficient in vitamin C you will not become ill easily.    True/False

5. Translation

If the teacher knows the mother tongue of the learners, translation is a useful way of providing a quick check of learning. The translation need not be exact. Understanding of word meanings develops as learners get more experience of English. The learners can be asked to translate underlined words presented in sentences or in a passage, or just to translate words in a list.

## WHAT SHOULD YOU DO WHEN LEARNERS DO NOT HAVE ENOUGH VOCABULARY TO READ THEIR SET TEXTS?

We have seen how it is necessary to have a vocabulary of a least 3000 headwords in order to be able to read unsimplified texts. However, many learners, especially those wanting to study at the university or technical institute level, may have less than this. What can be done?

It is necessary to look at the size of the task facing the learners. First, increasing a learner's vocabulary does not necessarily mean that there will be a big improvement in reading skills. Although vocabulary knowledge plays a large part in readability studies, it is partly a reflection of other factors like background knowledge and previous reading experience. Any increase in vocabulary size must be accompanied by many opportunities to put this vocabulary to use. Second, learners may need to learn several hundred words in order to be able to tackle unsimplified texts. This is not a hopeless task, but it is a big one.

The following suggestions are of two types—learning vocabulary by direct study and learning vocabulary through reading.

### Vocabulary Exercises

The direct teaching of vocabulary is best done on an individualized basis. There are several reasons for this. First, it takes account of the difficult circumstances under which most teaching of English as a foreign language is done, with few texts, high absenteeism, large classes, and learners with a wide range of proficiency (Nation, 1975). Second, analysis of the results of vocabulary tests shows that although the class average on a test may be 95 percent, in fact only 40 percent of the words are known by every student. If the teacher presents the remaining 60 percent of the words, at least half the learners will already know the words presented. This argues for an individualized teaching approach. Learners can go quickly over the already known material and can spend more time on the material that is new to them.

One way of doing this is to use an area approach. For example, the words that the learners are expected to learn are divided into various levels: 500 words, 1000 words, 1500 words, and so on. Where each learner begins and ends a level is unimportant as long as most of the material is covered. It is most convenient if each vocabulary teaching exercise occupies one typed over-sized page. Each word within the level could be presented in at least four different exercises. At least 30 words may be taught in each exercise. All the other words in the exercise would be from a lower level. Thus, to teach 500 words within any one level, approximately 70 exercises would be required. Each exercise can be sealed in a plastic bag and all of them put in a box. Learners use them in a similar way to a reading box. They work individually on different exercises at their own speed. Answer keys are used for self-correction. Each exercise takes an average of 20 minutes. During these 20 minutes the learner has paid close attention to 30 or more words, most of which are new.

Here are four examples of exercises for individual work which could be used in this way.

1. When the learners do this exercise they must try to guess the meaning of the new word by looking at the context. They show that they have guessed correctly by choosing the correct missing sentence.

---

### One More Sentence

Find the missing sentence from the group below. Write the number of the sentence and write the correct words next to it.

A boat is usually made of wood or iron.
People can travel in a boat.
A boat goes on the sea.

A car can carry four or five people.
A car has seats.
A car goes on the road.

Ice is made of water.
Ice is cold and hard.
The color of ice is like glass.

We do not like our enemy.
Our enemy usually does not like us.
Soldiers fight the enemy.

Electricity can kill people.
A light shines because there is electricity.
Electricity goes through wire.

Every person speaks a language.
Some people speak a foreign language.
We speak and write a language.

An officer is an important person.
There are officers in the army and the air force.
The soldiers listen to the officer.

People eat and drink at a party.
People are happy at a party.
When someone marries, there is a party.

We study history at school.
History is about the past.
We read about history in books.

A shed is one room.
A shed is usually near a house.
People keep tools and old things in a shed.

1. People teach it at the university.
2. This person watches the others carefully.
3. It is a small building.
4. It has words and sentences.
5. We have it on our birthday.
6. People put it in drinks.
7. He is not our friend.
8. It has four wheels.
9. Sometimes a stove or a machine uses it.
10. Sometimes the wind moves it.

---

Note that the words are presented in context and that reading for understanding and guessing from context clues are demanded.

When this exercise is used for teaching adjectives, verbs, or adverbs, the missing sentence has a blank space where the word should be.

2. Twenty words are taught on one page (Figure 8.1). They are not broken into smaller groups. When nonpicturable words are taught, the same type of context sentence is given, and instead of a picture a definition or translation is used. The sentence context of the word gives a part of the meaning and the picture adds to or checks the meaning.

3. Each exercise contains 35 items. All the coded words in an exercise make use of less than 14 different symbols, and each symbol occurs in at least 5 different words in the exercise (see Figure 8.2). five out of the

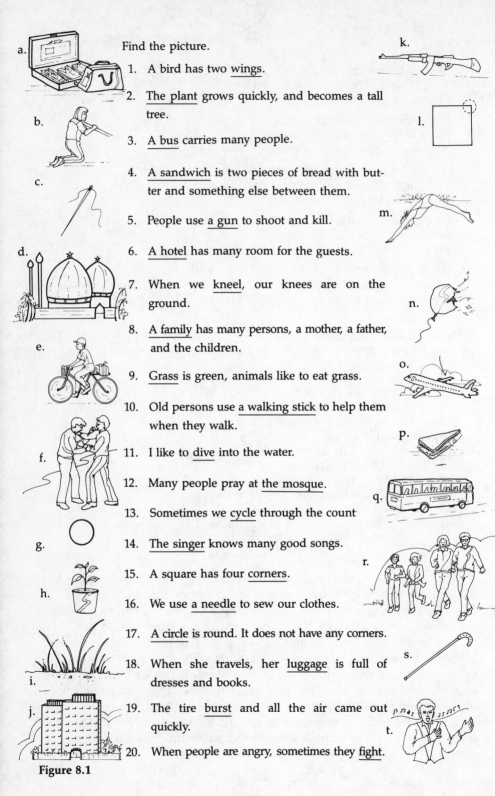

a.

b.

c.

d.

e.

f.

g.

h.

i.

j.

k.

l.

m.

n.

o.

p.

q.

r.

s.

t.

Find the picture.

1. A bird has two <u>wings</u>.

2. <u>The plant</u> grows quickly, and becomes a tall tree.

3. <u>A bus</u> carries many people.

4. <u>A sandwich</u> is two pieces of bread with butter and something else between them.

5. People use <u>a gun</u> to shoot and kill.

6. <u>A hotel</u> has many room for the guests.

7. When we <u>kneel</u>, our knees are on the ground.

8. <u>A family</u> has many persons, a mother, a father, and the children.

9. <u>Grass</u> is green, animals like to eat grass.

10. Old persons use <u>a walking stick</u> to help them when they walk.

11. I like to <u>dive</u> into the water.

12. Many people pray at <u>the mosque</u>.

13. Sometimes we <u>cycle</u> through the count

14. <u>The singer</u> knows many good songs.

15. A square has four <u>corners</u>.

16. We use <u>a needle</u> to sew our clothes.

17. <u>A circle</u> is round. It does not have any corners.

18. When she travels, her <u>luggage</u> is full of dresses and books.

19. The tire <u>burst</u> and all the air came out quickly.

20. When people are angry, sometimes they <u>fight</u>.

**Figure 8.1**

122

123

# Figure 8.2

Many words are in code. Find the words. The first word *:?)0 has five letters. Do your work very carefully.

1. He is at his office *:?)0 six o'clock, and then he goes home.

£ &£@?

2. This is an $0$&?@)& light.

£&*θ

3. My father's brother is my *:&0$

4. My mother and my £?(\$0

I 00$!$0''tea, but I like coffee too.

5. A person who is θ*:&?*£0 never comes late.

£: £%@*0£:&$

6. Our &(): moves when we talk.

I forgot his name. Do you 0$%$%@$0 it?

7. Be careful when you θ+*0 the water from the jug into the bottle.

8. £ ?0£):

9. What is the θ0)&$ of that shirt? Is it expensive?

10. £ ()00

11.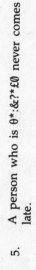

12.

13.

14.

15.

16. What &+0+0is it? Green.

17. Indonesia has a hot &0)%£$ and so has Thailand.

**Figure 8.2 (continued)**

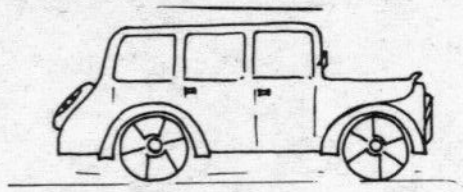

18.

This &£Ø is old but it is very expensive.

19.

At night, I sometimes ($£Ø the noise of the trains.

20.

!Ø*)? 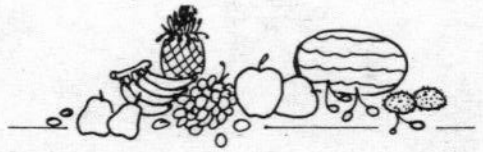

21.

The first %$£Ø of the day is breakfast.

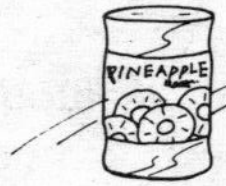



22.

A &£: of fruit is usually expensive.

23.

The ?)%$ is two o'clock.

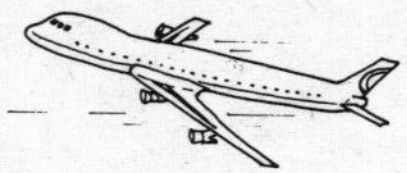

24.

£: £ØØØ£:$

25.

If he wants to do it, Ø$? him do it.

26.

This is the &+ØØ£Ø of the shirt. 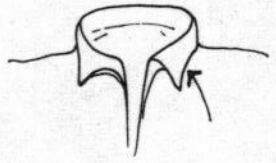

27.

In the battle the airplane dropped a big @+%@ 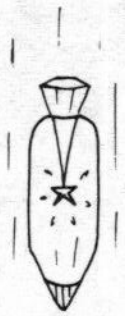

28.

A car engine burns θ$?Ø+Ø

This @£ØØ++: is full of air 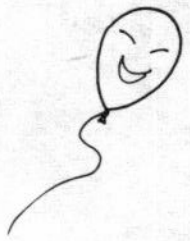

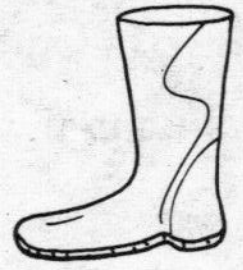

30.

£
@++?

31.

There is a good !)Ø% at the movies.

32.

!*Ø:)?*Ø$ 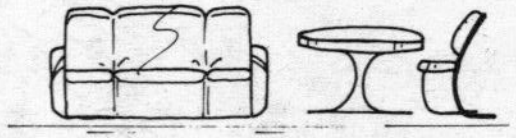

33.

The ?()$! stole a radio and a lot of clothes.

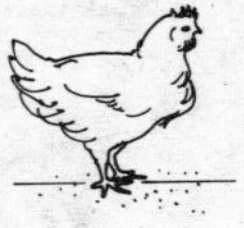

34.

£ ($:

35.

Before you drink the water, @+)Ø it for ten minutes.

30 coded words are from a lower level and should be known to the learners. By solving these easy words the learner is able to write the new words correctly. This exercise gets very close attention to the new words, especially their form, and presents them in context. Learners at all levels enjoy the challenge that this exercise presents to them.

A variation of this technique is to list difficult words, in code, with glosses under a reading passage. The learners decode the words by trying to find them in the passage. The glosses of the words help the learners to find them. Once a few words have been decoded, the rest are easy. This variation ensures attention to the glosses.

4. In learn-and-test exercises a variety of techniques of teaching words is used: labeled pictures, words with definitions, words in contexts, words and synonyms. On the back of each page the same words are tested using a different method. Thus, if the words are presented with definitions, then on the back the test requires insertion in contexts, and so on. If a labeled picture is used for presentation, then the words are tested using a different picture or matching words and written meanings. In the following exercise, the words are tested using a cloze exercise.

---

Some words are not in this story. You can find the words and their meanings above the story. Write the numbers on another piece of paper. Next to the correct number write the missing word. 3x means that the word *wings* is in three different places.

|     | before | in front of. | 1969 is *before* 1970. |
|-----|--------|--------------|------------------------|
|     | air    | the sky.     | The *air* was full of birds. |
| 3x  | wings  |              |                        |

|     | so     | because of this. | I hit him *so* he hit me. |
|-----|--------|------------------|---------------------------|
|     | moves  | goes from one place to another. | She wants to *move* this bed to another room. |
|     | ground | not the sky or the sea. | Children run on the *ground*, birds fly in the air. |
|     | flat   |                  |                           |

The top of his head is. *flat.*

His head is not *flat.*

|  | grow | become bigger.    When she is young, a child *grows* very quickly. |
|  | several | many.    I have *several* new books. |
| 2x | sometimes | not all the time.    I *sometimes* go to the movies. |
|  | along | |

He ran *along* the side of the road.

|  | spend | He *spends* $10 each week for food. |

A heavy bird cannot easily get into the __1__ . It __2__ its __3__ up and down, and __4__ it runs before it can fly. Because a lake or a river is __5__ , many big birds run __6__ the top of the water __7__ they fly. __8__ , many big birds __9__ a lot of time on the __10__ . __11__ , after many hundreds of years they cannot fly again. __12__ birds cannot fly at all. They still have __13__ . But their __14__ are very small and weak. Because they cannot fly, they __15__ bigger than most flying birds.

---

## Learning Words in Isolation

Learning lists of words has been unfashionable among many language teachers for quite a long time. However, learners working on their own frequently use this technique. In addition, for over a hundred years psychologists and researchers on language learning have investigated how such learning can be most efficiently carried out.

One of the great attractions of learning lists of words is that large numbers of words can be learned in a very short time. Without too much effort learners can master well over 30 foreign-word mother-tongue word associations per hour. Experiments have shown that some learners are capable of rates of over a hundred associations per hour. Moreover, most of this learning is still retained several weeks afterwards.

The research shows that some ways of learning from lists are more efficient than others, so there are many useful learning tips that teachers can pass on to their learners and give them practice in applying them.

1. Learning is more efficient if the foreign word form is associated with a word in the mother tongue rather than a foreign synonym or definition.

2. Each word form and its translation should be put on a small card with the foreign word form on one side and the translation on the other.

This is much more efficient than setting the words out in lists in a book or on a sheet of paper. First, the learners can look at the foreign word and make an effort to recall its translation without seeing the translation. It helps learning to say the foreign word while trying to think of its translation. Second, the learners can rearrange the cards so that they are not using the sequence of the words in the list to help recall. Third, they can put the words which give them the most difficulty at the beginning of their pile of cards so that they can give them extra attention.

Piles of these cards are easily carried around, and they can be studied whenever the learners have a free moment.

3. Much more important than the number of repetitions or the amount of effort put into the learning are the particular types of association made between the foreign word and its translation.

The keyword technique is one way (see Chapter 10). The use of word analysis by breaking the foreign word into prefix, root, and suffix is another. In such analysis it is often only necessary to know the meaning of the prefix in order to make a useful association between a foreign word and its mother-tongue translation. Instead of just trying to list the foreign word form with a mother-tongue word, the learners should try to imagine what the mother-tongue word represents. The more striking and unusual the image, the better the learning. Finally, the learners should look carefully at a foreign word they want to learn to see if the shape or sound of the word will provide a way of making a strong association with its translation. For example, a *pintu* is used when you go *into* a house. It needs to be stressed that learning words in lists is only the first step in mastering new vocabulary. Eventually the learners need to know much more about a word than can be learned from memorizing its mother-tongue translation, but learning the mother-tongue translation provides a useful basis for this future learning.

Nation (1982) gives a comprehensive review of experiments involving learning words in lists. The review examines issues such as these: How many words can be studied within a set time? Why are some words more difficult to learn than others? It presents the experimental findings on the relative effectiveness of various techniques for receptive and productive learning.

## Simplified Reading

Large quantities of simplified reading in conjunction with other vocabulary expansion approaches like those mentioned above can be a very effective way of increasing vocabulary size and developing reading skill. The disadvantage of simplified reading is that learners might feel that the activity is irrelevant to their needs, which are to read unsimplified texts.

This objection may be overcome by explaining the reasons for the simplified reading and by doing intensive reading of unsimplified texts as well. When the learners do large amounts of simplified reading they should not have to write book reports about what they have read. This writing would take time away from reading. Filling in a brief report form asking for the name of the book, its level, its interest for the reader, and any new vocabulary met would be sufficient. Chapter 11 looks at simplification.

## Intensive Reading of Unsimplified Texts

The exercises in this section are aimed not at improving reading skill but solely at learning vocabulary.

1. Written exercises on vocabulary can follow a reading text. There are many variations of these. Usually the exercise is a list of definitions, and the learners have to find the defined words in the text.

> _____ go after animals for food
> _____ not long ago

The exercise can be made easier by substituting a dash for each letter of the word, by putting the definitions in the same order as the words in the text, by putting the line number of the word next to the definition, by giving the first letter of the word, by underlining the words in the text, or by writing the words in code next to the definitions.

2. Many words like *too*, *like*, and *bear* have two or more different meanings. Sometimes the word has a different meaning when its grammar is different: *like*—a preposition, and *like*—a verb. Sometimes it is the context alone and not the grammar as well that is a signal of a different meaning: *light*—bright, and *light*—not heavy. This exercise gives learners practice in choosing the correct meaning when they read. Some of the sentences can be taken from a reading passage.

---

Choose the correct meaning and write (a) or (b) at the end of each sentence. The first two are done for you.

> a    fly = n. = a thing with wings and six legs
> b    fly = v. = move through the air
> 1    He killed a fly. (a)
> 2    The airplane did not fly fast. (b)

3    These flies were very old.
4    They were flying above the table.
5    One fly fell into the American's glass.
6    This bird flies south in the winter.
7    A person cannot fly by himself.
8    The American looked at the fly in his glass.
9    He flies to Singapore next week.
10    Flies are dirty.

(Nation, 1974)

Or, instead of explaining the meanings of *fly*, the directions just say:

When *fly* has the same meaning as in sentence 1, write (a) next to it. When *fly* has the same meaning as sentence 2, write (b) next to it.

## Semantic Mapping

There has been increasing interest in the use of semantic mapping as a way of increasing vocabulary (Stahl & Vancil, 1986). Semantic mapping involves the teacher and learners working together to build up diagrammatic maps showing the relationship between vocabulary suggested by the teacher, suggested by the learners, and found in a reading text. Stahl and Vancil (1986) suggest that discussion of the relationships between the words or the semantic map is a very important part of the procedure.

The semantic mapping procedure is subject to the same cautions as other procedures involving associative networks. Some associative relationships help learning, some interfere. Because semantic mapping is often text based, there is a high chance that the associative relationships will be positive.

## WHAT SHOULD YOU DO WHEN THERE ARE SOME UNKNOWN WORDS IN THE TEXTS?

When considering what to do about unknown vocabulary in a reading text, the teacher needs to decide what the purpose of the lesson is. If the purpose of the lesson is to develop reading skills or to master the content of a reading test, then time spent on vocabulary will be an unwanted interruption of the lesson. Any vocabulary work should be speedy and brief so that the learners are not distracted from the purpose of the lesson. If the purpose of the lesson is to develop learners' reading vocabulary, then the teacher can afford to spend some time on particular vocabulary and on vocabulary learning strategies. This will usually mean a frequent interruption of the reading process, but the interruptions are necessary so that the reading of future texts can proceed without interruption. The strategies of guessing from context, using word parts, and dictionary work require quite a lot of time while they are being learned, but once these strategies have been mastered they more than repay the time invested in them. When deciding if to spend time on a word the following factors should be considered.

1. Is the word itself worth learning? High-frequency words and specialized vocabulary are worth spending time on in their own right because the learners can be sure of meeting them again soon in their reading.

2. Does the word contain useful word parts, for example, *ad/voc/ate*? If it does, then although the word itself may not be very useful, the time spent reviewing or learning the word parts and relating their meaning to the meaning of the whole word will be repaid when learners meet words containing the same parts and when they relate word part meanings to whole word meanings. If the word contains known parts, then the effort of learning is small.

3. Does the word provide a good opportunity to practice guessing from context? Most unknown words in a text will provide this opportunity if there are not too many of them. Some adjectives may be difficult to guess. Guessing from context is the most important vocabulary learning technique and any time spent practicing it is well justified. It provides access to thousands of words. The early stages of practicing guessing are very time-consuming because the learner needs to be alerted to all the available clues. It is best if this practice is done separately from other reading skill practice because it interrupts reading considerably in terms of time and focus of attention. The ultimate aim of guessing, however, is that the learners can do it without interrupting reading.

Figure 8.3 summarizes the possibilities for dealing with unknown words.

Let us look at these possibilities.

## Guessing from Context

This is undoubtedly the most important vocabulary learning strategy. Its aim is for learners to be able to make a well-informed guess at the meaning of an unknown word in context without interrupting the reading too much. Developing skill in the strategy involves considerable

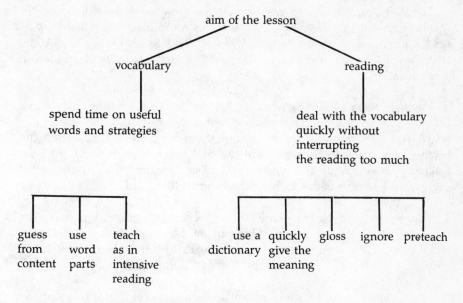

**Figure 8.3**  Dealing with unknown words.

time and interruption to the reading process, but this is well repaid by the usefulness of the strategy. This strategy is described in detail in Chapter 10.

## Using Word Parts

This is a strategy for learning new vocabulary after the meaning has been discovered by other methods, such as guessing, using a dictionary, or teacher explanation. It is not recommended as a way of finding the meaning of unknown vocabulary. About 60 percent of the low-frequency words of English are of Latin, French, or Greek derivation (Roberts, 1965), and many of these contain word parts that are found in other words. Using word parts is discussed in detail in Chapter 10.

## Spending Time on Words

When a teacher has decided it is worth spending time on a word, the next question is: What features of the word should be focused on? Chapter 3 examines this under several headings. These headings, to be found in Table 3.1, are listed below with some related techniques.

**Spoken Form**   The learners are given practice individually or together pronouncing the new word. If it has more than one syllable, particular attention is given to word stress. The teacher may also draw attention to regular features of the spelling that are reliable guides to pronunciation.

**Written Form**   The learners are given practice spelling the word. Here is one technique: The teacher writes several words on the blackboard and tells the learners to look at them for a short time. Then the teacher rubs out everything except the first letter of each word, and the learners have to write the words on a piece of paper. The first letter of each word provides clues to help them recall the words.

**Grammar**   The learners are shown what grammatical pattern the new word typically occurs in. This can be done by looking at the sentence in which it occurs in the reading text or by the use of outside examples. Chapter 9 presents several ways of doing this.

**Collocation**   The learners make or look at several examples of the words that typically occur with the new word. If possible, they draw some generalization about the types of words that collocate with the new word. Chapter 7 describes several collocation exercises.

**Frequency and Appropriateness**   The learners are told whether the word is commonly used or not and if it has any restrictions of use, such as being suitable only in formal contexts, or being used only with reference to children.

**Concept**   Using either deductive or inductive approaches, the teacher gets the learners to see the concept that runs through most uses of the word. An effective way is to get several examples of the word in context, including the one in the text, and get the learners to decide what the uses have in common.

**Association**   Sometime later it may be useful to do a grid, cluster, or cline exercise like those described in Chapter 7. This puts the word in its place with words of related meaning. It is best to delay this activity until the word is secure in the learners' knowledge so that interference between the word and related words does not occur.

The decision about what features of the new word to focus on should depend on an analysis of the learning burden of the word.

This approach to spending time on words can be turned into a learner strategy. The learners look at an unknown word in a text and then decide what questions they want to ask the teacher about it. When preparing them for this strategy, the teacher can show them the list of features described above (e.g., spoken form, written form, grammar). This teacher-questioning strategy encourages learners to look at what information is available in the text and sensitizes them to what they need to know in order to learn a new word. Preparation of the questions in pairs or small groups is a good introduction to the strategy.

There are ways in which learners can share their vocabulary knowledge with each other. Sandosham (1980) describes the setting up of "a word bank," which is like a dictionary on cards with one card for each word. Each card contains the word, its meaning, and several examples. The word bank is mainly the result of learners' work. Ndomba Benda (1983) suggests that as a part of presenting oral book reports, learners describe some of the new vocabulary they have met, giving its meaning and context, and how they found its meaning.

## Giving the Meaning Quickly

Chapter 4 details the various ways of getting the meaning of a word across quickly. In some situations translation will be the most effective way; in others a quick definition or simile will suffice. Usually the teacher will give a meaning that works in the context. If the word has useful parts, quick analysis of the word will not take much time and will have useful effects.

## Ignoring Unknown Words

It is often recommended that learners should be encouraged *not* to look up or puzzle over every unknown word that they meet in a reading text. Research with native speakers indicates that a good way to encourage learners not to do this is to have questions at the beginning of reading texts. Then learners read with a purpose and do not worry about not understanding a few words in those parts of the text that do not contain answers to the questions. Freebody and Anderson (1983) found that readers skipped unfamiliar words and even parts of sentences containing them if they did not seem to be necessary to follow the theme of the text or to do the task they were set. Putting a time limit on such reading will also make ignoring some unknown words an advantage (British Council Teachers, 1980).

## Preteaching Vocabulary

One way of stopping vocabulary work from interrupting reading is to preteach the unknown vocabulary in the text. This can be a useful procedure but there are several difficulties associated with it. First, research with native speakers (Nation & Coady, 1988) has not shown gains in comprehension as a result of preteaching vocabulary. One possible explanation for this is that giving the meaning of words that are in the text still does not make it easy for the learners to gain access to those meanings while reading. To help access, the words would need to be taught sometime before the learners read the text, and the teaching should be followed by collocation activities and others.

Second, preteaching takes away the opportunity for learners to use their guessing skill. Third, vocabulary teaching will be more meaningful for learners *after* they have met it in a text because then they have some experience to attach the teaching to.

## Glossing

One way of dealing with "one-timers" and other low-frequency words in a text is to provide a short definition somewhere near the text. This has several advantages. First, it allows the reader to follow the text without too much interruption. It is a way of dealing quickly with words which are important in the text but are not important in the language as a whole. Second, it gives the learner independence from the teacher. The learner does not have to wait for the teacher to supply the meanings of unknown words. Third, it individualizes attention to vocabulary. You look at the definition only if you need to. For this reason it is best if words which are glossed are not marked in any way in the text. Some form of marking in the text (the use of bold letters or an asterisk) would encourage learners to look at the definition when they did not need to. It would develop a sense of insecurity about vocabulary which would interfere with their reading.

Learners should be encouraged to use glosses as a way of confirming guessing from context. They should not look up the meaning of a word without first having a guess at its meaning. For this reason, glosses are best situated at the end of the text or in the back of the book.

The *Bridge Series* of simplified readers makes use of a glossary. In the books in this series, words above the 7000-word level have been replaced by more frequent words. "Words used which are outside the first 3000 of the [Thorndike and Lorge] list are explained in a glossary and are so distributed throughout the book that they do not occur at a greater density than 25 per running 1000 words" (Introduction to each *Bridge Series* book).

There have been only a few experiments on glossing. Brutten (1981) checked to see whether teachers' choices of words to gloss in a particular text agreed with learners' choices. Her experiment thus tried to answer the question: Can teachers accurately predict which words their learners do not know in a text? There was not perfect agreement between teachers and learners, but "The data suggest that experienced ESL teachers can, to a notable extent, read a passage and separate out the words that second-language students are likely to consider difficult when reading for meaning" (pp. 68–69). It seems likely that choosing words to gloss intuitively would be about as effective as using a word-frequency list as a guide. Holley and King (1971) experimented with three kinds of glosses—at the side of the page, at the bottom of the page, and in an attached list. Holley and King suggested that glosses could help vocabulary learning in two ways: by immediately giving the correct meaning of unknown words so that the learner repeats it, or by giving the learner the opportunity to repeat the form while looking for the meaning. "It seems possible that by positioning the gloss at the bottom of the page the benefits of both processes might be gained. A brief time for [repetition of the form] would be allowed while the student's eye moved to the bottom of the page, but the gloss would minimize erroneous guessing" (p. 214). Holley and King found no significant difference among the three types of glossing.

It still has to be shown that glossing helps vocabulary learning. The advantage of glossing may be that it helps reading by providing the meaning of words that are not easily guessed by using context clues.


## Referring to a Dictionary

*Choice of a Dictionary*    Dictionaries can serve several purposes, and the choice of a dictionary should depend on what it is to be used for. Studies of the use of dictionaries by both native speakers and second language learners show that dictionaries are used primarily to check meaning. The next most frequent uses are to check spelling and pronunciation (Bejoint, 1981; MacFarquhar & Richards, 1983).

If a dictionary is to be used as an aid to understanding in reading and perhaps listening, then it is important that it includes a large number of words and idioms, gives information about the meaning and appropriateness of words, and is easy to use. Research by MacFarquhar and Richards (1983) indicates that learners of English show a clear preference for a dictionary with definitions written within a limited vocabulary. The Longman *Dictionary of Contemporary English* uses a vocabulary of 2000 words. Dictionaries produced by West (1935) use an even more restricted vocabulary. This preference for definitions within a limited vocabulary applies both to low-proficiency and high-proficiency learners of English. Jain (1981) presents some of the arguments against such definitions, but the advantages clearly outweigh the disadvantages.

If a dictionary is going to help in the *learning* of vocabulary, it needs to show the form and meaning relationships between words and their uses so that the learning burden of words is reduced. Ilson (1983), for example, argues persuasively for the inclusion of etymological information in dictionaries for second language learners. Such information, if it is presented in a suitable way, could help learners relate new words with known words (*rank* with *arrange*), explain words and idioms so that they are easier to remember (*above-board*, *golly*), and encourage an interest in words. Dictionaries, in the interest of exactness, tend to increase the number of different meanings and uses a word has. Learning, however, is made easier if underlying concepts and relationships are made clear.

Bilingual dictionaries do not usually do this very well. Rather than give a definition, they give a translation. Baxter (1980) considers that the use of such dictionaries hinders the learners in developing the skill of using paraphrase to make up for words they do not know. Scholfield (1982a) gives useful guidelines for evaluating bilingual dictionaries.

Further discussion of the criteria to use in choosing a dictionary and reviews of dictionaries for second language learners can be found in Bauer (1980, 1981), Brown and Lynn (1976), Hartmann (1981, 1982), Jain (1981), Scholfield (1982a), Tomaszczyk (1981), and Yorkey (1974, 1979).

**Using the Dictionary**    In guessing words from context, reference to a dictionary was one of the steps used to check if a guess was correct. Efficient use of a dictionary to find the meanings of words in a passage for comprehension presupposes that the learner has already gathered some information about the word from the context. This information will probably include the part of speech of the word, its immediate context, some vague idea about its meaning, and knowledge of the wider context such as the theme of the passage. With this background knowledge, Scholfield (1982b) describes a dictionary use strategy involving seven steps.

1. Locate the word(s) or phrase you don't understand.
2. If the unknown word is inflected (e.g., *-er, -s, -ing*), remove the inflections to find the form to look up.
3. Search for the unknown word in the alphabetic list.
4. If you can't find at least one main entry for the unknown word, try looking in the addendum, look at nearby entries if the unknown word might be an irregular form, look up parts of the word or phrase.
5. If there are several senses or homographic entries, reduce them by elimination.
6. Understand the definition and integrate it into the context where the unknown word was met.

7. If none of the senses or entries seems to fit, attempt to infer one from the senses you have. If more than one fits, see further context clues in the passage to help you choose.

There are several exercises that can help learners prepare for this strategy. Practice with the alphabet is a useful activity. Breaking irregularly inflected words into parts is another. Analysis of typical dictionary entries to show the signs for part of speech and the ways of signaling collocations and sentence patterns is also useful.

Learners can do dictionary work in groups to learn new words in a reading passage. The class is divided into small groups. The reading passage is divided into parts so that there is one part for each group. Each group makes a list of the new words in its part of the passage. Then the teacher asks the leader of each group to name the words, and they are all written on the blackboard. Then the words are divided up among the groups, and each group uses a dictionary to find the meaning of the new words. Then the groups tell the meanings to the teacher, who writes them on the blackboard. The class can discuss the meanings while they are being written up.

Research on dictionary use has shown that allowing learners to use dictionaries while taking a reading comprehension test has no significant effect on their reading comprehension score (Bensoussan, Sim, & Weiss, 1984). Moreover, there are considerable obstacles to overcome before learners at all levels are able to make efficient use of a dictionary (Neubach and Cohen, in press). Research on dictionary use and comprehension has shown that allowing learners to use dictionaries while reading does not measurably increase their comprehension (Bensoussan, 1983; Bensoussan et al., 1984).

## Reviewing Words Met in Texts

The teacher keeps a record (or asks a learner to keep a record) of useful vocabulary which the class meets. Low-frequency vocabulary can be useful and worth attention for several reasons. The principle is that any attention given to these words will result in some *future* benefit to the learners. First, some low-frequency words may occur several times in a specialized area that is of relevance to the learners. Second, a low-frequency word may be a good example of some regular feature of the language. For example, a word may contain a prefix, root, or suffix that will be useful for the learners when dealing with other words. A low-frequency word may be an example of a useful spelling pattern, such as the doubling of consonants or the effect of final silent *e*. Or the word may be a collocation of a much more useful word.

Once or twice a week, the teacher can spend a few minutes reviewing these words in one or more of the following ways.

1. Dictate the words in sentences. Get one learner to write the words on the blackboard while you do this. This will help you get ready for the following techniques.

2. Put each word in a true/false statement as a way of quickly reviewing the meaning. For example, "When we show *reverence* toward something, we show our respect for it." Instead of doing this, the learners can be asked to suggest quickly synonyms or rough definitions for the words.

3. Ask the learners to break the words into prefix, root, and suffix where this is possible, and ask them to give the meanings of these parts.

4. Ask the learners to suggest words which collocate with those on the blackboard. For example, if the word is a verb, what words or types of words usually act as its subject, what words act as its object? If the word is a noun what adjectives go with it? What verbs can it collocate with?

5. Go around the class asking learners to pronounce any word on the blackboard that they are not sure about. Correct their pronunciation where necessary. Ask the learners to tell you how to break each word into syllables and where the stress is placed.

6. Erase all except the first letter of each word and then ask the learners to write the words on a piece of paper. Or tell the learners to look at the words for one minute, and then clean the blackboard. Ask the learners to write the words on a piece of paper exactly as they were on the blackboard—that is, in the same position, with the same capitalization, etc. About 14 to 20 words is a suitable number for this game.

## WHAT SHOULD YOU DO WHEN THERE ARE UNKNOWN WORDS IN AN ENGLISH FOR SPECIAL PURPOSES TEXT?

When learners have mastered the 2000 to 3000 words of general usefulness in English, it is wise to direct vocabulary learning to more specialized areas, depending on the aims of the learners. First, it is possible to specialize by learning the shared vocabulary of several fields of study—for example, academic vocabulary. Next, the specialized vocabulary of one particular field or part of that field can be studied. Let us look at each of these two in turn.

### Academic Vocabulary

There have been two types of frequency counts of university texts. One type assumes a basic vocabulary, like the *General Service List* (West, 1953), and counts words outside this basic vocabulary. The other type of frequency count does not count all the words in a set of university texts outside a basic group but counts only those words that cause difficulties for foreign students. The results of these counts overlap considerably.

The Campion and Elley (1971) and Praninskas (1972) counts were based on a range of first-year university textbooks. In the Campion and Elley count the textbooks and lectures covered 19 academic disciplines with the largest enrollment in New Zealand universities. The total words they inspected were 301,800. The Praninskas list was complied by using 10 basic university-level textbooks of first-year courses. The total words in her corpus were 272,466 running words from every tenth page of the 10 textbooks. The list was compiled for the students whose first language was not English but who planned to study in the English medium and would have to read textbooks written by and for native speakers of English.

The basic vocabulary found in any standard word count was excluded in the counts of university texts. Since the students for whom the lists were being prepared had studied English for several years at school, it could be assumed that the basic vocabulary should be familiar to more students entering universities. Campion and Elley excluded the words which can be found in the first 5,000 words in the *Teacher's Word Book of 30,000 Words* by E. L. Thorndike and I. Lorge (1944). In the Praninskas list, words appearing in the *General Service List of English Words* by Michael West (1953) were excluded. The range of the words in the count was recorded and considered when making the lists. The Campion and Elley list contains 500 words and the Praninskas list contains 507 headwords.

The Lynn (1973) and Ghadessy (1979) word lists were made by counting the words that foreign students wrote annotations above (usually mother-tongue translations) in their university textbooks. Thus, these were lists of words that learners found difficult during their reading. Lynn counted a total of 10,000 annotated words. He found that 120 headwords—for example, *relevant* (which includes *relevant, irrelevant, relevance*)—covered 20 percent of the lexical difficulties. Lynn's published list contains the top 197 headwords. Ghadessy went through 478,700 running words and made a list of 795 annotated word types.

Xue and Nation (1984) combined these four word lists so that the *General Service List* was the prerequisite for the combined list. The combined list contains almost 740 headwords (see Appendix 2). It was found that there was considerable overlap among the four lists. A revised version of the Xue and Nation list (Nation, 1984) incorporates words from Barnard and Brown's second 1000-word list.

Specialized word counts have several values. First, they provide a useful guide for teachers to help them focus on vocabulary in reading, writing, listening, and testing activities. Second, they can act as a checklist and a goal for learners. Learners can go through such lists, mark the words they do not know, and set about learning them. In this way these very important words are brought to the learners' conscious attention, and learning can proceed from there.

A word of caution is necessary. Specialized word counts which look at a *range* of material within a specialized area naturally end up with lists of words of general usefulness in that area. Lynn (1973, p. 26) puts it this way:

> "Perhaps the most striking feature of the resulting list is the absence of technical terms. One might expect to find terms like *debenture*, *blue-collar*, *inflation* and *debit*, and in fact terms of this type make up the bulk of the vocabulary items in nearly all TEFL texts for commercial students. But instead we find "textbook English" words—nontechnical terms from the academic register—presenting the greatest problems to our students. Even such apparently commercial terms as "appraise" and "compensate" were not, in fact, encountered in a commercial context, but in such academic phrases as "appraising the significance of . . . " and "factors which compensate for. . . . "

The research does *not* show that most of the words that learners do not know are nontechnical. It only shows that the words that *most* learners do not know are the middle-frequency words. It could not be any other way because technical words are, almost by definition, narrow range and *generally* infrequent. Therefore, when sampling a range of texts (and a range of learners), the technical words are likely to be one-timers and thus would not appear in a final list which took account of frequency and range. So, technical words as a group could still be a problem for second language learners.

The Vocabulary Levels Test (Appendix 8) contains a section based on the University Word List. If a learner intends doing academic study in English in an upper secondary school or at a university, then a score of at least 15 out of 18 is desirable. If a learner has a lower score than this, then study of the items in the University Word List will by very useful. This can be done in several ways. (a) The learners study the words out of context by using cards with the word on one side of the card and its translation on the other. Nation (1982) describes the justifications for such learning. (b) The learners use word-part analysis to help learn the vocabulary. Farid (1985) uses a word-part approach to words in the Praninskas list. Here is another possible word-part exercise.

---

Use the meaning of the underlined word parts to complete the sentences.

1. Things which are *simi*lar are the _____ in some ways.
        1    2

2. If a pen *con/sists* of three main parts, it means that these three parts __2__ __1__ to make the pen.
        1    2

3. When something is *pro/cess*ed, it __2__ __1__ through several steps in a factory.

---

## Technical Words and Low-Frequency Words

Technical words are usually considered to be the responsibility of the subject teacher rather than the English teacher. However, considering that large numbers occur in specialized texts, language teachers need to prepare learners to deal with them. Chapter 2 presents some information on the statistical nature of technical words.

If we look at technical words from the learners' point of view, the following information is revealed. Unknown technical words usually cannot be ignored during reading because they are closely connected to the topic being discussed. They are also difficult to guess from context if the reader does not already have a good background in that technical area. For the same reason, looking the word up in a dictionary does not bring much satisfaction. For example, a Chinese student reading a literary text on religious poetry found the words *liturgy* and *Eucharist* unguessable and still rather meaningless after looking them up because of her lack of experience with Christian worship. Clearly, learning technical words is closely connected with learning the subject.

Nagy, Herman and Anderson (1985) recognized the conceptual difficulty of unknown words using a 4-point scale: (a) The reader knows the concept and knows a one-word synonym. (b) The reader knows the concept but there is no one-word synonym—*apologize* means to say you are sorry. (c) The concept is not known but can be learned on the basis of experience and information already known to the reader. (d) The concept is not known and learning it requires new factual information or learning a related system of concepts.

Most technical vocabulary will be type (d), the most difficult to learn, or type (c) on this scale. Learners can usually decide if a word is technical or not when they meet it in a text.

For readers of specialist texts the advice "Learn every word you meet that you don't know" would not result in too much wasted effort. Li (1983) presents a slightly more sophisticated decision chart for low-frequency words (see Figure 8.4).

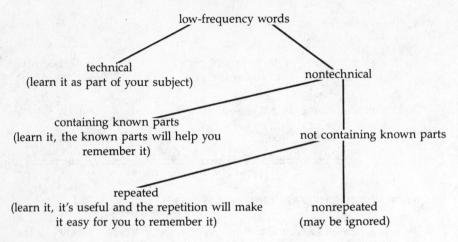

**Figure 8.4** Decision chart for dealing with low-frequency words in specialized texts.

The chart shows that when faced with unknown words the learner can ask three questions to help decide whether to make an effort to learn the new vocabulary. First, decide if the word is a technical word or not. If it is a technical word, it is worth learning because it is likely to occur again in this subject area, and learning the word is a part of learning the subject. If it is not a technical word, then decide if it contains known parts or not. If it has known parts, it is worth learning because this will review the strategy of using known parts, and the learning burden of the word will not be heavy. If the word does not contain known parts, do not worry about learning it unless you meet it again. If you meet it again, the repetition will help you learn it, and you know it is probably a useful word.

This focus on strategies for coping with vocabulary in texts is particularly suited to ESP texts. Bramki and Williams (1984) investigated the ways writers of specialized texts define (lexical familiarization) technical vocabulary. Their research shows that there are various clues that the writer is defining a word, and learners can be taught to recognize these. Williams (1985) suggests a variety of strategies for dealing with unknown words in ESP texts. These are inferring from context, identifying lexical familiarization, unchaining nominal compounds, searching for a synonym (lexical cohesion), and word analysis.

## APPLICATION

1. Get a learner to show you what vocabulary is unknown on two or three pages of a reading text. Which of the unknown words can the learner guess? What would you do about the unknown words?

2. Get a learner to guess some unknown words in a text (Appendix 4). What errors does the learner make? What learning is needed to avoid such errors?

3. Apply the decision chart (Figure 8.4) to the following passage.

What techniques would you use for those words you choose to spend time on?

Learners were given a passage from one of their school texts and were asked to (1) circle the words that they had never seen before, and (2) underline the words they had seen before but of which they felt unsure about the meaning. Here is one learner's response.

---

In another twelve or so countries, satisfactory progress had been made, although the campaign (was) not complete. One of these countries was Mexico. There, the battle against malaria got under way in 1957 with a series of surveys to find out where the disease was located. The country was then divided into fourteen (zones) and in 1958 <u>spraying</u> with <u>insecticide</u> began in each zone.

Teams travelled by <u>jeep</u>, on <u>horseback</u> and by boat. They moved through the inhabited areas (spraying) every house in every village. A record was kept of each spraying and the villagers were given instructions to call for assistance if the disease (flared) up. By 1964, three-quarters of the country, with a population of fifteen million people, was <u>rid</u> of the disease. However, in the most seriously affected areas it has proved very difficult to destroy the mosquito completely, and the struggle must continue.

The Malaria (campaign) has made least progress in Africa. In that continent, the disease has been a (stubborn) enemy. It remains very widespread in the countries surrounding the (Sahara) Desert and in those to the South, in the tropical <u>region</u>. One of the countries affected is <u>Togo</u> in West Africa. Togo is about half the size of the North Island, with slightly less population (1.8 million). But the great majority of its people, about 84 percent, suffer from malaria. The campaign began in Togo only as recently as 1964. First, a test area was selected to be a (site) for experimenting with ways of fighting the malarial mosquito. The area was small, about 650 square kilometres, but included one-tenth of Togo's population. The one large town <u>in the test</u> area was used as a base for the main health centre. Then, (dispensaries) were set up in the larger villages surrounding the town, and other teams were left to travel through the <u>outlying</u> districts. It was important, <u>of course</u>, that every person in the area was treated. There were many (obstacles) and they were not easily overcome. Movement was slow in the thick-wooded countryside, the hot(humid)climate made it difficult to work quickly. . . . (from *The United National and the Specialized Agencies* by B. J. Lynch. School Publications, New Zealand)

---

4. The section on vocabulary exercises at the beginning of the chapter has four kinds of exercises. Think of variations for each of these. For example, how could you make different checking items for the *One more sentence* exercise? How would you make an exercise like *Find the picture* for words which are not picturable? How many variations of *Learn-and-test* exercises can you think of?

5. Explain the meaning of these words using the meanings of their parts.

> *distraction, immerse, concentrate, ejected, exit, propulsion, decipher, discount, interfere, interpretation*

Here is one done for you.

> *intercept*—when someone intercepts a message, they get the message by coming *between* the sender and the receiver of the message. (*inter-* = between)

This contextual definition is a little clumsy but its aim is to make learning the new word, *intercept,* easier by relating it to a known part (*inter-*).

6. Apply the English for Special Purposes decision chart to the words in boxes in this text. The underlined words are in the University Word List. The words in boxes are the low-frequency and technical words. (They are not the first 2000 words of English and are not in the University Word List.)

---

### Ecosystems

The native forest, the man-made landscape and the rocky shore may on first appearance seem to consist of a jumble of plants and animals. Systematic examination, however, will reveal that each species present plays a definite role and has definite relationships with the others, and with its physical environment. Even more significantly, a comparative study of these relationships in forest, grassland, and rocky shore will reveal a pattern, or similarity common to them all. Such similarities found in widely differing sorts of ecological situations has led to the realization that the species concerned are participants in ordered, functioning systems. These are called ecosystems, a word which refers in a neat way to whole biological systems consisting of organisms and their physical surroundings involved together in the processes of living. Important features of organization are common to all ecosystems from the smallest to the largest.

The native forest, the grassland, and the rocky shore therefore represent three kinds of ecosystems. Comparable ecosystems are ponds, lakes, rivers, swamps, sand dunes, mud flats, sandshores, open ocean, alpine tussockland, exotic forest, and a large number of other definable ecological areas each with its characteristic selection of plants and animals. Commonly such ecosystems are named by their most obvious physical features, although some are recognized by their most obvious plant form as in the forest ecosystem, for example.

Ecosystems can be of any size, ranging from a decaying log or a piece of cattle dung to an extensive beech or pine forest. Collectively, all the ecosystems constitute the biosphere, that relatively thin layer over the surface of our planet within which all we know of life is found.

---

What would you do with each of the words in boxes?

Preteach.

Quickly give the meaning.

Let the learners look it up.

Help the learners use context to guess.

Do nothing about it.

Put it in a glossary.

Deal with it in an exercise after the passage.

Prepare a simplified version.

Spend time on it in class using word parts.

Spend time in class looking at its meaning and other features.

7. A new learner in your class is having great difficulty reading the set texts. You are not sure if vocabulary is a major part of the difficulty or not. How would you test to decide what to do?

# Chapter 9

# Vocabulary and Writing

This chapter looks at the following questions. What vocabulary is needed to write English? What should you do when learners do not have enough vocabulary to write? The activities looked at include giving attention to spelling, using vocabulary in sentences, using reading to help writing, using a dictionary, and using schematically related vocabulary.

## WHAT VOCABULARY IS NEEDED TO WRITE ENGLISH?

Work in simplification of texts has shown that a small number of words (around 2000 to 3000) can be used effectively to express an enormous number of ideas. As in the case with speaking, it is important to get learners to be able to make the best use of a small productive vocabulary. With writing, however, learners need to extend their productive vocabulary to include the specialized vocabulary of their areas of study and interest. In academic settings, writing is most often used as the form of assessment, and learners need to be able to show their knowledge of the field through the use of the specialized vocabulary. Raimes (1985, p. 248) stresses the need for an adequate vocabulary if learners are going to generate, develop, and present ideas in their writing. Raimes's studies show that the process of writing can be a contributor to vocabulary aquisition by making learners grapple with the meanings of words as they write.

## WHAT SHOULD YOU DO WHEN LEARNERS DO NOT HAVE ENOUGH VOCABULARY TO WRITE?

As with speaking, lack of vocabulary may be the result of a large enough receptive vocabulary but a very limited productive vocabulary, or it may be the result of a limited productive and receptive vocabulary. Learning to use a word productively in writing involves considerable learning that is not needed in listening, reading, or speaking. This learning includes spelling, the use of words in sentences, and the organization and signaling of written text. Spelling and the use of words in sentences are the most closely related to vocabulary, so we will look at them here. We will also look at the use of dictionaries in providing needed vocabulary. The sections in Chapter 7 on activities to improve access to vocabulary and paraphrase activities are also useful for writing. Particularly important among these are the techniques which make use of grids, clusters, and collocation.

## Spelling and Sound Patterns

Researchers on spelling (see e.g., Hanna, Hodges, & Hanna, 1971; Venezky, 1970) make the following points about English spelling: (a) There is a large amount of predictability of English spelling patterns. (b) This predictability must be based on a consideration of morphemic features such as stress and the effect of affixes, as well as on a consideration of graphemic and phonemic features. (c) The number of words with forms which are completely unpredictable are relatively few.

If a new word has a regular spelling, the teacher can say the word several times and the learner can try to write it without ever having seen it before. If this proves to be too difficult for the learners, the teacher can help them in the following ways.

1. The most useful technique is one which uses analogy. That is, the learners are encouraged to apply previously learned knowledge to help them learn new material. For example, if the learners have to spell the word *placidity*, the teacher can say, "You know how to spell *play*, *acid*, and *quantity*, so now spell *placidity*." In this technique the teacher uses words that the learners already know. These words contain spelling features that are the same as those in the new word. This technique can be used with beginners. For example, you know *stop* and *play*, so write *stay*.

2. The learners can be taught various spelling rules, such as those concerning short and long vowels, the doubling of consonants, final silent *e*, and *i* before *e* (West, 1955). When learners are asked to write a word that they have not seen before, the teacher says the word several times and reminds learners of the appropriate spelling rule. For example, "Write *transmitter*. /T/ is a short sound so the following letter is doubled." Spelling rules are also useful when helping learners correct spelling errors.

Words which do not follow common spelling patterns may cause difficulty for learners. The following techniques direct learners' attention to these words as individual words rather than as examples of rules.

1. When learners make several spelling mistakes in their written work, they should keep a list of the words which they spell incorrectly.

They can practice spelling the words in the following way. They write 12 or more of the words in a list down the left-hand side of a page. Then, after each word they write the first letter of the word.

divide     d
parallel   p
. . .

Then they cover the words with a piece of paper and use the first letters to remind them of the words as they try to write the words correctly. After they write a word, they can uncover the word on the left to check if they spelled the word correctly.

divide     divide
           p

Then they write the first letters again and carry on across the page.

2. The teacher writes the letters of a new word on the blackboard in the wrong order. *Book*, for example, would be written as

o k o b

Then the teacher asks a learner to come to the blackboard and guess the first letter of the word. For this exercise, the teacher does not say the word, and the learners have not seen it before. The learner points at the letters until he or she manages to point to the right one, *b.* Then the teacher says, "Yes, now try to point to the second letter in the new word." This continues until the learners know the correct order of the letters and thus can spell the word correctly. Other learners can try to write the word by guessing what it will be. When a learner thinks he or she has the correct answer, that learner puts a hand up. The aim is to beat the person who is pointing. When the word is known, it is written correctly on the blackboard.

3. The teacher writes about 12 words on the blackboard, not in a list, but arranged something like this:

reduce          believe     consider        agreement
    arrangement         in time     delivery        fine
as soon as          the result          opposed

The teacher says, "You have one minute to look at these words. Then I will erase them from the blackboard and you must write them in exactly the same position on your piece of paper." This gives a very strong challenge to the learners to pay close attention to the words and to use their memory. The exercise is marked by asking learners to come to the blackboard and rewrite the words in exactly the same place they were before.

## Using Vocabulary in Sentences

The following techniques show learners how a word fits into known patterns. These techniques can be used deductively or inductively. When an item is presented deductively, the lesson moves from attention to a rule to applying the rule to examples. For example, the teacher tells the learners that the new word *prevent* is used in the pattern "*prevent* someone or something *from* doing something." Then the learners are helped to make examples based on this pattern. The motivation in this kind of technique comes from the challenge of making correct sentences based on the pattern. The teacher needs to be able to control the amount of help given to the learners so that the activity is a challenge but is not too difficult. For this reason it is useful to know a range of techniques for providing help for the learners.

When an item is presented inductively, the learners are given examples and try to discover the rule by examining the examples. For example, the teacher provides several sentences containing *prevent* and verbs with similar patterns, and the learners try to see what is similar in all of the sentences. The motivation in this kind of technique comes from the challenge to observe and analyze the material. If the challenge is too difficult, the teacher can provide help for the learners by guiding them toward the features of the pattern.

When using these techniques, the teacher should help the learners draw on their previous experience of English by associating the new word with known words which follow the same patterns. Thus, when introducing *prevent*, it might help the learners to see that *stop* shares some of the same patterns.

1. The learners repeat a sentence that the teacher says or make sentences from a substitution table.

2. The teacher tells the learners that the new word behaves like a known word. For example, "*Instance* is used in much the same way as *example*."

3. The teacher gives the learners a model sentence containing the new word and helps them make ones following the same pattern. Here is an example with the verb *overlook*. "Here is a sentence with the word *overlook*. *I will overlook your bad behavior.* Now you make a similar sentence. Here is a word to help you, *mistakes*." If the teacher provides cue words, as in the example, it will be easier for the learners to make sentences. Or

the teacher asks a question. The answer requires the use of the new word. This is made easier by having the answer follow a given model.

TEACHER: How can we distinguish sugar from salt?
LEARNERS: We can distinguish sugar from salt by tasting it.

4. The teacher says a sentence and the learners paraphrase it using the new word.

TEACHER: You can tell the difference between p and t by watching the position of the tongue.
LEARNERS: You can distinguish p from t by . . .

5. The teacher helps the learners find the grammatical pattern that the new word fits into. The learners use this information to make sentences using the word. Here are some examples using a deductive approach.

*Insanity* is usually an uncountable noun.

*Inhabit* is usually followed by an object.

*Inoculate* often follows the pattern *inoculate someone against an illness*.

Here are some examples using an inductive approach.

Look at the word *insanity* in this sentence. What part of speech is it? . . . Is it countable or uncountable? How do you know this?

Look at *inhabit* in this sentence. What is it followed by?

When learners know the grammar of a word, they can try to make a sentence using the word.

6. The teacher makes half a sentence containing the new word and the learners complete the sentence. Here are some examples practicing *interfere*.

Bad weather interferes with television reception.

Lack of sleep interferes . . .

The airline strike interfered . . .

The accident . . .

Several exercise types can be used to test as well as practice the use of vocabulary in sentences.

a. Complete these sentences using the words given. In the case of nouns and verbs you may change the form of the word.

1. In the middle of the lecture the lights went out.

   This _____ .
   (confusion)

2. The economic crisis has _____ .
   (create)

3. Dark objects and surfaces _____ .
   (absorb)

b. Choose a word from the list to replace the underlined words in each sentence.

| | |
|---|---|
| He listed all the possibilities. | reinforced |
| All sections worked together well. | devastated |
| The area was ruined. | contradicted |
| Whatever I said, he said the opposite. | enumerated |
| They made the bridge stronger by adding steel bars. | integrated |

c. Change the word in front of each sentence so that it will fit the sentence.

propose     The committee put forward a _____ .

disagree     There was considerable _____ among the members.

d. Match the words or phrases in Column A with a sensible word or phrase from Column B. The first one has been done for you.

| A | B |
|---|---|
| 1. a main road | intention |
| 2. perform _____ | principles |
| 3. a slight _____ | attention |
| 4. a vertical _____ | a function |
| 5. a great variety _____ | distribution |
| 6. a series _____ | line |
| 7. to pay _____ | pressure |
| 8. a practical _____ | of techniques |

9. the basic _____     improvement

10. to serve _____     current

11. internal _____     a purpose

12. uneven _____     road

13. a national _____     of events

14. to exert _____     injuries

15. a serious _____     suggestion

16. an alternating _____     sport

## Using Reading to Help Writing

The following detailed series of steps can be introduced gradually to learners. Although most attention is focused on grammar, some attention is given to meaning. The information learners can get by following this strategy is particularly useful for advanced students who have to write reports or assignments after reading. By examining the grammar of technical terms and other useful vocabulary in the reading material, they have a greater chance of using that vocabulary correctly in their writing.

When you find a new word in a book or a passage that you are reading, follow these steps.

Step 1. Look carefully at the word in the sentence. Decide if it is a noun, a verb, an adjective, or an adverb in that sentence.

Step 2. I. If it is a noun,
      a. see if it is countable (c) or uncountable (u). You do this by looking to see if it is plural or if it has *a* or *each*, etc., in front of it.
      b. see what adjective it has in front.
  II. If it is a verb,
      a. see what type of word comes in front of it and what type of word comes after it. For example, is it followed by a noun, or is it followed by a preposition group or an adverb? Does it have the verb *to be* in front?
  III. If it is an adjective,
      a. see what noun follows it.
  IV. If it is an adverb,
      a. see where it is in the sentence. Is it after a verb or in front of it or at the beginning or end of the sentence?

Step 3.  See if it is possible to break the word into parts that have different meanings. What are the meanings of these parts? What do
the prefix, the suffix, and the root mean?

Step 4.  I.  Look for the word in the dictionary. If the dictionary gives an
example of the word in a sentence, see if the grammar is the
same as the grammar you discovered. If the dictionary tells
you about the grammar of the word, look at that carefully and
compare it with the grammar you discovered.

II. Find the meaning of the word.

Step 5.  In your notebook, write

I.  the word (if it is a singular countable noun, write *a* in front of
it).

II. its grammar.

III. its meaning.

IV. the sentence or the part of the sentence containing the word,
plus the sentence you found in the dictionary (if there was
one).

V. a new sentence containing the word. Get the teacher or a
friend to check if your sentence is correct.

Step 6.  I.  Learn the meaning of the word

a. by covering the meaning of the word with a piece of paper
and by looking at the word while trying to guess the meaning.

b. by writing the word on a small card and the meaning on
the other side. Look at the word and try to guess the meaning. When you can do this, look at the meaning and try to
guess the word. You should carry around a pile of cards
like this and look at them when you have nothing to do for
a few minutes.

II. Learn the spelling of the word by looking at a list of words
you are learning, then cover them with a piece of paper and
try to write them from memory. Then check to see if you are
correct. Before you cover the words, you can write the first
letter of each word in the list to help you remember.

***An Example:***  He wanted a *meal* and there was a good hotel on the
*main* street. He found a place for his car and walked *slowly* toward the
hotel. His hands were in his pockets and he was *staring* at the ground.
(The dictionary used is the *Advanced Learners' Dictionary.*)

| | |
|---|---|
| I. a meal | n.c. (n = a noun, c = countable) |
| | occasion of eating (the meaning) |
| | He wanted a meal. (the example in the passage) |
| | three meals a day (from the dictionary) |
| | He eats two meals a day. (the new sentence) |
| II. main | adj. |
| | chief, most important |

the main street
the main line of a railway, the main point of my argument (from the dictionary)
This is the main building in our town.

III. slowly    adv.   It comes after the verb.
not quick, slow + ly, -ly = an adverb
He walked slowly toward the hotel. (There is no example
in the dictionary.)
He moved slowly to the door.

IV. staring    vb. vb + at + n VP 24 (from the dictionary)
look fixedly, stare + ing
He was staring at the ground.
Do you like being stared at? (from the dictionary)
He stared at me.

The collocation techniques described in Chapter 7 are also very useful for developing a writing vocabulary.


## Using a Dictionary

If a dictionary is to be used for productive purposes, to help in writing and perhaps speaking, then it needs to contain a great deal of information which would not usually appear in a dictionary for native
speakers. This information includes syllabification, meaning, grammar,
collocations, register appropriateness, frequency, and advice on common
errors involved with a particular item. Items like phrasal verbs also need
to be dealt with. Research on dictionary use shows that most learners do
not make use of most of this information, and that they have not usually
studied the introduction to the dictionary which explains how to make
the best use of such information (Bejoint, 1981). In order to do something
about this, some publishers of dictionaries for second language learners
have published accompanying booklets to guide learners (Underhill,
1980; Whitcut, 1979). The best dictionaries for productive purposes are
monolingual—that is, the meaning and extra information is given in the
same language as the word. There is a need for productive bilingual dictionaries (Tomaszczyk, 1981) where learners can look up a word by beginning with a word in their mother tongue and then find an English
word with information about its grammar, collocations, etc., to guide its
use.

The dictionary can also be used to correct errors in writing and
eventually prevent such errors (Scholfield, 1981). The procedure is
simple, but the learning required to perform it is considerable. The
teacher underlines suitable errors in the learner's written work. The

learners look up the items in the dictionary to correct them. As the learners practice, they can look up words while they are writing. The teacher needs to choose the errors carefully and must make sure that the dictionaries deal with them. Typical errors would include word building, meaning, collocation, appropriateness, inflections, grammar, and spelling. The value of this activity is that it does two things at the same time. It teaches vocabulary and gives effective, realistic practice in dictionary use. Monolingual dictionaries are most suitable for this activity because of the wealth of information they contain. Some writers, however, suggest that two dictionaries may occasionally be necessary—a bilingual dictionary going from the mother tongue to English and a monolingual dictionary.

## Using Schematically Related Vocabulary

The vocabulary which conveys the most information in a text is not usually composed of the words which are common in the language as a whole. Usually they are the words which we recognize as being closely related to the subject matter of the text and that area of knowledge of which the text makes up one part. Even if we see the words out of context we can tell what subject area they are from—for example, *input data, program, compiler.*

These narrow-range words typically have a very small set of collocations and may occur with a predictable group of other narrow-range words: *manipulate input data, execute a program, the compiler translates, store input data.*

The exercises on grids, clines, clusters, and collocation in Chapter 7 are particularly relevant for writing as well. They help learners relate vocabulary which typically occurs together and which is at a similar level of formality.

## APPLICATION

1. One of your learners writes very fluently, with good grammar and organization, but misspells two or three words in almost every line. This learner mastered English through speaking. What would you do?

2. Look at the following piece of writing. What vocabulary-related problems does the writer have? What would you do about them?

In most of Indonesian family, mother is always looks after their children and their family until they grown up, not forgetting until they married, they still under family attention.

Household is always done and taken care by mother, like early morning breakfast, cleaning up etc. Some family have a maid, which help to clean up the blouse too. Since an Indonesian family is considered a very large family, which some family have more than 5 children. But they always believe that the larger the family the more prosperity there is. This thing still found in some family, but modern family does not believe in this thing.

Most woman in Indonesia like to be educated, so woman that work is always bright and happy going person. 85% woman in Indonesia is working 15% just to be a house wife.

3. Choose two or more dictionaries and compare them for the help they give a learner to use the word productively. How much information does each give? How accessible is this information? Choose some low-frequency words and see if a learner can use the information in one of the dictionaries to use each word in a sentence.

4. Drawing learners' attention to words in reading texts can be a useful preparation for writing. Brainstorm the various ways a teacher could draw attention to a word in a text so that this word could be made a part of learners' productive vocabulary. It is best if you do this exercise with a text in front of you.

5. Look at the following vocabulary errors in second language learners' writing. Why did they occur?

Nobody will *say* you what to do.

Using picture and maps will *avoid* people of tiring of reading.

The advertisements tempt people to *consume* their money.

Altogether there will be six people *containing* you.

Dogs are blamed for the *spreading* diseases.

This gives an opportunity for *late* students to develop themselves.

This language has thirteen *alphabets*.

The claws of the dog *crash* the wooden door.

# Chapter 10

# Learner Strategies

In this chapter it is argued that because of the large number of low-frequency words and because of their infrequent occurrence and narrow range, it is best to teach learners strategies for dealing with these words rather than to teach the words themselves. Three strategies are described—guessing from context, mnemonic techniques, and word parts.

Low-frequency words have several characteristics. First, there are many of them. There are between two and three thousand high-frequency words and several hundred thousand low-frequency words. Second, learners will meet many of these words only once or twice. Kucera and Francis (1967) found in a study of fifty 2000-word passages that the percentage of the words (types) occurring once ranged from 56 percent to almost 80 percent. That is, in each 2000-word text over one-half to three-quarters of the words were not repeated. In large counts of 1 million words or more, approximately 40 percent of the words occur only once. Any effort spent learning them will not be repaid by meeting them on other occasions. Third, words which are infrequent in the language as a whole may be reasonably frequent in a very specialized area or in a particular text. That is, they have a very narrow range.

It is clear that if a teacher wants to help learners cope with low-frequency vocabulary, particularly in their reading, it is far better to spend time on strategies that the learners can use to deal with these words than to spend time on individual words.

Additional support for this comes from an analysis of the results of a vocabulary test (Saragi et al., 1978). Although the class average on a vocabulary test based on the 1000 most frequent English words may be 89 percent, in fact only 40 percent of the words are known by every learner. If the teacher presents the remaining 60 percent of the words, at least half the learners will already know the words presented. As Table 10.1 shows, the amount of common knowledge of vocabulary decreases as the word level increases.

Even with a common coursebook there is considerable variety in the nature (and size) of the vocabulary learned by different individuals. Thus, dealing with low-frequency words with the class as a whole will be wasting some learners' time. They will already know some of the words.

Table 10.1    RESULTS OF FOUR 100-ITEM MULTIPLE-CHOICE VOCABULARY TESTS
WITH TEACHERS' TRAINING COLLEGE STUDENTS

|  | Average of scores | % of words known by all students | Range of scores |
|---|---|---|---|
| 1st 1000 | 89% | 40% | 70–100% |
| 2nd 1000 | 74% | 20% | 45–100% |
| 3rd 1000 | 52% | 8% | 20–95% |
| 4th 1000 | 38% | 0% | 0–75% |

*Source:* The 1000-word levels are based on Thorndike and Lorge (1944).

We will look at three strategies for dealing with unknown vocabulary. They are (1) guessing words in context, (2) using mnemonic techniques to remember word meanings, and (3) using prefixes, roots, and suffixes.

## GUESSING WORDS IN CONTEXT

Once learners know around two or three thousand words, they can use the reading skills they have developed to infer the meanings of unknown words that they meet. Some readers can do this without any particular training, but those who cannot do it can easily be taught a strategy which will quickly enable them to guess most of the unknown words they meet. The range of achievement on the first passage used in one of our classes was 0 to 80 percent. After working on five passages in this way, each with 10 to 15 words to be guessed, the range was 50 to 85 percent. In theory, at least, if one learner can find enough clues in a passage to guess 80 percent of the previously unknown words, then every learner can achieve a similar score with training. In any passage, very few of the unknown words cannot be guessed from context. The few studies of guessing words from context indicate that a large proportion of the unknown words (at least 80 percent) can be successfully dealt with in this way (Liu Na & Nation, 1985; Saragi et al., 1978; Seibert, 1945).

### Clues to Help Guessing

Several writers describe various types of clues that can provide information to help in guessing. Brown (1980) lists definition, learners' experience of the world, contrast, inference, and analysis. Kruse (1979) has a similar list, with a lot of attention given to word building. Steinberg (1978) lists grammar, punctuation, definition, contrast, connectives, reference words, word analysis, and the learner's experience and common sense. What these approaches lack, however, is a systematic procedure for learners to follow. Chandrasegaran (1980) uses a questioning procedure to guide learners in their guessing, but this is very dependent on the teacher's choice of questions. There seems to be no generalizable arrangement to the questions which would give learners independence in guessing.

## Strategies

The strategy described by Bruton and Samuda (1981) in Figure 10.1 does not suffer from this weakness. It differs from the procedure described by Clarke and Nation (1980) below in that it is based more on a

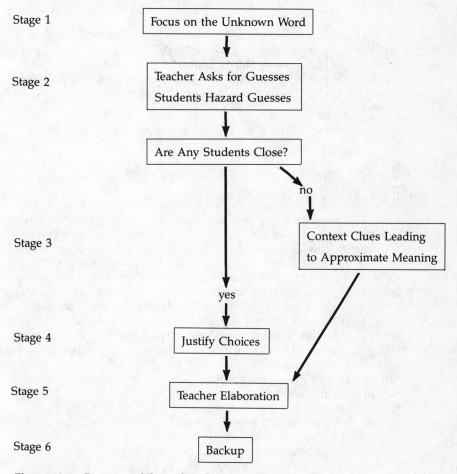

**Figure 10.1**  Bruton and Samuda's Guessing Procedure.

trial-and-error approach, with guessing occurring very early in the procedure and being followed by justification and elaboration.

Clarke and Nation's (1980) strategy is basically very simple. It begins by getting the learner to look closely at the unknown word, next to look at its immediate context, and then to take a much broader view of how the clause containing the word relates to other clauses, sentences, or paragraphs. After guessing, there is a simple system of checks to make sure that the guess is the best possible. Once learners have mastered the steps of the strategy and have practiced guessing words by systematically going through the steps, it is no longer necessary to apply all the steps. That is, the strategy is just a means of acquiring the unconscious skill that an efficient reader already has.

Let us look at the steps involved in the strategy and then apply them.

Step 1. Look at the unknown word and decide its part of speech. Is it a noun, a verb, an adjective, or an adverb?

Step 2. Look at the clause or sentence containing the unknown word. If the unknown word is a noun, what adjectives describe it? What verb is it near? That is, what does this noun do, and what is done to it?

If the unknown word is a verb, what nouns does it go with?

Is it modified by an adverb?

If it is an adjective, what noun does it go with?

If it is an adverb, what verb is it modifying?

Step 3. Look at the relationship between the clause or sentence containing the unknown word and other sentences or paragraphs. Sometimes this relationship will be signaled by a conjunction like *but, because, if, when,* or by an adverb like *however, as a result.* Often there will be no signal. The possible types of relationship include cause and effect, contrast, inclusion, time, exemplification, and summary. (See Appendix 6 and Halliday & Hasan, 1967, for a fuller list.) Punctuation may also serve as a clue. Semicolons often signal a list of inclusion relationships; dashes may signal restatement. Reference words like *this, that,* and *such* also provide useful information.

Step 4. Use the knowledge you have gained from Steps 1–3 to guess the meaning of the word.

Step 5. Check that your guess is correct.

    a. See that the part of speech of your guess is the same as the part of speech of the unknown word. If it is not the same, then something is wrong with your guess.

    b. Replace the unknown word with your guess. If the sentence makes sense, your guess is probably correct.

c. Break the unknown word into its prefix, root, and suffix, if possible. If the meanings of the prefix and root correspond to your guess, good. If not, look at your guess again, but do not change anything if you feel reasonably certain about your guess using the context.

Experience has shown that using affixes and roots alone as a means of guessing meanings is not very reliable. Also, once a word has been analyzed according to its parts, this guess at its meaning is more likely to result in twisting the interpretation of the context than allowing interpretation of the context to modify the guess of the meaning. So, by leaving the use of affixes and root until the last step in the strategy, the learner is more likely to approach interpretation of the context with an open mind.

Let us apply the strategy to guess the meanings of two infrequent words. The following paragraph is taken from Mackin and Carver (1968, pp. 45–50).

[Chinese spectacles] were regarded as objects of *reverence* because the rims of tortoise-shell came from a sacred and symbolic animal, and the lenses were made from sacred stones. People wore them at first not so much to aid eyesight, or for curing eye-ailments, as for good luck, or for the dignity which they *bestowed* on the wearer. Sometimes even empty frames were worn as a mark of distinction.

*reverence* (line 2)

Step 1. *reverence* is a noun.
Step 2. spectacles are objects of reverence. If, because of the *-ence* suffix, we guess that *revere* might be a verb, we could say

People revere spectacles.

Step 3. *because* indicates a cause–effect relationship. The causes are *The rims of tortoise-shell came from a sacred and symbolic animal* and *the lenses were made from sacred stones.* The effect is *Chinese spectacles were regarded as objects of reverence.*
Step 4. *reverence* seems related to *sacred* and *symbolic* so it probably means something like *religion* or *holiness.*
Step 5. a. Like *reverence*, *religion* and *holiness* are nouns.
　　　 b. Spectacles were regarded as objects of holiness. Spectacles were regarded as objects of religion. The first substitution seems the best.
　　　 c. re- -ver- -ence, -ence indicates that the word is a noun. The prefix and root do not help at all.

The dictionary says that *reverence* means *feelings of deep respect. Holiness* is close enough to this: 95 percent correct.

*bestowed* (line 6)

Step 1. *bestowed* is a verb.

Step 2. Spectacles bestow dignity on the wearer.

Step 3. *or* indicates that there are alternatives. The other alternatives are *good luck*, and *curing eye-ailments* which are desirable things, so we can conclude that *bestowing dignity* is also a desirable thing.

Step 4. *bestowed* probably means *gave* or *put*.

Step 5. a. *gave* and *put* are verbs.

        b. Spectacles put dignity on the wearer. Spectacles gave dignity on the wearer. Except for the awkwardness of *on*, both words seem suitable.

        c. *be- -stow- -ed*. No help here.

The dictionary gives *put, place*: 100 percent correct.

The errors that learners make when guessing words from context give interesting insights into their grasp of the strategy and also into difficulties they encounter while reading. One of the commonest errors in using the strategy was to guess a meaning that was a different part of speech from the word in the passage. Faulty analysis of word parts also led to errors (*laterally* = coming after or later). Failure to understand the context produced some errors. Most learners did not infer *sparse* correctly in the sentence *Desert areas owe their aridity to sparse rainfall*. After talking to some learners it was found that they did not interpret *owe* correctly. When it was explained to them that the sentence means *The aridity of desert areas is caused by sparse rainfall*, most were able to find the meaning correctly.

Our experience coincides with that of Bright and McGregor (1970, p. 31): "Perhaps the most important thing of all is to remember that the ability to infer in this way is a skill that can only be acquired by practice. Every time we tell a pupil what a word means we are robbing him of a chance to practice this skill."

The various steps needed in the strategy—namely part of speech, immediate context, wider context, word parts—can be practiced separately before being combined into a strategy (Long & Nation, 1980). So learners can practice recognizing the part of speech of various words in context. They can do the *What does what?* exercise with various nouns, verbs, adjectives, or adverbs in a text. In this exercise the teacher gives the learners a word and the line number of that word in the text. The learners must ask themselves questions like "What does what? Who does what?" if the word is a noun or verb, or "What is what?" if it is an adjective, or "What does what how?" if it is an adverb. They answer these questions by reference to the text. The learners can also practice using the wider context as a separate exercise by analyzing sentences to find the conjunction relationships.

The guessing strategy can be used in cooperative class exercises or for individual work such as homework. When the strategy is being introduced, the teacher can demonstrate the steps to the learners using a word from the passage. The steps are put up on the board. Then one word is chosen from the passage for the whole class to guess. The teacher then calls on different learners to do each step. So one learner has the task of saying what part of speech the word is, and then another looks at the immediate grammar of the word, and so on. After doing a few words like this the learners can work in pairs and then on their own.

When the learners work in pairs, they work on the steps together and then describe the steps to the rest of the class. The teacher gives them a percentage grade for correctness, as in the examples above.

The research of van Parreren and Schouten-van Parreren (1981) supports the value of an organized system for guessing, with the grammar level being one of the lowest and then meaning and word analysis being higher levels—"a subject can act correctly on a certain level only if there is no problem on one of the lower levels" (p. 238). They found that making a good guess did not involve going through all the levels but involved "estimating how many difficulties guessing a certain word would present and then entering on the apparently most appropriate level. Sometimes however this estimation proved to be wrong and in that case the skilled guesser went down or moved up to the appropriate level" (p. 240).

Guessing words in context obviously leads on to dictionary work. Unless the learners already have a reasonable idea of what a word means, they will be unable to choose the most suitable meaning from those given in the dictionary. Using the dictionary could be the fourth way of checking in Step 5.

Honeyfield (1977a) suggests three types of exercise for practicing guessing words from context. The first is a cloze exercise where gaps are made which must be filled by context words. Such an exercise involves many of the requirements of guessing from context. The major disadvantage is the lack of a form which must be largely ignored while guessing but is useful when checking. The second type of exercise provides multiple-choice answers either for the meaning of the unknown word or for the clues which give the meaning. Finally, he describes a context-enrichment exercise where gradually increasing information is revealed.

All the guessing procedures described so far focus on linguistic information that is present within a text. There are other important sources of information (Drum and Konopak, 1987). These include knowledge that learners already have about particular words through having met them before, knowledge of the subject that they are reading about (this may be knowledge gained through the learner's first language), and knowledge of the conceptual structure of the topic.

To help readers make the most effective use of these other clues to guess words, it may be necessary to show them ways of stimulating this knowledge before or as they begin reading a text.

## USING MNEMONIC TECHNIQUES

When learners meet an unknown word and discover its meaning, they may wish to make an extra effort to remember the word. The key-word technique is an effective way of doing this. In this technique the learners create an unusual association between the word form and its meaning. Let us imagine that an Indonesian learner of English wants to remember the meaning of the English word *parrot*. First, the learner thinks of an Indonesian word that sounds like *parrot* or like a part of *parrot*—for example, the Indonesian word *parit*, which means "a ditch." This is the keyword. Second, the learner imagines a parrot lying in a ditch! The more striking and unusual the image, the more effective it is. (see Figure 10.2).

This image, then, is the linking association between *parrot* and its meaning because it contains a clue or key to the sound of the foreign word (*parrot–parit*) and it contains the key to the meaning of *parrot* (see Figure 10.3).

Here is another example. If English-speaking learners want to master the Thai words *khaaw saan*, meaning "uncooked rice," they would think of an English word (the keyword) which sounds like *khaaw saan*,—for example, *council*. Then they would form a mental image of a council and uncooked rice interacting with each other (see Figure 10.4).

**Figure 10.2**

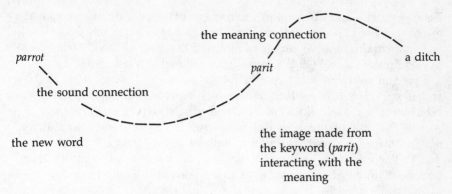

the meaning connection

parrot                                                          a ditch

*parit*

the sound connection

the new word

the image made from
the keyword (*parit*)
interacting with the
meaning

**Figure 10.3**   The keyword technique.

The keyword technique, while being very effective for learning foreign vocabulary, is best considered as only one of several learning techniques that can be used to master foreign vocabulary. Other possible techniques which try to develop both form and meaning associations are the use of analysis into affixes and roots, and mnemonics like "A *pintu* (door) is used for going *into* something" (i.e., the partial homophony of *pintu* and *into*). The general principle of the "levels of processing" theory (Craik & Lockhart, 1972) is that the more that words are analyzed and are enriched by associations or images, the longer they will stay in the memory. Although the keyword technique seems rather bizarre at first sight, its effectiveness lies in its association of both formal and meaning elements of the new word by the use of aural and imagery cues. The analysis of words into Latin affixes and roots is similar to the keyword technique in this association of form and meaning. Pressley, Levin, and

**Figure 10.4**

Delaney (1982) and Paivio and Desrocher (1981) provide comprehensive reviews of the experimental research on the keyword technique.

In a comprehensive survey of almost 50 studies of the keyword technique, Pressley et al. (1982) reached the following conclusions.

1. The keyword technique helps the learning of foreign vocabulary and is superior to other techniques, such as rote repetition, placing vocabulary in a meaningful sentence, and using pictures or synonyms.

2. The use of the keyword technique is not restricted to concrete nouns but can be used with verbs, abstract nouns, and adjectives.

3. The use of the keyword technique is not restricted to adults. It can be used with children as young as three years if they are helped a lot in using the technique.

4. It is still not clear if it is best for the teacher to provide the keywords or for learners to make their own. Where learners need help, it will of course be best if the teacher provides it. It seems to be best for the teacher to provide the linking picture if possible. There are difficulties in doing this, however, particularly if learners think of their own keywords.

5. The keyword technique does not slow down recall of the meaning of foreign words.

6. Very little experimentation has been done on the effect of the keyword technique on pronunciation and spelling. No negative effects have yet been found. Pressley et al. point out that there is no reason to expect the keyword technique to help spelling or pronunciation because the technique does not have any in-built mnemonic tricks to help spelling or pronunciation.

7. Most experiments with the keyword technique have looked at receptive vocabulary learning (being able to recall the meaning when the foreign word is supplied). To use the keyword technique for productive vocabulary learning (being able to recall the foreign word when the meaning is supplied), the form of the keyword must have a close connection with the form of the foreign word. If care is taken with this, then the keyword technique is good for productive vocabulary learning.

8. One difficulty with the keyword technique is that it is often difficult to think of keywords that sound like the foreign word. The more imagination you have, the more useful the technique.

## USING PREFIXES, ROOTS, AND SUFFIXES

A knowledge of Latin affixes and roots has two values for an advanced learner of English. It can be used to help the learning of unfamiliar words by relating these words to known words or to known prefixes and suffixes, and it can be used as a way of checking whether an unfamiliar word has been successfully guessed from context.

Some Latin prefixes occur in many different words. For example, the prefix *ad-* in its various forms occurs in 433 of the 20,000 most frequent words in *The Teacher's Word Book* by Thorndike and Lorge (Stauffer, 1942; see also Bock, 1948). *Circum-* occurs in only 8 words. The root *dur-* (as in *endure*) occurs in fewer words than the root *duc-* (as in *reduce*). Stauffer (1942) counted prefixes in the Thorndike word list. Almost one-quarter of the 20,000 words in the list had prefixes. Stauffer found that 15 prefixes accounted for 82 percent of the total number of occurrences of prefixes used in words in the list. Table 10.2 contains most of the common Latin prefixes found in English.

Brown "tabulated the most important prefixes and root elements and compiled a list of 20 prefixes and 14 root elements which pertain to over 14,000 words in *Webster's Collegiate Dictionary* and a projected 100,000 words in an unabridged dictionary. These have been combined into 14 master words" (Thompson, 1958, p. 62). By learning the master words and the meaning of their parts, learners will know the most useful prefixes and roots (see Table 10.3).

Saragi (1974) studied the frequency, regularity of meaning, regularity of translation into Indonesian (as a check on regularity of meaning), and regularity of spelling of all the suffixes found in the words in the *General Service List* (West, 1953). Those derivational suffixes which best fit the criteria given above were *-ness* (n.), *-en* (v.), *-ty/-ity* (n.), *-less* (adj.), *-er/-or* (n.), *-al* (adj.), *-ion* (n.), *-y* (adj.), *-ful* (adj.), *-ance/-ence* (n.), and *-ment* (n.). Each of these occurs in more than 30 words. Less frequent suffixes, but having a high regularity of meaning, translation and spelling, were *-ise/-ize* (v.), *-ward* (adj.), and *-ern* (adj.). These 14 suffixes are found in over 60 percent of the words with derivational suffixes in the *General Service List*. Other suffixes occurring more than 10 times in the *General Service List* were *-able* (adj.), *-ous* (adj.), *-ant/-ent* (adj.), *-ive* (adj.), *-al* (n.), *-ure* (n.), *-ery/-ary* (n.), *-th* (n.), *-y* (n.), *-age* (n.), and *-ic* (adj.).

To make use of prefixes and roots, learners need three skills. They need to be able to break new words into parts so that the affixes and roots are revealed, they need to know the meanings of the parts, and they need to be able to see a connection between the meaning of the parts and the dictionary meaning of the new word. These skills can be learned in various ways.

## Recognizing Word Parts

1. The learners are given words which they must break into parts. The learners can either rewrite the word in parts, *pro duct ion*, or underline the words to show the parts pro/duct/ion. If the learners analyze

**Table 10.2    A LIST OF USEFUL LATIN PREFIXES**

| Prefix | Meaning | Word | Other forms |
|---|---|---|---|
| ab-[b] | from, away | abstract | a-, abs- |
| ad- | to(ward) | advertise, attention | a-, ab-, ac-, af-, ag-, al-, an-, ap-, aq-, ar-, as-, at- |
| com- | with, together | complicated, confuse, contain | co-, col-, con-, cor- |
| de-[1d] | down | describe | |
| de-[2d] | away | deduct | |
| dis-[1c,d] | not | dislike | |
| dis-[2c,d] | apart, away | distance | di-, dif- |
| ex- | out, beyond | express | e-, ef- |
| in-[1] | not | inconsistent | ig-, il-, im-, ir- |
| in-[2] | in (to) | instruct | il-, im-, ir- |
| inter-[c] | between, among | intermittent | |
| mis-[c] | wrong(ly) | misinform | |
| non-[c] | not | nonviolent | |
| ob-[1c,d] | against | oppose | o-, oc-, of-, op- |
| ob-[2c,d] | to(ward) | obtain | o-, oc-, of-, op- |
| over-[c] | above | overpower | |
| per-[a,b,c] | through | perfect | |
| pre- | before | predict | |
| pro-[1d] | forward | prospect | pur- |
| pro-[2d] | in favor of | pro-Western | |
| re-[1d] | back | reduce | |
| re-[2d] | again | reorganize | |
| sub- | under | support, subscribe | suc-, suf-, sug-, sum-, sur-, sus- |
| trans-[c] | across, beyond | transfer | tra-, tran- |
| un- | not | unable | |

[a] *per-* is included in the list because it combines with many useful roots.
[b] Not in Thompson (1958).
[c] Not in Stauffer (1942).
[d] Not distinguished by Stauffer or Thompson.

several words in this way, they can then bring together the words with the same prefix or root.

2. The learners are given words that contain different forms of the prefixes *ad-*, *com-*, *ex-*, *dis-*[2], *in-*, *ob-*, and *sub-* (*com-* for example has the forms *co-*, *col-*, *com-*, *con-*, and *cor-*). The learners group the different forms of the same prefix together.

**Table 10.3    THE FOURTEEN WORDS (KEYS TO THE MEANINGS OF OVER 14,000 WORDS)**

| | | Derivations— | | |
|---|---|---|---|---|
| Words | Prefix | Common meaning | Root | Common meaning |
| 1. precept | pre- | (before) | capere | (take, seize) |
| 2. detain | de- | (away, down) | tenere | (hold, have) |
| 3. intermittent | inter- | (between, among) | mittere | (send) |
| 4. offer | ob- | (against) | ferre (Lat.) | (bear, carry) |
| 5. insist | in- | (into) | stare | (stand) |
| 6. monograph | mono- | (alone, one) | graphein | (write) |
| 7. epilogue | epi- | (upon) | legein | (say, study of) |
| 8. aspect | ad- | (to, toward) | specere | (see) |
| 9. uncomplicated | un- com- | (not) (together, with) | plicare | (fold) |
| 10. nonextended | non- ex- | (not) (out, beyond) | tendere | (stretch) |
| 11. reproduction | re- pro- | (back, again) (forward, for) | ducere | (lead) |
| 12. indisposed | in- dis- | (not) (apart, not) | ponere (pos) | (put, place) |
| 13. oversufficient | over- sub- | (above) (under) | facere | (make, do) |
| 14. mistranscribe | mis- trans- | (wrong) (across, beyond) | scribere | (write) |

3. The game **Wordmaking and Wordtaking** using affixes and roots is a very amusing way of seeing how affixes and roots combine to make words. In this game, about 300 small cards are used. On each card there is either a prefix, a root, or a suffix. The cards are turned face down, and then one by one the learners turn the cards over and try to make words by combining the affixes and roots on the cards. Fountain (1979) gives detailed instructions for preparing, playing, and scoring the game.

4. The game **Stemgo** (Bernbrock, 1980) is an amusing way of practicing prefixes and stems. The learners have a sheet like the one in Figure 10.5. There is a prefix or stem written at the head of each square. Learners work in pairs to write three words for each prefix or stem. For each square the teacher announces and explains two words of his or her own that contain the prefix or stem. If one of the pairs of learners has these two words on its sheet, it ticks that square. When a pair has four ticks in a line down, across, or diagonally, it wins.

| anthro | | auto | | cosm | | dic, dict | |
|---|---|---|---|---|---|---|---|
| 1. | 1. | | 1. | | 1. | | |
| 2. | 2. | | 2. | | 2. | | |
| 3. | 3. | | 3. | | 3. | | |
| duc, duct | | geo | | homo | | medi | |
| 1. | 1. | | 1. | | 1. | | |
| 2. | 2. | | 2. | | 2. | | |
| 3. | 3. | | 3. | | 3. | | |
| pater, patri | | pathy | | scrib, script | | voc, vok | |
| 1. | 1. | | 1. | | 1. | | |
| 2. | 2. | | 2. | | 2. | | |
| 3. | 3. | | 3. | | 3. | | |
| form | | sequ, secut | | man, manu | | pan | |
| 1. | 1. | | 1. | | 1. | | |
| 2. | 2. | | 2. | | 2. | | |
| 3. | 3. | | 3. | | 3. | | |

**Figure 10.5**  Stemgo.

## Learning the Meanings of Prefixes and Roots

1. The learners are given lists of affixes and roots to memorize. One way of doing this is to write the root or affix on one side of a small card, and its meaning on the other side.

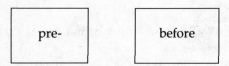

The learners carry a pile of these cards around in their pockets. When they have free time, they take them out and look at each root or affix and try to recall its meaning. If they cannot remember, they turn the card over to see the meaning on the back. When they can go through the pile twice without any errors, they can start on a new pile.

2. The learners can use "master words" (Thompson, 1958) to help them remember the meanings of the affixes and roots (see Table 10.3). This technique involves using a few words to help remember several prefixes and roots. *Uncomplicated*, for example, contains *un*, *com*, and *plic*, so this word can be used as the master word for these items. The master words should be words that the learners are already familiar with. The teacher should always refer to the master words when explaining new

words to the learners. If cards are used to learn the affixes and roots, the master word can be written on the back of the cards next to the meaning.

| pre- |
|---|

| before<br>(predict) |
|---|

3. The learners can study the lists of prefixes and roots in class. This can be done in pairs. The following description is based on the learning of the list in Table 10.2.

One learner has a list folded so that only the list of meanings can be seen. The other learner acts as the teacher. This "teacher" can see all of the list. The teacher says a prefix—for example, *com-*. The learner looks at the list of meanings and tries to guess which meaning goes with *com-*. If the guess is correct, the teacher says, "Good," and goes on to another item. If the guess is incorrect, the teacher says, "No. *Com-.*" If the learner still cannot guess after three attempts, the partner-teacher gives the answer. This type of testing-teaching exercise continues until the learner can quickly give the meaning of all the prefixes. Then the learners change roles. When both learners in a pair know the meaning of the prefixes, one learner acts as the teacher and says a word from the list— for example, *confuse*. The other learner, without looking at the sheet, has to repeat the word, say the prefix, and say the meaning of the prefix. So the learner says, *"Confuse, com-, together."*

## Using Prefixes and Roots

1. The teacher explains how the meanings of affixes and roots are connected to the meanings of particular words. The learners use words they already know to practice describing the connection between the meaning of the affixes and roots in a word and its meaning. From here the learners move to describing new words that the teacher chooses.

2. When guessing words from context it is not wise to use prefixes and roots as a guide for guessing. Clarke and Nation (1980) describe a strategy that learners can follow. The first step asks the learners to decide what part of speech the unknown word is. The second and third steps look at the word's immediate content and wider context. The fourth step is the guess, and the fifth step includes three checking procedures. The checking procedures involve comparing the part of speech of the guess with the part of speech of the unknown word to check that they are the same, breaking the unknown word into parts to see if the meanings of the prefix and root agree with the guess, and substituting the guess in place of the unknown word.

The analysis of the prefix and the root is left until after a guess has been made using context clues so that misinterpretation of the prefix and root does not lead to misreading of the context in order to suit the faulty prefix and root analysis. By leaving prefix and root analysis until last, all the options are kept open.

Strategies which learners can use independently of a teacher are the most important of all ways of learning vocabulary. For this reason it is worthwhile ensuring that learners are able to apply the strategies and that they get plenty of help and encouragement in doing so. By mastering a few strategies learners can cope with thousands of words. Any time spent on these strategies is well repaid. It is worth testing to see if learners have mastered the necessary information and steps involved in these strategies. A good way to test if learners can apply a strategy is to sit next to them while they use it and get them to explain, in English or in their mother tongue, what they are doing. Research like this done on guessing words from context has yielded interesting results. Wilford (1982) found one learner who, when faced with a repeated occurrence of an unknown word, said, "I couldn't guess this word when I met it earlier in the passage, so I won't try again." She also found that the second language learners in her study made much less use of the wide context clues than a native speaker did. This type of information, gained through investigation of individuals using introspection, provides useful information to guide teaching.

The text containing nonsense words in Appendix 4 can be used as a test. Learners should guess at least 6 or 7 of the 10 words correctly if they have mastered the skill of guessing from context.

## APPLICATION

1. Learners used context clues to guess the meaning of the underlined words in a continuous text. They had never met the underlined words before. Many learners made correct guesses but some made the following wrong guesses.

| Context | Wrong Guesses |
|---|---|
| The question of water supplies of the <u>arid</u> lands is of great significance | run away |
| develop their economy by providing export crops of meat, <u>hides</u> and skins, gum, animal's body | bone<br>a kind of crop<br>inner part of fruit |

| | |
|---|---|
| arid countries owe their aridity to <u>sparse</u> rainfall | (all said it was a verb) absorb, control make, distribute cannot keep water |
| The arid lands include some of the best and most extensive <u>grazing</u> areas of the world | important, useful, special land |
| ground-waters . . . percolate <u>laterally</u> | come later, come after the first one, after |

Prepare an explanation for the various wrong guesses. What would you do to help these learners to improve their skill at guessing? Support your answer by using data from the wrong guesses.

2. Which of the following underlined words could be broken into parts and could have their meaning explained by including the meaning of a part? Find others like them in the text.

For over two thousand years language has intrigued scholars, not only because it is an <u>intricate</u> and powerful tool for human <u>communication</u>, but also because it seems to <u>reflect</u> the very nature of human thought. Traditionally, philosophers and linguists have paid most <u>attention</u> to the structure and function of language. In the psychology of language, however, we are <u>concerned</u> with three <u>processes</u>: <u>comprehension</u>, <u>production</u>, and <u>acquisition</u>.

Structurally, the basic unit of language is the sentence. It has roughly two levels: a <u>surface</u> structure <u>consisting</u> of sounds, words, phrases, and clauses—surface <u>constituents</u> of various sizes—<u>arranged</u> so that they form a linear succession of units; and an underlying representation consisting of propositions combined with each other by coordination, relativization, or complementation. These propositions, woven together in complex patterns, bear an indirect, but specifiable, relation to the constituents in surface structure. In effect, the surface structure says how the sentence is to be pronounced, and the underlying representation indicates what ideas it was meant to convey.

Functionally, the sentence has three relatively separate aspects: speech acts, propositional content, and thematic structure. Speakers utter sentences in order to perform speech acts—to ask questions, assert facts, promise favors, make bets, and the like. The speech act that a sentence is meant to express is reflected directly or indirectly in its structure. In performing speech acts, speakers also convey propositional content—to indicate the objects, states or events, and facts their speech acts are about.

The sentences they use express propositions, and these denote objects, states or events, and facts in particular ways. Finally, speakers are careful to use their sentences in cooperation with their listener. In each sentence they indicate given and new information (what they judge their listener does and doesn't know), subject and predicate (what they are talking about and what they are saying about it), and frame and insert (the framework of their ideas and its contents). In short, different aspects of a sentence fulfill different functions.

# Chapter 11

# Simplification of Reading Material

This chapter deals with the reasons and procedures for simplifying written and spoken language. Several reasons are given for using simplified reading material and the distinction between simplifying usage and simplifying use is explained and justified.

Simplification is an essential feature of all language learning. Adults simplify their speech when they talk to children. Course designers introduce vocabulary and structures gradually into their courses so that learners are not faced with a confusing quantity of items. When lessons are prepared, previous learning is considered and manageable quantities of unknown materials are introduced.

Teachers of English as a second language are probably most aware of simplification as it applies to reading. There are hundreds of different titles of simplified reading books available for learners of English. They can read *Robinson Crusoe* in different versions in a vocabulary of 750, 1000, or 2000 words. Most of the English classics like *A Tale of Two Cities*, *Emma*, *Silas Marner*, and *Ivanhoe* can be read in simplified versions written in a vocabulary of 2000 words or less. Simplified English versions of French, German, and Russian novels are also available. In addition, there is an increasing amount of original material, both fact and fiction, written in limited vocabularies as small as 300 words. Bright and McGregor (1970, Chapter 2) provide very useful information about simplified books and their use.

## WHY SIMPLIFY?

There are several reasons for producing simplified material, but they all share the primary aim of removing or reducing the number of low-frequency words and constructions so that some kind of learning or related activity can occur. Without simplification, there would be too many unknown words and constructions, and the learners would need to give all their attention to them.

## Presenting New Vocabulary and Constructions

In direct vocabulary learning, a conscious effort is made to learn vocabulary either in context or in isolation—for example, by learning lists of word forms and their meanings, by doing vocabulary learning exercises, or by studying affixes and roots. In indirect vocabulary learning, new words are learned incidentally while reading or listening, usually as the result of information provided by the context.

By far the bulk of vocabulary learning is indirect. Because of the amount of vocabulary involved and the complexity of the learning, it is not possible for a language course to teach all of the vocabulary required to read unsimplified material with ease (Honeyfield, 1977b). In addition, there is some experimental evidence to show that large quantities of vocabulary can be learned indirectly. Saragi et al. (1978) found that after reading a novel, learners could recognize the meanings of 76 percent of the 90 new words tested, although learners had not been able to refer to a dictionary while reading and were not expecting a vocabulary test.

Indirect vocabulary learning can thus be encouraged by exposure to large amounts of reading and listening material. A well-organized extensive program of graded simplified reading is an important vocabulary component of a language course. Concurrently, learners can be given practice in the strategies of guessing the meanings of words from context. Clarke and Nation (1980), Honeyfield (1977a), and Seibert (1945) give useful advice on this.

There is a growing amount of evidence to show that an increase of interesting reading material—simple but not too carefully controlled—results in very significant increases in vocabulary growth (Elley, 1981).

Simplification is used as a way of controlling the presentation of unknown words and constructions so that they are learned. The material is simplified so that only a few unknown items appear at a time. In his *New Method Readers* West (1932) controlled the introduction of unknown vocabulary so that 1 unknown word appeared in about every 25 known words. Here is a short section from Reader 2 of the *New Method Readers* (pp. 79–80).

---

*Mistake*                    *(Up-side-down)*                    *Sail*

"But it is not finished," you say, "for I do not know what it is a picture of!"

Perhaps we have made a *mistake*.—Yes, we have made a mistake! How very foolish of us! The picture is *up-side-down*!—But we can soon put that right. Turn the book round the other way.

Now you will see that it is a picture of the sea: there are two mountains at the back, and two little ships in front. The ships have *sails*: they are sailing on the sea. Near the foot of the mountain there is a little tent: the letter V makes the tent for us.

If you have colours, you should finish the picture by colouring it. Colour the mountains green; colour the sky and the sea blue; and leave the tent and the sails white.

*You now know the first 500 Commonest Words in English.*

You now know 742 words.

---

In supplementary readers West considered that the ratio of unknown words to known should be 1 : 50 (West, 1955, p. 21). Holley (1973) tried to find the best ratio experimentally. She investigated the relationship between new-word density (that is, the ratio of unknown words to the total length of a text) on the one hand and vocabulary learning, reading time, comprehension, and student ratings of difficulty and enjoyment on the other, using a 750-word text with a glossary. Instead of finding a favorable new-word density beyond which learning suffered, Holley found that "vocabulary learning continues to increase even up to a new vocabulary density of one new word per fifteen known words" (p. 343). Scores on reading time, comprehension, and student ratings of difficulty and enjoyment were not significantly related to new-word density.

A reason for Holley's finding may be that her text was short (750 words) compared with the length of most simplified reading books, which are several thousand words long. In Holley's short text a high ratio of unknown words to known may be acceptable because the total number of unknown words is not high. In a longer simplified reading book this high ratio would result in an unacceptably high total number of unknown words.

West's rule for the introduction of an unknown word was that "each new word on its first appearance should occur at least three times in the paragraph and as often as possible in the rest of the lesson or story" (West, 1955, p. 22). In the Longman Structural Readers, content words not in the basic list but "required for the subject matter may be used provided each is repeated within a few lines, and again a few pages later" (Handbook, p. 1).

   *Advanced English Vocabulary* by Helen Barnard (1972) is an example of another type of text that is simplified to control the introduction of unknown vocabulary. An important feature of this text, like the West readers, is that particular attention is given to repetition of the introduced words. Each unit contains a list of the new vocabulary, programmed learning to explain and exemplify it, and dictation and reading exercises to help establish it.

> . . . the course has as its goal the acquisition of a specified vocabulary. Each target word has a long "life" in the course. It is initially defined or explained in simple terms, or with the aid of a diagram. It is then practiced or encountered in a variety of contexts, at first frequently and later less frequently. These planned repetitions are sometimes read or written and sometimes spoken or listened to.
>
> The first exercises involving a target word are usually sentences or short passages in which a blank space represents a typical occurrence of the word. Students write or say it to themselves as they read. For certain words, especially verbs, the "filling-in-the-blanks" exercises are followed by exercises giving practice in the grammar of the word, i.e. its typical syntactic or structural uses.
>
> *The word is now in circulation.* It will be used throughout the course in defining other words and in the examples and exercises following their definitions. It will be used as a focus of aural attention in dictation exercises and dictations; it may also enter into a pronunciation drill. It will appear in the vocabulary list of the unit in which it is first taught. It will occur in one or more of the reading passages at the end of that unit and will be given further attention in tests and comprehension exercises on the passages. In subsequent units it will be systematically repeated in varying but typical contexts.
>
> It will appear in at least ten places* in the workbooks—often much more frequently.
>
> *In the case of a few words having a narrow range, e.g. "piston," the number of contexts may be less. (Barnard, 1971, p. 11)

   The Longman Bridge series of adapted readers is prepared so that words between the 3000- and 7000-word levels do not occur at a greater density than 25 per 1000 running words, which is a ratio of 1 : 40. Words above the 7000-word level have been simplified.

## Establishing Familiar Vocabulary

   Simplified reading texts can be used to establish familiar vocabulary by repeated use in context; "it reviews and fixes vocabulary already learned" (West, 1955, p. 69). The control of vocabulary increases the chances of repetition because a small number of words must perform many functions. Most simplified reading books—for example, the Ladder series, Longman's Structural Readers, and the Oxford Delta series—do not have the introduction of unknown vocabulary as a major aim but allow the learner to gain further experience of known and partly known vocabulary and structures. West's supplementary readers were like this, and his other name for them was "plateau" readers. They allowed the learner to increase familiarity with what was known rather than continue the process of adding new vocabulary. According to West (1955, p. 69), the supplementary reading book

> . . . serves four purposes. It gives extra practice in reading; it reviews and fixes the vocabulary already learned; it "stretches" that vocabulary so that the learner is enabled to give a greater width of meaning to the words already learned; and lastly, by showing the learner that what he has learned so far really enables him to do something, it encourages him to press on with his study of the language.

Research on the statistical behavior of vocabulary in graded reading texts (Wodinsky & Nation, 1987) indicates that as long as the graded reader is long enough or the learners read two or three readers at the same level, almost all the words used in the books will be repeated several times.

The main requirement of such texts is that they stay as much as possible within the limits of the learners' command of vocabulary and structures. Each series of graded readers has its own graded word list, which is often accompanied by a graded list of structures.

## Getting Pleasure from Reading

An important feature of simplified reading books is that they should bring pleasure and a feeling of success to the reader. Both Palmer (quoted in Bongers, 1947) and West saw this as a necessary aim. "The child should at the earliest moment derive pleasure and a sense of achievement from his study" (West, 1955, p. 20). For this reason, the reading should not be often interrupted by the need to look up an unknown word. For reading for pleasure, "new words should not be introduced more frequently than one new in every fifty running words of the text" (West, 1955, p. 21). Fluency and quantity are features of this type of reading, which is often called extensive reading.

In order to satisfy this aim of simplified material, the content of the texts should be interesting to the reader, and they should be well written. They should also contain few difficulties and should not result in the learner having to do large quantities of comprehension exercises.

## Improving Reading Skills

Some simplified texts are written to give readers a taste of the real thing and to prepare them for dealing with similar material in an unsimplified form. In these cases, unknown vocabulary and structures are avoided so that learners can give their attention to other features of the text or to strategies for dealing with the text. One example of this is simplified speed reading courses (Quinn & Nation, 1974). In such a course, because the vocabulary and structures present no difficulty, learners can concentrate on the techniques of reading faster. Similarly, simplified science texts can introduce learners to the ways in which scientific findings are presented. A requirement of such texts is that although they are simplified, they should contain the important features of similar unsimplified texts. Mountford (1976) discusses this in detail.

## Serving as Models

Some simplifications are intended to act as models for learners' production. That is, learners using those materials could write or speak using the vocabulary and structures of the simplified material. Simplifications of this kind will avoid written imitations of strong dialects ('e died in 'orspital . . . 'cause I bought 'arf his kit) and bookish language.

## Understanding the Content

Some simplifications are not intended to be models of language or opportunities for learning vocabulary but are written solely to make it easier for readers to understand the ideas. They are written in simple English so that readers for whom English is not the mother tongue can easily understand the content. This book is written in that way. Such simplifications include technical terms that will be known or should be learned by the readers in that field of study but avoid other low-frequency vocabulary.

## HOW TO SIMPLIFY

We can divide simplification into two types: (1) simplification of the language and (2) simplification of the use. Here we are most concerned with simplification of the language because that involves vocabulary control, but simplification of use will be discussed because a combination of the different types is common, and they can both play a part in increasing vocabulary knowledge.

## Simplification of the Language

Simplification of vocabulary is done by finding simpler vocabulary to substitute for less frequent words, by using a paraphrase instead of a substitution, by leaving in a word but explaining it in the text, and by leaving out parts of the text containing unwanted vocabulary. Usually simplification is done according to a word list, and most publishers of books for learners of English have their own graded vocabulary lists. Writers preparing simplified material have to work within the vocabulary of the chosen level of the list, but they can introduce outside vocabulary under certain conditions.

Let us compare a simplified text with the unsimplified original to see the processes involved in simplification.

The original:

> Candy and Lennie stood up and went toward the door. Crooks called:
> "Candy!"
> "Huh?"
> " 'Member what I said about hoein' and doin' odd jobs?"
> "Yeah," said Candy. "I remember."
> "Well, jus' forget it," said Crooks. "I didn' mean it. Jus' foolin'. I wouldn't want to go no place like that."
> "Well, O.K., if you feel like that. Good night."
> The three men went out of the door. As they went through the barn the horses snorted and the halter chains rattled.
> Crooks sat on his bunk and looked at the door for a moment, and then he reached for the liniment bottle. He pulled out his shirt at the back, poured a little liniment in his pink palm and, reaching around, he fell slowly to rubbing his back. (Steinbeck, 1949, p. 77)

The simplification:

> Candy and Lennie stood up and went towards the door. Crooks called, "Candy!"
> "Yes?" Candy replied.
> "Do you remember what I said about coming and helping you?" asked Crooks.
> "Yes," said Candy, "I remember."
> "Well, just forget it. I didn't mean it, I was only talking. I wouldn't want to go to a place like that."

"O.K.," said Candy, "You needn't come if you don't want to. Goodnight."

The three men went out of the door and they walked through the barn, past the horses, to the bunk-house.

Crooks sat on his bunk and looked at the door for a moment. Then he reached for the bottle of medicine. He pulled his shirt out of his jeans, poured a little of the medicine into his hand and slowly started rubbing his back. (Steinbeck, 1975, p. 61)

**Regularization**    The most notable feature of the simplified text is the way it has been altered to make it more like the English of schoolbooks. In the second line, the colon (:) is changed to a comma (,). Colloquial items are replaced (*Huh* becomes *Yes*), and dialect forms are changed to standard English ('*Member* becomes *Do you remember; no place* in *I wouldn't want to go to no place like that* becomes *a place*). With these changes the language in the simplified text becomes suitable as a model for production. What is lost, however, is the extra information which is carried by the colloquial and dialect forms. They tell us that the speaker has little education and perhaps remind us of the sound of such speakers.

**Explicitness**    In some places items have been added in order to make the story easier to follow. In line 3, for example, the words *Candy replied* are added. *O.K., if you feel like that* is changed to *O.K. . . . you needn't come if you don't want to*. The meaning is stated rather than implied.

**Removal of Low-Frequency Words**    Words outside the basic list are avoided (*the horses snorted and the halter chains rattled* is not in the simplified version) or are replaced by known words (*hoein' and doin' odd jobs* becomes *coming and helping you; liniment* becomes *medicine; his pink palm* becomes *his hand; fell . . . to* becomes *started*). In these examples, words with very specific meanings are replaced by more general words. This loss in specificity is more than made up for by the ease in reading. Blum and Levenston (1979) examine the strategies and processes involved in removal or avoidance of words in more detail.

**Repetition**    Near the end of the text, *at the back* in the original is replaced by *out of his jeans* in the simplified version. This seems to make the simplified version more difficult, but a likely reason for the change is that *jeans* is a word which has occurred earlier in the story and the simplifier wants to make sure that the word is repeated so that it is learned.

*Of Mice and Men* is a short novel so there is no need to shorten it. In many simplifications of novels, parts of the story are removed so that the story is not too long for learners at that level and so that large sections of unwanted vocabulary are avoided. Davies and Widdowson (1974) compare simplified versions of part of *David Copperfield* and look at this point.

Simplification also involves simplifying structure and rhetoric. Most series of graded reading books have a graded list of grammatical structures to accompany their vocabulary list. In general, complex and compound sentences are replaced by simpler sentences. Unfortunately, the relative frequency of the structures does not seem to be a major consideration in the grading. Low-frequency structures like the present continuous and present perfect are introduced early. The reason for this is that the grading schemes are matched to various English courses. Simplification of the rhetoric usually involves adding explicit markers to show how the text is organized.

Honeyfield (1977b) suggests that for intermediate learners the criteria for simplification should not be too strict so that learners have plenty of opportunity to develop skills for dealing with unknown words.

Simplification of the language of a text can have bad effects. First, the changes in vocabulary and sentence structure might bring the text within the learners' language knowledge but it may make it less readable. This happens when the sentences do not follow each other smoothly and there is a loss of linking words. Second, the message of the text may become less clear. This can occur because the simplifier comes between the original writer and reader and the simplifier's interpretation may be different from the original writer's intention. The language of the text is also likely to be much less specific than the language of the original.

Third, as a result of simplification, the text may no longer be a true piece of writing. Honeyfield (1977b) and Bhatia (1983) argue that simplification can result in a flattening out of the normal information distribution of the text. Thus, instead of the main points of information being concentrated in different parts of the text, they are spread evenly through the text. They suggest that this can result in the development of faulty reading strategies and expectations.

## Simplification of Use

Mountford (1976) divides simplifications into two types—simplification of usage (vocabulary and grammar), which creates an alternative version of the original text, and simplification of use, which changes the nature of the whole text by aiming it at a different audience, by adding interpretation, explanation, and summary, and by providing diagrams and illustrations. Mountford calls the first type of simplification *adaptation* and the second type *re-creation*. He argues that for learners of English for special purposes, adaptations are unsuitable because they are no longer "authentic." That is, they do not represent the genuine use of language in science. Re-creations, however, can be authentic because they are written for a special audience with the genuine aim of communicating the content. Adaptations, on the other hand, present useful vocabulary and grammar but not genuine language use.

The re-creations that Mountford describes are usually written in simple language. Mountford is very careful to stress that simplifications of use can involve simplifications of usage. The simplification of the content that occurs is a result of audience to which the text is directed.

Widdowson (1979) says that "the simplifying of usage does not necessarily result in the simplification of use, that is to say, it does not necessarily facilitate communication. On the contrary it very often makes communication less effective" (p. 197).

If we want learners to master the conventions of communication which are typical in a particular branch of science or any other field of study, then we must select our material from that field. The learner needs to be able to respond to the conventions of communication in a process of active interpretation. If the material has been simplified so that these conventions have been lost or hidden, then the text is no longer authentic because the learner cannot respond to it in the way the writer intended. Simplification of use, *which includes and controls simplification of usage*, tries to bring the text within the learner's language ability without losing its authenticity—that is, without removing those conventions of communication.

What are some of these typical conventions? They include the typical propositions and their functions expressed in that field, such as definition, generalization, the description of processes, and the ways in which these are put together to communicate ideas. Widdowson (1979, pp. 185–189) and Mountford (1976) present analyzed examples.

Simplification of the use can occur in the following ways. Difficult ideas in the text are explained and extra examples may be given. The simplifier can interpret parts of the text so that the readers will understand more clearly. Other parts may be summarized.

Bhatia (1983) suggests an interesting alternative to simplification for advanced learners which he calls "easification." In easification the text is not changed, but it is accompanied by an extra source of information that guides the learner through the text. Bhatia uses illustrations and short questions as examples of easifying. The illustrations are flow diagrams or decision charts of the information in the text. They provide a picture which helps make sense of the organization of the ideas. When short questions are used instead of illustrations, the questions are added to different parts of the text to help learners check and direct their understanding. Bhatia argues that the use of such techniques helps learners develop similar strategies to guide their understanding of texts.

## APPLICATION

1. Choose a passage, simplify it, and describe the principles you followed. What word list did you use? What changes did you make in the passage?

2. Compare a simplified text with its unsimplified original. What has been lost as a result of the simplification? Are the losses important? Is the simplified text fluent and readable? Does it seem too simple?

3. What simplified material can you find which is suitable for your learners? What criteria will you use to decide if it is suitable or not? Bamford (1984) is a useful starting point. Publishers' catalogues are also a useful source.

Chapter **12**

# Directions in Vocabulary Studies

This chapter looks briefly at directions in research on vocabulary which are of current interest to researchers. At present, research on teaching and learning vocabulary is focusing on several areas, some of which continue previous research and some which break new ground.

## VOCABULARY LEARNING GOALS

Researchers have continued to look at the size and nature of the task facing learners, particularly in reading unsimplified texts. Laufer (1987b) investigated the vocabulary coverage of text needed to make a significant difference to second language learners' comprehension of the text. She found that a 95 percent vocabulary coverage had this effect while a 90 percent coverage did not. In Chapter 2 we looked at the effect of vocabulary size on coverage of academic texts finding that a 2000-headword vocabulary plus the University Word List (Appendix 2) provides around 95 percent coverage of academic texts. If specialized word lists are not used the amount of vocabulary needed will be larger. Work in progress by Laufer (personal communication) provides experimental evidence that mastery of the 2000–3000 word level as measured by the levels test (see Appendix 8) is critical for comprehension of unsimplified texts.

Research by Hwang and Nation (forthcoming) on newspaper stories found that, if learners read a series of related stories, the vocabulary load was reduced compared with if they read a similar number of unrelated newspaper stories. If proper nouns were added to the first 2000 words, learners would have a 95 percent coverage of the vocabulary from the second story on in a set of follow-up stories. This 95 percent coverage figure agrees with that found by Liu Na and Nation (1985) for the text coverage needed to guess unknown words from context.

Recent work on the estimation of total vocabulary size confirms the suggestion in Chapter 2 that the smaller estimates are most likely to be correct (Goulden et al., in press). According to these estimates the vocabulary of English-speaking university students is likely to be around 15,000 word families.

Chall (1987) argues that when native-speaking children are learning to read, the greatest vocabulary growth from about 5 years old until 11 years old is in learning to recognize the written forms of words that are already a part of their oral vocabulary. At around 11 years old there is a shift to learning the forms *and meanings* of unknown words especially those met in books.

> Thus the primary grades may be characterized as overcoming a gap
> in word recognition, whereas the intermediate grades and beyond
> may be characterized as overcoming a gap in word meanings (Chall,
> 1987, p. 9).

Chall says that research evidence indicates that, for both word recognition and learning word meanings, direct teaching apart from context is a useful addition to contextual learning.

## ORGANIZING VOCABULARY LEARNING

There has been considerable interest in the quality of vocabulary learning with most attention on associative networks or semantic fields as a way of enriching vocabulary knowledge. Crow (1986) and Crow and Quigley (1985) present evidence for superior achievement in vocabulary learning using a semantic field approach. Other supporters of this kind of approach (Harvey, 1983; Maiguashca, 1984; Stieglitz, 1983) have drawn on evidence from recall experiments in verbal learning studies and word association studies. However, much caution is needed in applying the findings of these studies to second language teaching. There are two reasons for this. First, the verbal learning studies have investigated recall of words that are already part of the subjects' vocabulary. There is a very big difference between recall of known items and learning new items. Words that are closely related to each other are easier to recall than unrelated words, but as Higa (1963) has shown, some kinds of relationships help learning and some have a very strong negative effect on learning (see Chapter 3). Second, the word association studies look at the result of learning and language use. The network of associations between words in a native speaker's brain may be set as a goal for second language learners, but this does not mean that directly teaching these associations is the best way to achieve this goal. In fact, there is clear evidence that it can make learning more difficult. Research on verbal behavior and verbal learning (e.g., Osgood, 1949) has looked closely at the effects of learning related items together. Learning is helped if a group of related items require the learner to make the same response. The experiment by Crow and Quigley (1985) is an example of this. In this experiment, learners had to provide the same synonym for closely related words. However, learning is made more difficult if each item in a group of closely related items requires the learner to make a different response. That is, if learners are presented with a group of words like

*limit, restrict, confine, constrict*

the meaning relationships among these words and their presentation together will encourage their association and the differences between the words will interfere with each other. So the learners will have difficulty in remembering if *constrict* can refer to limiting the number of people or if *restrict* does that job. Higa (1963) found that synonyms like these were the most difficult to learn together. There are therefore strong reasons for being skeptical about suggestions for teaching new vocabulary in associative networks. It is necessary to look first to see if the particular networks suggested will help or interfere with learning.

Research on vocabulary errors (Laufer, 1987a; Zimmerman, 1987) has verified Henning's (1973) finding that formal similarity between words can be a major source of interference in recall and learning.

## VOCABULARY AND READING

It is tempting to expect that an increase in vocabulary size will have noticeable effects on reading comprehension. However, a variety of studies have failed to show this relationship consistently. Bensoussan et al. (1984) studied the effect of allowing learners to use dictionaries while doing reading tests. They found no significant difference between learners using a dictionary and learners not using a dictionary. The temporary increase in vocabulary size provided by the dictionary did not result in a measurable increase in comprehension. A survey of mainly native-speaker studies by Nation and Coady (1988) showed the difficulty in experimentally demonstrating a clear connection between vocabulary manipulations and comprehension. The major cause of this difficulty is that reading involves much more than vocabulary recognition. In addition, vocabulary knowledge is only one of a range of ways for coping with the vocabulary in a text. Other ways include guessing from context, making greater use of background knowledge of the content, and ignoring unimportant parts of the text. Williams (1985) also suggests other possibilities of looking for a synonym in the text (lexical cohesion) and using word parts.

Reviews by Nagy and Herman (1987), Kameenui et al. (1987), and Beck et al. (1987) agree in saying that if vocabulary learning is to have a positive effect on reading comprehension, then this learning not only requires "accuracy of word knowledge, but also fluency of access to meanings in memory, and rich decontextualized knowledge of words" (Beck et al., 1987, p. 148). Nagy and Herman (1987) suggest

> Vocabulary instruction that does improve comprehension generally has some of the following characteristics: multiple exposures to instructed words, exposure to words in meaningful contexts, rich or varied information about each word, the establishment of ties between instructed words and students' own experience and prior knowledge, and an active role by students in the word-learning process (p. 33).

These conditions can be filled by rich instruction (Beck et al., 1987) or by substantial quantities of regular sustained reading (Nagy and Herman, 1987).

## QUALITY OF VOCABULARY KNOWLEDGE

There are now many reasons to believe that the earlier neglect of vocabulary in theorizing and research is now being replaced by a vigorous interest (Laufer, 1986a). Most of this research focuses on immediately practical aspects of learning and coping with vocabulary. However, the most exciting area of vocabulary research is likely to be research into quality of vocabulary knowledge. This research attempts to answer such questions as the following: What increases speed of access to word meanings or forms? How can we tell if one word is better known than another word? How can we tell if learners have improved their knowledge of a word? What stages do learners go through in truly mastering a vocabulary item? Do these stages depend on the type of word, the age of the learners, individual learning styles? Answers to these questions will undoubtedly result in an improvement in the quality of vocabulary teaching.

# Bibliography

A Guide to Collins English Library. 1984. Collins, Glasgow.

Abberton, Evelyn 1963. Some persistent English vocabulary problems for speakers of Serbo-Croatian. English Language Teaching Journal 22:167–172.

Aborn, M. and Rubenstein, H. 1956. Word class distribution in sentences of fixed length. Language 32:666–674.

Aborn, Murray et al. 1959. Sources of contextual constraint upon words in sentences. Journal of Experimental Psychology 57, 3:171–180.

Abramovici, Shimon 1984. Lexical information in reading and memory. Reading Research Quarterly 19, 2:173–187.

Adams, M. J. and Huggins, A. W. F. 1985. The growth of children's sight vocabulary: A quick test with educational and theoretical considerations. Reading Research Quarterly 20, 3:262–281.

Adams, Shirley J. 1982. Scripts and the recognition of unfamiliar vocabulary: Enhancing second language reading skills. Modern Language Journal 66, 2:155–159.

Adams, Sidney and Powers, Francis F. 1929. The measurement of language capacity: The psychology of language. Psychology Bulletin 26:241–260.

Adil Al-Kufaishi 1988. A vocabulary-building program is a necessity not a luxury. English Teaching Forum 26, 2:42.

Akirov, A. and Salager, F. 1985. Difficulty analysis and reading comprehension: An experimental study with Venezuelan science students. English for Specific Purposes (Oregon State University) 94:8–11.

Alderson, C. and Alvarez, G. 1978. The development of strategies for the assignment of semantic information to unknown lexemes in text. ERIC:ED177863.

Alexander, F. and Chamberlain, I. C. 1904. Studies of a Child. Pedagogical Seminary 11:263–291.

Alexander, Richard J. 1984. Fixed expressions in English: Reference books and the teacher. English Language Teaching Journal 38, 2:127–134.

Allen, E. D. and Valette, R. M. 1972. Modern Language Classroom Techniques. Harcourt Brace Jovanovich, New York: Chapter 7.

Allen, Virginia French 1983. Techniques in Teaching Vocabulary. Oxford University Press, New York.

Aly, Anwar Amer. 1986. Semantic field theory and vocabulary teaching. English Teaching Forum 24, 1:30–31.

Amery, H. and Cartwright, S. 1979. The First 1,000 Words—A Picture Word Book. Usborne, London.

Ames, Wilbur S. 1966. The development of a classification scheme of contextual aids. Reading Research Quarterly 2, 1:57–82.

Ames, Wilbur S. 1970. The use of classification schemes in teaching the use of contextual aids. Journal of Reading 14, 1:5–8, 50.

Ammerlaan, T. Lexical retrieval in dormant bilinguals. Department of Psychology, Russian and Language Studies, University of Melbourne.

Andersen Elaine S. 1975. Cups and glasses: Learning that boundaries are vague. Journal of Child Language 2:79–103.

Anderson, J. P. and Jordan, A. M. 1928. Learning and retention of Latin words and phrases. Journal of Educational Psychology 19:485–496.

Anderson, Janet I. 1980. The lexical difficulties of English medical discourse for Egyptian students. English for Specific Purposes (Oregon State University) 37:4.

Anderson, R. C. and Shifrin, Z. 1980. The meaning of words in context. In Spiro et al. (eds.): 330–348.

Anderson, R. C. and Nagy, W. E. Word meanings. Handbook of Reading Research, 2nd edition (forthcoming).

Anderson, R. C., Stevens, K. C., Shifrin, Z. and Osborn, J. H. 1978. Instantiation of word meanings in children. Journal of Reading Behavior 10, 2:149–157.

Anderson, Richard C. and Kulhavy, Raymond W. 1972. Learning concepts from definitions. American Educational Research Journal 9, 3:385–390.

Anderson, Richard C. and Ortony, Andrew 1975. On putting apples into bottles—a problem of polysemy. Cognitive Psychology 7:167–180.

Anderson, Richard C. and Freebody, Peter 1981. Vocabulary knowledge. In Comprehension and Teaching: Research Reviews, John T. Guthrie (ed.). International Reading Association, Newark: 77–117.

Anderson, Richard C. and Freebody, Peter 1983. Reading comprehension and the assessment and acquisition of word knowledge. Advances in Reading/Language Research 2:231–256.

Anglin, J. M. 1977. Word, Object and Conceptual Development. W. W. Norton, New York.

Anthony, Edward 1955. The importance of the native language in teaching vocabulary. Language Learning V:3 and 4.

Anthony, Edward M. 1952–1953. The teaching of cognates. Language Learning IV:3 and 4.

Anthony, Edward M. 1975. Lexicon and vocabulary. RELC Journal 6, 1:21–30.

Anton, H. 1980. Calculus. Wiley, New York.

Arlin, Marshall 1976. Causal priorities between comprehension subskills: Word meaning and paragraph meaning. Journal of Reading Behavior 8, 4:351–362.

Arnaud, Pierre J. L. 1982. A study of some variables linked to the English vocabulary proficiency of French students. Journal of Applied Language Study I, No. 1.

Arnaud, Pierre J. L. 1987. Enseignement/apprentissage du lexique en français langue étrangère. Presented to L'Association Nationale des Enseignants de Français Langue Etrangère, Strasbourg.

Arnaud, Pierre J. L. 1980. L'Enseignement du vocabulaire. Linquistique et Enseignement des Langues, Linguistique et Semiologie, Lyon: Presses Université, Lyon: 83–107.

Arnaud, Pierre J. L. 1984. A practical comparison of five types of vocabulary tests and an investigation into the nature of L2 lexical competence. Paper read at 7th World Congress of Applied Linguistics, August, Brussels.

Arnaud, Pierre J. L., Bejoint, Henri and Thoiron, P. 1985. A quoi sert le programme lexical, l'apprentisage du lexique. Les Langues Modernes 3/4.

Artley, A. Sterl 1943. Teaching word-meaning through context. Elementary English Review 20, 1:68–74.

Asher, James J. 1963. Evidence for "genuine" one-trial learning. IRAL 1, 2:98–103.

Aston, Paul and Christian, Carol (eds.) 1974. Guide to Rangers. Macmillan, London.

Atkinson, R. C. 1972. Optimizing the learning of a second-language vocabulary. Journal of Experimental Psychology 96:124–129.

Atkinson, R. C. 1975. Mnemotechnics in second-language learning. American Psychologist 30:821–828.

Atkinson, R. C. and Raugh, M. R. 1975. An application of the mnemonic keyword method to the acquisition of a Russian vocabulary. Journal of Experimental Psychology: Human Learning and Memory 1:126–133.

Aulls, M. 1971. Context in reading: How it may be depicted. Journal of Reading Behavior 3:61–73.

Babbit, E. H. 1907. A vocabulary test. Popular Science Monthly 70:378.

Baddeley, Alan. Reading and working memory. Best of SET Reading, Item 10, NZCER, Wellington, New Zealand.

Baddock, Barry, 1979. Vocabulary development through describing pictures. Modern English Teacher 6, 5:9–10.

Bagster-Collins, E. W. 1918. A brief study showing the relation between the vocabulary and treatment of the annotated reading text. Modern Language Journal 2, 8:341–351.

Bailey, Charles, James, N. and Shuy, Roger W. 1973. The boundaries of words and their meanings. In New Ways of Analyzing Variation in English, William Labov (ed.), Georgetown University Press, Washington, DC.

Baker, Katherine E. and Sonderegger, Theo B. 1964. Acquisition of meaning through context. Psychonomic Science 1:75–76.

Bamford, J. 1984. Extensive reading by means of graded readers. Reading in a Foreign Language 2, 2:218–260.

Barnard, Helen 1961. A test of P.U.C. students' vocabulary in Chotanagpur. Bulletin of the Central Institute of English 1:90–100.

Barnard, Helen 1971. Teachers' Book for Advanced English Vocabulary. Newbury House, New York.

Barnard, Helen 1972. Advanced English Vocabulary. Newbury House, New York.

Barnard, Helen 1980. Advanced English Vocabulary Workbook I. Newbury House, New York: Revised edition.

Barnard, Helen and Brown, Dorothy 1984. The E.L.I. little language. In Nation, 1984.

Barnhart, C. L., Steinmetz, S. and Barnhart, R. K. 1980. The Second Barnhart Dictionary of New English. Barnhart/Harper & Row, New York.

Barr, A. S. and Gifford, C. W. 1929. The vocabulary of American history. Journal of Educational Research 20, 2:103–121.

Barrett, Martyn D. 1982. Distinguishing between prototypes: The early acquisition of the meaning of object names. In Language Development, Stan A. Kuczaj II (ed.). Erlbaum, Hillsdale, NJ: 313–334.

Barron, R. F. and Stone, F. 1974. The effect of student constructed graphic post organizers upon learning vocabulary relationships. In Nacke: 172–175.

Bateman, W. G. 1914. A child's progress in speech. Journal of Educational Psychology 5, 6:307–320.

Bateman, W. G. 1915. Two children's progress in speech. Journal of Educational Psychology 6:475–493.

Bauer, Laurie 1980. Review of the Longman Dictionary of Contemporary English. RELC Journal II, 1:104–109.

Bauer, Laurie 1981. Review of Chambers Universal Dictionary. RELC Journal 12, 2:100–103.

Baxter, James 1980. The dictionary and vocabulary behaviour: A single word or a handful?. TESOL Quarterly 14, 3:325–336.

Bear, Robert M. and Odbert, Henry S. 1941. Insight of older pupils into their knowledge of word meanings. School Review:754–760.

Beck, I. L., Perfetti, C. A. and McKeown, M. G. 1982. The effects of long-term vocabulary instruction on lexical access and reading comprehension. Journal of Educational Psychology 74:506–521.

Beck, Isabel L. et al. 1983. Vocabulary: All contexts are not created equal. Elementary School Journal 83, 3:177–181.

Beck, I. L. et al. 1984. Improving the comprehensibility of stories: The effects of revisions that improve coherence. Reading Research Quarterly, 19, 3:263–277.

Beck, I. L., McKeown, M. G. and Omanson, R. C. 1987. The effects and uses of diverse vocabulary instructional techniques. In McKeown and Curtis: 147–163.

Becka, J. V. 1972. The lexical composition of specialized texts and its quantitative aspect. Prague Studies in Mathematical Linguistics 4:47–64.

Becker, Wesley C. et al. 1980. Morphographic and Root Word Analysis of 26,000 High Frequency Words. University of Oregon, Follow Through Project, College of Education, Eugene, Oregon.

Beheydt, Ludo 1987. The semantization of vocabulary in foreign language learning. System 15, 1:55–67.

Bejoint, Henri 1981. The foreign student's use of monolingual English dictionaries: A study of language needs and reference skills. Applied Linguistics 2, 3:207–222.

Bellezza, F. S. 1983. Mnemonic-device instruction with adults. In Cognitive Strategy research, M. Pressley and J. R. Levin (eds.), Springer-Verlag, New York: 51–74.

Bendix, Edward Herman 1966. Componential analysis of general vocabulary. International Journal of American Linguistics 32, 2.

Bensoussan, Marsha 1983. Dictionaries and tests of EFL reading comprehension. ELT Journal 37, 4:341–345.

Bensoussan, Marsha and Laufer, Batia 1984. Lexical guessing in context in EFL reading comprehension. Journal of Research in Reading 7, 1:15–32.

Bensoussan, M., Sim, D. and Weiss, R. 1984. The effect of dictionary usage on EFL test performance compared with student and teacher attitudes and expectations. Reading in a Foreign Language 2, 2:262–276.

Bergman, Jerry R. 1977. Reducing reading frustration by an innovative technique for vocabulary growth. Reading Improvement 14, 3:168–171.

Bernbrock, Chris 1980. Stemgo: A word-stems game. E.T. Forum 18, 3:45–46.

Bhatia, V. K. 1983. Simplification v. easification—The case of legal texts. Applied Linguistics 4, 1:42–54.

Bialystock, Ellen and Frohlich, Maria 1980. Oral communication strategies for lexical difficulties. Interlanguage Studies Bulletin, Utrecht 5, 1:3–30.

Blair, Cyrus E. and Burke, Edmund V. 1980. Vocabulary/contextual/spelling interdependency in specific reading and writing tasks for the elementary school student. Guidelines 3:95–103.

Bloom, Kristine C. and Shuell, Thomas J. 1981. Effects of massed and distributed practice on the learning and retention of second-language vocabulary. Journal of Educational Research 74, 4:245–248.

Blum, S. and Levenston, E. 1979. Lexical simplification in second-language acquisition. Studies in Second Language Acquisition 2, 2:43–63.

Blum, Shoshana and Levenston, E. A. 1978. Universals of lexical simplification. Language Learning 28, 2:399–415.

Bock, Carolyn 1948. Prefixes and suffixes. Classical Journal 44:132–133.

Bohn, William E. 1914. First steps in verbal expression. Pedagogical Seminary 21:579–595.

Bongers, H. 1947. The History and Principles of Vocabulary Control. Wocopi, Woerden.

Bower, G. H. 1970. Analysis of a mnemonic device. American Scientist 58:496–510.

Bower, Gordon H. 1973. How to . . . Uh . . . Remember. Psychology Today 7, 5:63–69.

Boyd, William 1914. The development of a child's vocabulary. Pedagogical Seminary 21:95–123.

Bramki, D. and Williams, R. C. 1984. Lexical familiarization in economics text, and its pedagogic implications in reading comprehension. Reading in a Foreign Language 2, 1:169–181.

Brandenburg, George C. 1914. The language of a three-year-old child. Pedagogical Seminary 22:89–120.

Brandenburg, G. C. and Brandenburg, Julia 1919. Language development during the fourth year: The conversation. Pedagogical Seminary 26, 1:27–40.

Bridges, Robert 1919. English Homophones. SPE Tract No. 2, Clarendon Press, London.

Bright, J. A. and McGregor, G. P. 1970. Teaching English as a Second Language. Longman, London.

Briones, I. T. 1937. An experimental comparison of two forms of linguistic learning. Psychological Record 1:204–214.

British Council Teachers 1980. Six aspects of vocabulary teaching. Guidelines 2:80–94.

Broeder, P. 1987. Measuring lexical richness and variety in second language use. Polyglot 8, 1:1–16.

Bromage, Bruce K. and Mayer, Richard E. 1986. Quantitative and qualitative effects of repetition on learning from technical text. Journal of Educational Psychology 78:271–278.

Brown, Dorothy F. 1974. Advanced vocabulary teaching: The problem of collocation. RELC Journal 5, 2:1–11.

Brown, Dorothy F. 1980. Eight Cs and a G. Guidelines 3:1–17.

Brown, D. and Barnard, H. 1975. Dictation as a learning experience. RELC Journal 6, 2:42–62.

Brown, J. 1971. Programmed Vocabulary. New Century, New York: 2nd ed.

Brown, Jim 1979. Vocabulary: Learning to be imprecise. Modern English Teacher 7, 1:25–27.

Brown, Lesley A. and Lynn, Robert 1976. Review of the Oxford Advanced Learner's Dictionary of Current English. RELC Journal 7, 1:77–79.

Brown, R. and McNeill, D. 1966. The "tip of the tongue" phenomenon. Journal of Verbal Learning and Verbal Behaviour 5, 4:325–357.

Brown, Roger 1978. A new paradigm of reference. In The Psychology and Biology of Language and Thought, G. A. Miller and Elizabeth Lenneberg. Academic Press, New York: 151–166.

Bruce, B., Rubin, A., Starr, K. and Liebling, C. 1983. Vocabulary bias in reading curricula. Technical Report No. 280, Center for the Study of Reading, Bolt Beranek and Newman.

Bruce, Nigel J. (ed.) 1985. Newsletter: English for Medical Paramedical Purposes. The Medical Study Skills Division, Health Sciences Centre, Kuwait University 2, 2.

Bruton, Anthony 1984. Review of Wallace (1982). ELT Journal 38, 1:58–60.

Bruton, Anthony and Samuda, Virginia 1981. Guessing words. Modern English Teacher 8, 3:18–21.

Bruton, J. G. 1964. Overlap. ELT 18, 4:161–166.

Brutten, Sheila R. 1981. An analysis of student and teacher indications of vocabulary difficulty. RELC Journal 12, 1:66–71.

Bryan, Fred E. 1953. How large are children's vocabularies? Elementary School Journal 54:210–216.

Buckingham, R. R. and Dolch, E. W. 1936. A combined word list. Ginn, Boston.

Bullard, Nick 1985. Word-based perception: a handicap in second language acquisition? English Language Teaching Journal 39, 1:28–32.

Burling, Robins 1983. A proposal for computer-assisted instruction in vocabulary. System II, 2.

Burns, D. G. 1951. An investigation into the extent of first-year vocabulary in French in boys' grammar schools. British Journal of Educational Psychology 21:36–44.

Burridge, Shirley and Adam, Max, no date. Using a Learner's Dictionary in the Classroom. Oxford University Press, Oxford.

Bush, Arthur 1914. The vocabulary of a three-year-girl. Pedagogical Seminary 21:125–142.

Cahen, L. S., Craun, M. J., and Johnson, S. K. 1971. Spelling difficulty—A survey of the research. Review of Educational Research 41, 4:281–301.

Campion, Mary E. and Elley, Warwick B. 1971. An Academic Vocabulary List. NZCER, Wellington.

Carey, Susan 1978. The child as word learner. In Linguistic Theory and Psychological Reality, M. Halle, J. Bresnan and G. A. Miller (eds.). M.I.T. Press, Cambridge, MA: 264–293.

Carnine, Douglas et al. 1984. Utilization of contextual information in determining the meaning of unfamiliar words. Reading Research Quarterly 19, 2:188–204.

Carroll, B. and Drum, P. A. 1982. Effects of context in facilitating unknown word comprehension. In New enquiries in reading, J. A. Niles and L. A. Harris (eds.), National Reading Conference, Rochester, NY: 89–93.

Carroll, B. A. and Drum, P. A. 1983. Definitional gains for explicit and implicit context clues. In Niles and Harris: 158–162.

Carroll, J. B. 1940. Knowledge of English roots and affixes as related to vocabulary and Latin study. Journal of Educational Research 34, 2:102–111.

Carroll, J. B. 1976. Modern languages. In Encyclopaedia of Educational Research, R. L. Ebel (ed.), 4th ed.

Carroll, J. B., Davies, P. and Richman, B. 1963. Research on teaching foreign languages. In Handbook of Research on Teaching, N. L. Gage (ed.). Rand McNally, Chicago: 1060–1100.

Carroll, John B. 1964. Language and Thought. Prentice-Hall, Englewood Cliffs, NJ.

Carroll, John B. 1964. Words, meanings and concepts. Harvard Educational Review 34, 2:178–202.

Carroll, John B. 1972. A new word frequency book. Elementary English 49:1070–1074.

Carroll, John B., Davies, P. and Richman, B. 1971. The American Heritage Word Frequency Book. Houghton Mifflin, Boston; American Heritage, New York.

Carroll, John Miller and Roeloffs, Robert. July 1969. Computer selection of keywords using word-frequency analysis. American Documentation: 227–233.

Carter, R. 1987. Is there a core vocabulary? Applied Linguistics 8:178.

Carter, R. 1987. Vocabulary. Allen & Unwin, London.

Carter, Ronald 1986. Core vocabulary and discourse in the curriculum—A question of the subject. RELC Journal 17, 1:52–70.

Carter, Ronald 1988. Vocabulary, cloze and discourse. In Carter and McCarthy: 161–180.

Carter, Ronald and McCarthy, Michael (eds.) 1988. Vocabulary and Language Teaching. Longman, London.

Carton, A. S. 1971. Inferencing: A process in using and learning language. In The Psychology of Second Language Learning, Paul Pimsleur and Terrence Quinn (eds.). Cambridge University Press, Cambridge: 45–58.

Cassels, J. R. T. and Johnstone, A. H. 1985. Words That Matter in Science: A Report of a Research Exercise. The Royal Society of Chemistry, London.

Chall, J. 1958. Readability: An Appraisal of Research and Application. Ohio State Bureau of Education Research Monographs.

Chall, J. S. 1987. Two vocabularies for reading: recognition and meaning. In McKeown and Curtis: 7–17.

Chamberlain, A. F. and I. C. 1904. Studies of a child. 1 and 2. Pedagogical Seminary 11:263–291.

Chandrasegaran, Antonia 1980. Teaching the context clue approach to meaning. Guidelines 3:61–68.

Channell, Joanna 1981. Applying semantic theory to vocabulary teaching. English Language Teaching Journal 35, 2:115–122.

Channell, Joanna 1988. Psycholinguistic considerations in the study of L2 vocabulary acquisition. In Carter and McCarthy: 83–96.

Chapman, F. L. and Gilbert, L. C. 1937. A study of the influence of familiarity with English words upon the learning of their foreign language equivalent. Journal of Educational Psychology 28:621–628.

Chaudron, Craig 1982. Vocabulary elaboration in teachers' speech to L2 learners. Studies in Second Language Acquisition 4, 2:170–180.

Christopher, John 1972. In the Beginning. Longman, London.

Chun, Ann E. et al. 1982. Errors, interaction and correction: A study of native-non-native conversations. TESOL Quarterly 16, 4:537–547.

Clackson, Janet 1977. Interference and vocabulary learning, the influence of cross-language homonymy. TESL Honors Course, course paper. Victoria University of Wellington, New Zealand.

Clark, E. V. 1971. On the acquisition of the meaning of "before" and "after." Journal of Verbal Learning and Verbal Behavior 10:266–275.

Clark, E. V. 1973. What's in a word? On the child's acquisition of semantics in his L1. In Cognitive Development and the Acquisition of Language, T. E. Moore (ed.). Academic Press, New York.

Clark, H. H. and E. V. 1977. Memory for Prose: Psychology and Language, Harcourt Brace Jovanovich, New York: 154.

Clarke, D. F. and Nation, I. S. P. 1980. Guessing the meanings of words from context: Strategy and techniques. System 8, 3:211–220.

Clarke, M. J. (ed.) 1964. English Studies Series I. Oxford University Press, London.

Clifford, Geraldine Joncich 1978. Words for schools: The applications in education of the vocabulary researches of Edward L. Thorndike. In Impact of Research on Education, Some Case Studies, P. Suppes (ed.), University of California at Berkeley.

Coady, J. M. 1979. A psycholinguistic model of the ESL reader. In Reading in a Second Language, R. Mackay et al. (eds.). Newbury House, New York: 5–12.

Coady, James 1988. Research on L2 vocabulary acquisition: Putting it in context. Unpublished paper, Ohio University.

Coady, James, Carrell, Pat and Nation, Paul 1986. The teaching of vocabulary in ESL from the perspective of schema theory. Unpublished paper.

Cohen, A. and Hosenfield, C. 1981. Some uses of mentalistic data in second language research. Language Learning 31, 2:285–313.

Cohen, Andrew, to appear. Attrition in the productive lexicon of two Portuguese third-language speakers. Studies in Second Language Acquisition.

Cohen, Andrew D. 1984. The use of verbal and imagery mnemonics in second language learning. Unpublished paper.

Cohen, Andrew D. and Aphek, Edna 1980. Retention of second-language vocabulary over time: Investigating the role of mnemonic associations. System 8, 3:221–235.

Colvin, Cynthia M. 1951. A re-examination of the vocabulary question. Elementary English 28:350–356.

Cook, J. M., Heim, A. W. and Watts, K. P. 1963. The word-in-context: A new type of verbal reasoning test. British Journal of Psychology 54, 3:227–237.

Cook, Vivian 1981. Teaching vocabulary. Modern English Teacher 8, 3:16–18.

Cornu, Anne-Marie 1979. The first step in vocabulary teaching. Modern Language Journal 63:262–272.

Corson, D. J. 1985. The Lexical Bar. Pergamon Press, Oxford.

Corson, David 1983. Measures of lexical difficulty: The lexical bar. Working Papers in Language and Linguistics, Tasmanian College of Advanced Education.

Corson, David 1983. The priority of words in meaning. University of Wollongong Working Papers.

Corson, David 1983. Social dialect, the semantic barrier, and access to curricular knowledge. Language and Society 12:213–222.

Corson, David 1984. The case for oral language in schooling. Elementary School Journal (University of Chicago) 84, 4:458–467.

Corson, David 1984. The lexical bar: lexical change from 12 to 15 years measured by social class, region and ethnicity. British Educational Research Journal 10, 2:115–133.

Corson, David 1984. Lying and killing: Language and the moral reasoning of 12 and 15 year olds by social group. (Libra Publishing Inc., 391 Willets Rd, Roslyn Heights, New York 11577) No. 74.

Corson, David, in press. Social group lexes in the Illawarra: the register of the secondary school. The Australian and New Zealand Journal of Sociology 26, 1.

Corson, David J. 1982. The Graeco-Latin (G-L) instrument: A new measure of semantic complexity in oral and written English. Language and Speech 25, Pt. 1.

Corson, David J. 1983. The Corson measure of passive vocabulary. Language and Speech 26, 1:3–20.

Cowan, J. R. 1974. Lexical and syntactic research for the design of EFL reading materials. TESOL Quarterly 8, 4:389–400.

Cowie, A. P. 1988. Stable and creative aspects of vocabulary use. In Carter and McCarthy: 126–139.

Cowie, A. P. 1982. Problems of syntax and the design of a pedagogic dictionary. Rassegna Italiana di Linguistica Applicata 10, 2:255–264.

Craik, F. I. M. and Lockhart, R. S. 1972. Levels of processing: A framework for memory research. Journal of Verbal Learning and Verbal Behavior 11:671–684.

Craik, F. I. M. and Tulving, E. 1975. Depth of processing and the retention of words in episodic memory. Journal of Experimental Psychology 104:268–284.

Cripwell, Kenneth and Foley, Joseph 1984. The grading of extensive readers. World Language English 3, 3:168–173.

Crist, Robert L. 1981. Learning concepts from contexts and definitions: A single subject replication. Journal of Reading Behaviour 13, 3:271–277.

Croft, Kenneth and Brown, Billye Walker 1966. Science Readings. McGraw-Hill, New York.

Cronbach, Lee J. 1942. An analysis of techniques for diagnostic vocabulary testing. Journal of Educational Research 36, 3:206–217.

Cronbach, Lee J. 1943. Measuring knowledge of precise word meaning. Journal of Educational Research 36, 7:528–534.

Crothers, E. and Suppes, P. 1967. Experiments in Second-Language Learning. Academic Press, New York.

Crow, John T. 1986. Receptive vocabulary acquisition for reading comprehension. Modern Language Journal 70, 2:242–250.

Crow, John T. and Quigley, June R. 1985. A semantic field approach to passive vocabulary acquisition for reading comprehension. TESOL Quarterly 19, 3:497-513.

Crystal, David 1987. How many words? English Today 12.

Cuff, Noel B. 1930. Vocabulary tests. Journal of Educational Psychology 21, 3:212–220.

Cummins, Jim 1980. Age on arrival and immigrant second language learning in Canada: a reassessment. Applied Linguistics 11, 2:132–149.

Curtis, M. E. 1987. Vocabulary testing and vocabulary instruction. In McKeown and Curtis: 37–51.

Cziko, Gary A. 1978. Differences in first- and second-language reading: the use of syntactic, semantic and discourse constraints. Canadian Modern Language Review 34:473–489.

D'Agostino, P. R., O'Neill, B. J. and Paivio, A. 1977. Memory for pictures and words as a function of level of processing: Depth or dual coding? Memory and Cognition 5:252–256.

Dagut, M. B. 1977. Incongruencies in lexical "gridding"—An application of contrastive semantic analysis to language teaching. IRAL 15, 3:221–229.

Dagut, M. and Laufer, B. 1985. Avoidance of phrasal verbs—a case for contrastive analysis. Studies in Second Language Acquisition 7:73–80.

Dale, E. 1956. The problem of vocabulary in reading. Educational Research Bulletin 25:113–123.

Dale, E. and O'Rourke, J. 1971. Techniques of Teaching Vocabulary. Field Enterprises, Chicago.

Dale, Edgar 1931. Difficulties in vocabulary research. Educational Research Bulletin 10, 5:119–122.

Dale, Edgar 1965. Vocabulary measurement: Techniques and major findings. Elementary English 42:895–901.

Dale, Edgar and Razik, Raher 1963. Bibliography of Vocabulary Studies. Bureau of Educational Research and Service, Ohio State University 2nd ed.

Dale, Edgar and O'Rourke, Joseph 1976. The Living Word Vocabulary. Field Enterprises (distributed exclusively by DOME, Inc., 1169 Logan Ave, Elgin, IL 60120).

Dale, Philip S. 1976. Language Development. Holt, Rinehart & Winston, New York 2nd ed.

Daneman, Meredith and Green, Ian 1986. Individual differences in comprehending and producing words in context. Journal of Memory and Language 25:1–18.

Darnell, Donald K. and Howes, D. H. 1971. Review of Carroll et al. Research in the Teaching of English 6, 2:222–246.

Davies, Alan and Widdowson, H. G. 1974. Reading and writing. In Techniques in Applied Linguistics: The Edinburgh Course in Applied Linguistics. Oxford University Press, London 3:176–177.

Davies, Pat and Williams, Phillip 1974. Growth of word recognition skills. In Aspects of Early Reading Growth: A Longitudinal Study. Schools Council Research and Development Project in Compensatory Education, Blackwell, Oxford: 13–53.

Davis, F. B. 1968. Research in comprehension in reading. Reading Research Quarterly 4:499–545.

Davis, F. B. 1972. Psychometric research on comprehension in reading. Reading Research Quarterly 7:628–678.

Davis, Frederick B. 1944. The interpretation of frequency ratings obtained from "The Teacher's Word Book." Journal of Educational Psychology 35:169–174.

Davis, Nancy B. 1973. Vocabulary Improvement. McGraw-Hill, New York: 50–51.

Deighton, L. C. 1959. Vocabulary Development in the Classroom. Columbia University Press, New York.

Deno, S. L. 1968. Effects of words and pictures as stimuli in learning language equivalents. Journal of Educational Psychology 59:202–206.

Diack, Hunter 1970. Standard Literacy Tests. Hart–Davis Educational.

Diack, Hunter 1975. Test Your Own Wordpower. Paladin, St. Albans.

Dickinson, David K. 1984. First impressions: Children's knowledge of words gained from a single exposure. Applied Psycholinguistics 5:359–373.

Dietrich, T. G. and Freeman, C. 1979. A Linguistic Guide to English Proficiency Testing in Schools. CAL/ERIC: 13–14.

Diller, Karl Conrad 1978. The Language Teaching Controversy. Newbury House, New York: Chapter 12.

Dolby, J. L. and Resnikoff, H. L. 1967. The English Word Speculum. Mouton, The Hague.

Dolch, E. W. 1936. How much word knowledge do children bring to grade one? Elementary English Review xiii:177–183.

Dolch, E. W. 1951. The use of vocabulary lists in predicting readability and in developing reading materials. Elementary English 28:142–149, 177.

Dolch, E. W. and Leeds, D. 1953. Vocabulary tests and depth of meaning. Journal of Educational Research 47:181–189.

Dollerup, Cay 1982. An analysis of some mechanisms and strategies in the translation process based on a study of translations between Danish and English. The Incorporated Linguist, the Journal of the Institute of Linguists 21, No. 4.

Dollerup, Cay, Glahn, Esther and Hansen, C. R. 1982. Reading strategies and test-solving techniques in an EFL-reading comprehension test: A preliminary report. Journal of Applied Language Study 1, 1.

Dollerup, Cay, Glahn, Esther and Hansen, C. Rosenberg 1988. Issues Raised by Studies of Passive Vocabularies in Reading Comprehension with Advanced EFL-Learners.

Doran, E. W. 1907. A study of vocabularies. Pedagogical Seminary 14, 4:401–438.

Drake, Richard M. 1940. The effect of teaching the vocabulary of algebra. Journal of Educational Research 33, 8:601–610.

Draper, A. G. and Moeller, G. H. 1971. I/we think with words. Phi Delta Kappan 52, 8:482–484.

Dresher, Richard 1934. Training in mathematics vocabulary. Educational Research Bulletin 13, 8:201–204.

Drum, P. A. and Konopak, B. C. 1987. Learning word meanings from context. In McKeown and Curtis: 73–87.

Drum, Priscilla A. 1983. Vocabulary knowledge: History. In Searches for meaning in reading/language processing and instruction. J. A. Niles and L. A. Harris (eds.), 32nd yearbook of the National Reading Conference, Rochester, NY: 163–171.

Duin, A. H. and Graveas, M. F. 1987. Intensive vocabulary instruction as a pre-writing technique. Reading Research Quarterly 22, 3:311–330.

Dulin, K. 1970. New research on context clues. Journal of Reading 12:33–38.

Dulin, Kenneth L. 1970. Using context clues in word recognition and comprehension. Reading Teacher 23, 5:440–445.

Dulin, Kenneth La Marr 1969. New research on context clues. Journal of Reading 13, 1:33–38, 53.

Duncan, Carl P. 1970. Thinking of a word under different retrieval constraints. Journal of Verbal Learning and Verbal Behaviour 9:356–361.

Dupuy, Harold J. 1974. The Rationale, Development and Standardization of a Basic Word Vocabulary Test. U.S. Government Printing Office, Washington, DC.

Durkin, K., Crowther, R., Shire, B., Riem, R. and Nash P. 1985. Polysemy in mathematical and musical education. Applied Linguistics 6, 2:147–161.

Durkin, K., Crowther, R. D. and Shire, B. 1986. Children's processing of polysemous vocabulary in school. In Language Development in the School Years, K. Durkin (ed.). Croom Helm, London.

Eaton, Helen S. 1940. An English-French-German-Spanish Word Frequency Dictionary. Dover Publications, New York.

Eaton, Helen S. 1951–1952. Vocabulary building. Language Learning IV, 1 and 2:54–60.

Ebel, R. L. (ed.). Encyclopaedia of Educational Research, 4th ed.

Edwards, R. P. A. and Gibbon, Vivian 1973. Words Your Children Use. Burke Books, London.

Eichholz, Gerhard and Barbe, Richard 1961. An experiment in vocabulary development. Educational Research Bulletin 40, 1:1–7, 28.

Elivian, J. 1938. Word perception and word meaning in student reading in the intermediate grades. Education 59:1–56.

Ellegard, Alvar 1960. Estimating vocabulary size. Word 16:219–244.

Ellegard, Alvar 1978. On dictionaries for language learners. Moderna Sprak 72, 3:225–242.

Elley, Warwick 1985. What do children learn from being read to? SET 1, NZCER.

Elley, Warwick B. 1981. The role of reading in bilingual contexts. In Comprehension and Teaching: Research Reviews, John T. Guthrie (ed.). International Reading Association, Newark: 227–254.

Elley, Warwick B. 1988. New vocabulary: How do children learn new words? Set–Research Information for Teachers, Item 10, No. 1. NZCER, Wellington.

Elley, Warwick B. 1989. Vocabulary acquisition from listening to stories. Reading Research Quarterly 24, 2:174–187.

Elley, Warwick B. and Mangubhai, Francis 1981. The long-term effects of a book flood on children's language growth. Directions 7:15–24.

Elshout-Mohr, M. and van Daalen-Kapteijns, M. 1987. Cognitive processes in learning word meanings. In McKeown and Curtis: 53–71.

Emans, Robert and Fisher, Gladys Mary 1967. Teaching the use of context clues. Elementary English 44, 3:243–246.

Engels, L. K. 1968. The fallacy of word counts. IRAL 6, 3:213–231.

Erdmenger, Manfred 1985. Word acquisition and vocabulary structure in third-year EFL-learners. IRAL 23, 2:159–164.

Farid, Anne 1985. A Vocabulary Workbook. Prentice-Hall, Englewood Cliffs, N.J.

Faust, G. W. and Anderson, R. C. 1967. Effects of incidental material in a programmed Russian vocabulary lesson. Journal of Educational Psychology 58:3–10.

Feeny, Thomas P. 1976. Vocabulary teaching as a means of vocabulary expansion. Foreign Language Annals 9, 5:485–486.

Feifel, Herman and Lorge, Irving 1950. Qualitative differences in the vocabulary responses of children. Journal of Educational Psychology 41, 1:1–18.

Feldman, K. V. and Klausmeier, H. J. 1974. Effects of two kinds of definition on concept attainment of fourth and eighth graders. Journal of Educational Research 67, 5:219–223.

Fiks, A. E. and Corbino, J. P. 1967. Course density and student perception. Language Learning 17:3–8.

Finkenstaedt, T., Leisi, E. and Wolff, D. 1970. A Chronological English Dictionary. Carl Winter, Universitets Verlag, Heidelberg.

Finn, P. J. 1977–1978. Word frequency, information theory, and cloze performance: A transfer theory of processing in reading. Reading Research Quarterly 13:508–537.

Flood, W. E. 1957. The Problem of Vocabulary in the Popularization of Science. University of Birmingham, Institute of Education.

Flood, W. E. and West, M. P. 1950. A limited vocabulary for scientific and technical ideas. English Language Teaching 4, 4 & 5:104–128.

Forlano, G. and Hoffman, M. 1937. Guessing and telling methods in learning words in a foreign language. Journal of Educational Psychology 28:632–636.

Fountain, R. L. 1979. Word making and word taking: A game to motivate language learning. RELC Journal: Guidelines 1:76–80.

Fountain, Ron 1980. Word learning games with vocabulary cards. Guidelines 3:104–110.

Fountain, Ronald 1974. A Case for Dictation Tests in the Selection of Foreign Students for English Medium Study in New Zealand. Paper offerd for Dip. Applied Linguistics at the University of Edinburgh.

Fox, Jeremy 1984. Computer-assisted vocabulary learning. English Language Teaching Journal 38, 1:27–33.

Fox, Jeremy and Mahood, John 1982a. Lexicons and the ELT materials writer. English Language Teaching Journal 36, 2:125–129.

Fox, Jeremy and Mahood, John 1982b. Review of "The Longman Lexicon of Contemporary English." English Language Teaching Journal 36, 4:275–277.

Freebody, Peter and Anderson, Richard C. 1983. Effects on text comprehension of differing propositions and locations of difficult vocabulary. Journal of Reading Behavior 15, 3:19–39.

Fries, C. C. 1945. Teaching and Learning English as a Foreign Language. University of Michigan Press, Ann Arbor, MI.

Fries, Charles C. and Traver, A. Aileen 1960. English Word Lists. George Wahr, Ann Arbor, MI.

Frith, Uta (ed.) 1980. Cognitive Processes in Spelling. Academic Press, London.

Fry, E. B. 1960. A study of teaching machine response modes. In Teaching Machines and Programmed Learning, A. A. Lumsdaine and R. Glaser (eds.). National Education Association, Washington, DC: 469–474.

Fuentes, E. J. 1976. An investigation into the use of imagery and generativity in learning a foreign language vocabulary. Dissertation Abstracts International 37:2694A.

Fulcher, Glenn 1987. "Contextual hyponymy": A communicative approach to teaching lexis in context. Modern English Teacher 14, 3:14–17.

Fulcher, Glenn 1988. Teaching vocabulary for writing. Modern English Teacher 15, 3:25–30.

Gale, M. C. and H. 1902. Children's vocabularies. Popular Science Monthly 61:45–51.

Gale, M. C. and H. 1902. The vocabularies of three children in one family at two and three years of age. Pedagogical Seminary 9:422–435.

Gansl, Irene 1939. Vocabulary: Its measurement and growth. Archives of Psychology, NY 33, No. 236.

Gary, J. D. and Gary, N. G. 1981. Caution: Talking may be dangerous for your linguistic health. IRAL 19, 1:1–13.

Gates, A. I., Bond, G. L. and Russell, D. H. 1938. Relative meaning and pronunciation difficulty of the Thorndike 20,000 words. Journal of Educational Research 32:161–167.

Gefen, Raphael 1987. Increasing vocabulary teaching in Israel schools. English Teachers Journal (Israel) 35:38–44.

Gentner, Dedre 1982. Why nouns are learned before verbs: Linguistic relativity versus natural partitioning. Technical Report No. 257, Center for the Study of Reading, Bolt Beranek and Newman Inc.

George, H. V. 1962. On teaching and "unteaching." English Language Teaching Journal, 17, 1:16–20.

George, H. V. 1972. Common Errors in Language Learning. Newbury House, New York.

George, H. V. 1978. Teaching from a Structural Syllabus. English Language Institute, Victoria University of Wellington.

George, H. V. 1983. Classification, Communication, Teaching and Learning. English Language Institute, Victoria University of Wellington.

Gerlach, Fred M. 1917. Vocabulary Studies: Studies in Education and Psychology, J. V. Brentweiser (ed.). Colorado College.

Gershman, S. J. 1970. Foreign language vocabulary learning under seven conditions. Dissertation Abstracts International 31:3690B.

Ghadessy, Mohsen 1979. Frequency counts, word lists, and materials preparation: A new approach. English Teaching Forum 17, 1:24–27.

Gibbons, Helen 1940. The ability of college freshmen to construct the meaning of a strange word from the context in which it appears. Journal of Experimental Education 9, 1:29–33.

Gipe, Joan 1979. Investigating techniques for teaching word meanings. Reading Research Quarterly 14, 4:625–644.

Gipe, Joan P. 1980. Use of a relevant context helps kids learn new meanings. The Reading Teacher 33, 4:398–402.

Gipe, Joan P. and Arnold, Richard D. 1979. Teaching vocabulary through familiar associations and contexts. Journal of Reading Behavior II, 3:282–285.

Godman, A. and Payne E. M. F. 1981. A taxonomic approach to the lexis of science. In English for Academic and Technical Purposes: Studies in Honor of Louis Trimble, Larry Selinker, Elaine Tarone, and Victor Hanzeli (eds.). Newbury House, New York: 23–39.

Goethals, M., Engels, L. K. and Leenders, T. 1987. Automated analysis of the vocabulary of English texts. . . . AILA paper, Sydney: 37.

Goldfus, Carol 1987. Teaching vocabulary for production—oral and written—in the Upper Division. English Teachers Journal (Israel) 35:53–57.

Golebiowska, Aleksandra 1986. Review of Gairns, Ruth and Redman, Stuart: Working with Words. Cambridge University Press, Cambridge.

Goodman, K. S. 1976. Reading: A psycholinguistic guessing game. In Theoretical Models and Processes of Reading, H. Singer and R. Ruddell (eds.). International Reading Association, Newark 2nd ed.

Goodman, K. S. and Bird, L. B. 1984. On the wording of texts: A study on intra-text word frequency. Research in the Teaching of English 18:119–145.

Goulden, R., Nation, I. S. P., and Read, J. A. S., in press. How large can a receptive vocabulary be? Applied Linguistics.

Gove, P. B. (ed.) 1963. Webster's Third New International Dictionary. G. & C. Merriam Co., Springfield, MA.

Graham, C. Ray, Belnap, A. D., and Kirk, R. 1986. The acquisition of lexical boundaries in English by native speakers of English. IRAL 24, 4:275–286.

Graves, M. F. 1987. The roles of instruction in fostering vocabulary development. In McKeown and Curtis: 165–184.

Graves, M. F. 1985. A Word is a Word. Scholastic, New York.

Graves, M. F. and Duin, A. L. 1985. Building students' expressive vocabulary. Educational Perspectives 23, 1:4–10.

Graves, M. F., Ryder, R. J. and Slater, W. H. 1983. Family frequency as a predictor of word knowledge. In Searches for Meaning: Reading/Language Processing and Instruction, J. A. Niles and L. A. Harris. Yearbook of the National Reading Conference, Rochester, N.Y.

Graves, Michael F. et al. 1980. Word frequency as a predictor of students' reading vocabularies. Journal of Reading Behavior 12, 2:117–127.

Green, Georgia M. 1984. Some remarks on how words mean. Technical Report No. 307, Center for the Study of Reading, Bolt, Beranek and Newman.

Greenfield, Norman and Prindle, Anthony 1966. Acquisition of a foreign language vocabulary as influenced by meaning (m) and reinforcement. Psychological Reports 19:585–586.

Gregory, C. A. 1923. The reading of third-grade children. Journal of Educational Research 7, 2:127–131.

Grinstead, W. J. 1915. An experiment in the learning of foreign words. Journal of Educational Psychology 6:242–245.

Grinstead, W. J. 1924. On the sources of the English vocabulary. Teachers College Record 26:32–46.

Haastrup, Kirsten 1987. Using Thinking Aloud and Retrospection to Uncover Learners' Lexical Inferencing Procedures. Multilingual Matters, Avon.

Hafner, Lawrence E. 1965. A one-month experiment in teaching context aids in fifth grade. Journal of Educational Research 58, 10:472–474.

Hafner, Lawrence, E. 1967. Using context to determine meanings in high school and college. Journal of Reading 10, 7:491–498.

Hague, Sally A. 1987. Vocabulary instruction: What L2 can learn from L1? Foreign Language Annals 20, 3:217–225.

Halff, Henry M. et. al. 1976. A context-sensitive representation of word meanings. Memory and Cognition 4, 4:378–383.

Hall, David with Bowyer, Tim 1980. Nucleus: Mathematics. Longman, London.

Hall, W. S., Nagy, W. E. and Linn, R. 1984. Spoken words: Effects of situation and social group on oral word usage and frequency. Hillsdale, NJ.

Hall, Winfield S. 1896. The first five hundred days of a child's life. Child Study Monthly 2:586–608.

Halliday, M. A. K. and Hasan, R. 1967. Cohesion in English. Longman, London.

Hanna, Paul R., Hodges, Richard E. and Hanna, Jean 1971. Spelling: Structure and Strategies. Houghton Mifflin, Boston.

Harlech-Jones, Brian 1983. ESL proficiency and a word frequency count. English Language Teaching Journal 37, 1:62–70.

Harris, A. J. and Jacobson, M. D. 1972. Basic Elementary Reading Vocabularies. Macmillan, New York.

Harris, David P. 1969. Testing English as a Second Language. McGraw-Hill, New York.

Hartmann, George W. 1941. A critique of the common method of estimating vocabulary size, together with some data on the absolute word knowledge of educated adults. Journal of Educational Psychology 32:351–358.

Hartmann, George W. 1946. Further evidence on the unexpected large size of recognition vocabularies among college students. Journal of Educational Psychology 37:436–439.

Hartmann, R. R. K. 1982. Reviews of Chambers dictionaries. System 10, 1:85–86.

Hartmann, Reinhard 1981. Dictionaries, learners, users: Some issues in lexicography. Applied Linguistics 2, 3:297–303.

Harvey, P. D. 1983. Vocabulary learning: The use of grids. ELT Journal 37, 3:243–246.

Hatch, E. M. 1983. Psycholinguistics: A Second Language Perspective. Newbury House, New York: Chapter 4.

Hatch, Evelyn and Farhady, Hossein 1982. Research Design and Statistics for Applied Linguistics. Newbury House, New York.

Hayes-Roth, B. and F. 1977. The prominence of lexical information in memory representations of meaning. Journal of Verbal Learning and Verbal Behaviour 16:119–136.

Haynes, Margot 1984. Patterns and perils of guessing in second language reading. In On TESOL '83: The Question of Control, J. Handscombe, R. A. Orem and B. P. Taylor (eds.). TESOL: 163–176.

Heaton, J. B. 1975. Writing English Language Tests. Longman, London: Chapter 4.

Heilig, Mathias R. 1913. A child's vocabulary. Pedagogical Seminary 20:1–16.

Hendon, Rufus S. 1961. Review of an Indonesian-English dictionary, Echolls, John M., and Shadily, Hassan. Language 37, 3:433–453.

Henning, G. H. 1973. Remembering foreign language vocabulary: Acoustic and semantic parameters. Language Learning 23:185–196.

Henzl, Vera M. 1973. Linguistic register of foreign language instruction. Language Learning 23, 2:207–222.

Herdan, G. 1960. Type-Token Mathematics. Mouton, S-Gravenhage.

Herman, P. and Dole, J. 1988. Theory and practice in vocabulary learning and instruction. Elementary School Journal 89, 1:43–54.

Herman, P. A., Anderson, R. C., Pearson, P. D. and Nagy, W. E. 1987. Incidental acquisition of word meaning from expositions with varied text features. Reading Research Quarterly 22, 3:263–284.

Hess, Carla W., Ritchie, Kelley P. and Landry, R. G. 1984. The type-token ratio and vocabulary performance. Psychological Reports 55:51–57.

Heyer, Sandra 1984. A technique for teaching vocabulary. TESOL Newsletter 18, 2:8–9.

Higa, Masanori 1963. Interference effects of interlist word relationships in verbal learning. Journal of Verbal Learning and Verbal Behaviour 2:170–175.

Higa, Masanori 1965. The psycholinguistic concept of "difficulty" and the teaching of foreign language vocabulary. Language Learning 15, 3 & 4:167–179.

Hill, A. A. 1958. The use of dictionaries in language teaching. In Readings in Applied Linguistics, H. B. Allen (ed.). Appleton-Century-Crofts, New York.

Hill, David A. 1985. Variations on Kim's Game. Modern English Teacher 12, 4:14–17.

Hill, David R. and Thomas, Helen Reid 1988. Survey review: Graded readers (Part 1). English Language Teaching Journal 42, 1:44–52.

Hill, L. A. 1965. A Picture Vocabulary. Oxford University Press, London.

Hill, L. A. and Popkin, P. R. 1968. A First Crossword Puzzle Book. Oxford University Press, London.

Hindmarsh, R. 1980. Cambridge English Lexicon. Cambridge University Press, Cambridge.

Holley, F. M. 1973. A study of vocabulary learning in context: The effect of new-word density in German reading materials. Foreign Language Annals 6:339–347.

Holley, Freda M. 1971. The mental lexicon: Vocabulary acquisition as a problem of linguistics and of human memory. In Proceedings of the Pacific Northwest Conference on Foreign Languages, 22nd Annual Meeting, Idaho: 266–276.

Holley, Freda M. and King, Janet K. 1971. Vocabulary glosses in foreign language reading materials. Language Learning 21, 2:213–219.

Homburg, Taco Justus and Spaan, Mary C. 1982. ESL reading proficiency assessment: Testing strategies. In On TESOL '81, M. Hines and W. Rutherford (eds.). TESOL, Washington DC.

Honeyfield, J. 1977a. Word frequency and the importance of context in vocabulary learning. RELC Journal 8, 2:35–42.

Honeyfield, John 1977b. Simplification. TESOL Quarterly 11, 4:431–440.

Horowitz, Leonard M., and Gordon, Alice M. 1972. Associative symmetry and second language learnings. Journal of Educational Psychology 63, 3:287–294.

Howards, M. 1964. How easy are "easy" words? Journal of Experimental Education 32, 4:377–382.

Howes, D. 1966. A word count of spoken English. Journal of Verbal Learning and Verbal Behaviour 5:572–604.

Hubbard, P., Coady, J., Graney, J., Mokhtari, K. and Magoto, J. 1986. Report on a pilot study of the relationship of high frequency vocabulary knowledge and reading proficiency in ESL readers. Ohio University Papers in Linguistics and Language Teaching 8:48–57.

Hutchings, Geoffrey 1970. Colourless green ideas: Multiple-choice vocabulary tests. English Language Teaching Journal 25:68–71.

Hwang, Kyongho and Nation, Paul 1989. Reducing the vocabulary load and encouraging vocabulary learning through reading newspapers. Unpublished paper.

Ilson, Robert 1983. Etymological information: Can it help our students? English Language Teaching Journal 37, 1:76–82.

Ilson, Robert (ed.) 1985. Dictionaries, Lexicography and Language Learning. Pergamon Press, Oxford.

Ilson, Robert (ed.) 1987. EURALEX: BULLETIN. 4, No. 1: London, England.

Irujo, Suzanne 1986. A piece of cake: Learning and teaching idioms. English Language Teaching Journal 40, 3:236–242.

Jain, Mahavir P. 1981. On meaning in the foreign learner's dictionaries. Applied Linguistics 2, 3:274–286.

James, Peter 1985. Word trees. Modern English Teacher 12, 4:31–34.

James, Vaughan 1981. Review of Collins Dictionary of the English Language. English Language Teaching Journal 35, 4:471–472.

Jamieson, Penelope 1976. The Acquisition of English as a Second Language by Young Tokelau Children Living in New Zealand. Unpublished Ph.D. thesis, Victoria University of Wellington.

Jamieson, Penny 1977. Acquisition of communicative competence by children learning a second language. Paper presented to AULLA, XVIIIth Congress, VUW.

Jamieson, Penny 1977. Second Language Education of Young Children. Set 77, No. 1, NZCER, Wellington, New Zealand.

Jeffries, Lesley and Willis, Penny 1982. Review of Longman Lexicon of Contemporary English. ELT Journal 36, 4:277–278.

Jegi, John I. 1901. The vocabulary of a two year old child. Child Study Monthly 6, 7:242–261.

Jenkins, J. J. 1974. Language and memory in psychology and communication, G. A. Miller (ed.). Voice of America, Forum Series: 181–193.

Jenkins, Joseph R. and Dixon, Robert 1983. Vocabulary learning. Contemporary Educational Psychology 8:237–260.

Jenkins, Joseph R. et al. 1984. Learning vocabulary through reading. American Educational Research Journal 21, 4:767–787.

Jespersen, Otto 1928. Monosyllabism in English. Biennial Lecture on English Philology.

Johansson, Stig 1978. Some Aspects of the Vocabulary of Learned and Scientific English. Gothenburg Studies in English, Acta Universitas Gothoburgensis 42.

Johns, W. B. 1939. The growth of vocabulary among university students with some consideration of methods of fostering it. Journal of Experimental Education 8, 1:89–102.

Johnson, D. and Pearson, P. D. 1984. Teaching Reading Vocabulary. Holt, Rinehart & Winston, New York.

Johnson, Donald M. and Stratton, R. Paul 1966. Evaluation of five methods of teaching concepts. Journal of Educational Psychology 57, 1:48–53.

Johnson, D. Barton 1972. Computer frequency control of vocabulary in language learning reading materials. Instructional Science 1:121–131.

Johnson, George Barry 1980. Lexis through learning. Guidelines 3:69–72.

Johnson, Patricia 1982. Effects on reading comprehension of building background knowledge. TESOL Quarterly 16, 4:503–516.

Johnson-Laird, P. N. 1987. The mental representation of the meaning of words. Cognition 25:189–211.

Johnson-Laird, P. N. and Quinn, J. G. 1976. To define true meaning. Nature 264:635–636.

Johnson-Laird, P. N., Herrmann, D. J. and Chaffin, R. 1984. Only connections: A critique of semantic networks. Psychological Bulletin 96, 2:292–315.

Jones, Lyle V. and Wepman, Joseph M. 1966. A Spoken Word Count: Adults. Western Psychological Services, Los Angeles.

Jones, S. and Sinclair, J. McH. 1974. English lexical collections. Cahiers de Lexicologie 24:15–61.

Judd, Elliot L. 1978. Vocabulary teaching and TESOL: A need for re-evaluation of existing assumptions. TESOL Quarterly 12, 1:71–76.

Kachroo, J. N. 1962. Report on an investigation into the teaching of vocabulary in the first year of English. Bulletin of the Central Institute of English 2:67–72.

Kalivoda, T. B. 1987. Extra linguistic support—a crucial element in F. L. teaching. English Teaching Forum 25, 2:2–6.

Kameenui, Edward J. et al. 1982. Effects of text construction and instructional procedures for teaching word meanings on comprehension and recall. Reading Research Quarterly 17, 3:367–388.

Kameenui, E. J., Dixon, R. C. and Carnine, D. 1987. Issues in the design of vocabulary instruction. In McKeown and Curtis: 129–145.

Kankashian, A. K. 1979. College-level instruction: A new approach. English Teaching Forum 17, 2:38–41.

Keil, F. C. and Batterman, N. 1984. A characteristic-to-defining shift in the development of word meaning. Journal of Verbal Learning and Verbal Behaviour 23:221–236.

Kellar, Howard H. 1978. New Perspectives in Teaching Vocabulary. Language in Education, Center for Applied Linguistics, Virginia.

Kelley, Victor H. 1933. An experimental study of certain techniques for testing word meanings. Journal of Educational Research 27, 4:277–282.

Kellogg, G. S. and Howe, M. J. A. 1971. Using words and pictures in foreign language learning. Alberta Journal of Educational Research 17:89–94.

Kennon, Laura Hall Vere 1926. Appendix A, B, C in Tests of Literary Vocabulary for Teachers of English. Teachers College, Columbia University, Contributors in Education. 223:37–57.

Kercuk, Nadia 1984. My pictionary. Modern English Teacher II, 4:27–30.

Kibby, M. E. W. 1977. A note on the relationship of word difficulty and word frequency. Psychological Reports 41:12–14.

King, Janet K., Holley, Freda M. and Weber, Betty 1975. A new reading. In Perspective: A New Freedom. ACTFL Review 7:169–217.

King, P. S. and Son 1936. Interim report on vocabulary selection. London.

Kirkpatrick, E. A. 1907. A vocabulary test. Popular Science Monthly 70:157–164.

Kirkpatrick, J. J. and Cureton, E. E. 1949. Vocabulary item difficulty and word frequency. Journal of Applied Psychology 33:347–351.

Klare, G. R. 1963. The Measurement of Readability. Iowa State University Press, Ames, IA: 164–169.

Klare, G. R. 1974–1975. Assessing readability. Reading Research Quarterly 10:62–102.

Klein, H., Klein, G. A. and Bertino, M. 1974. Utilization of context for word identification in children. Journal of Experimental Child Psychology 17:79–86.

Koh Moy Yin 1980. What does knowing an item of vocabulary mean? Guidelines 3:76–79.

Kopstein, F. F. and Roshal, S. M. 1954. Learning foreign vocabulary from pictures vs. words. American Psychologist 9:407–408.

Kopstein, F. F. and Roshal, S. M. 1955. Method of presenting word pairs as a factor in foreign vocabulary learning. American Psychologist 10:354.

Krakowian, Bogdan 1984. The teacher's mediation in students' vocabulary learning. English Teaching Forum 22, 3:26–29.

Krashen, S. D. 1981a. The "fundamental pedagogical principle" in second language teaching. Studia Linguistica 35, 1 & 2:50–70.

Krashen, S. D. 1981b. The theoretical and practical relevance of simple codes in second language acquisition. In Second Language Acquisition and Second Language Learning 119–137.

Kressel, Rivka 1987. Teaching "active vocabulary in the foreign language." English Teachers Journal (Israel) 35:48–53.

Kruglov, L. P. 1953. Qualitative differences in the vocabulary choices of children as revealed in a multiple-choice test. Journal of Educational Psychology 44:229–243.

Kruse, Anna Fisher 1979. Vocabulary in context. ELT Journal 33, 3:207–213.

Kucera, H. 1982. The mathematics of language. In The American Heritage Dictionary. Houghton Mifflin, Boston 2nd ed.

Kucera, H. and Francis, W. N. 1967. A Computational Analysis of Present-Day American English. Brown University Press, Providence, RI.

Kuczaj, S. A. 1982. Acquisition of word meaning in the context of the development of the semantic system. In Verbal Processes in Children, C. J. Brainerd and M. Pressley (eds.), Springer-Verlag, New York: 95–123.

Kundu, M. 1988. Riddles in the ESL/EFL classroom: Teaching vocabulary and structure. Modern English Teacher 15, 3:22–24.

Lado, R., Baldwin, B. and Lobo, F. 1976. Massive Vocabulary Expansion in a Foreign Language Beyond the Basic Course: The Effects of Stimuli, Timing and Order of Presentation. U.S. Department of Health, Education and Welfare 5–1095.

Lado, Robert 1956. Patterns of difficulty in vocabulary. Language Learning 6, 1 & 2:23–41.

Lakoff, George and Johnson, Mark 1980. Conceptual metaphor in everyday language. Journal of Philosophy LXXVII, 8.

Langenbeck, Mildred 1914. A study of a five-year-old child. Pedagogical Seminary 22:65–88.

Larrick, Nancy 1954. How many words does a child know? Education Digest 19, 6:42–44.

Larson, Donald N. and Smelley, William A. 1972. Practicing for vocabulary in becoming bilingual: A guide to language learning. Practical Anthropology (Box 1041, New Canaan, CT 06840).

Laufer, Batia 1981. A problem in vocabulary learning—Synophones. English Language Teaching Journal 35, 3:294–300.

Laufer, Batia 1985. Vocabulary acquisition in a second language: The hypothesis of 'synforms' (similar lexical forms). Ph.D., University of Edinburgh.

Laufer, Batia 1986a. Possible changes in attitude towards vocabulary acquisition research. IRAL 24, 1:69–75.

Laufer, Batia 1986b. What percentage of text-lexis is essential for comprehension? Paper delivered at LSP symposium, Vaasa.

Laufer, Batia 1987a. Words you know: How they affect the words you learn. In Further Insights into Contrastive Linguistics, J. Fisiak (ed.). Benjamins, Holland.

Laufer, Batia 1987b. The lexical perspective of reading comprehension. English Teachers Journal (Israel) 35:58–67.

Laufer, Batia 1987c. A case for vocbulary in EAP reading comprehension materials. In Beads or Bracelet? How do we approach ESP? A. M. Cornu et al. (eds.), Oxford University Press, Oxford: 284–291.

Laufer, Batia 1988. The development of L2 lexis in the expression of the advanced language learner. Unpublished paper.

Laufer, Batia 1989. Why are some words more difficult than others?—Some intra-lexical factors that affect the learning of words. IRAL 27, 3.

Laufer, Batia, in press. Knowing a word: What is so difficult about it? English Teachers Journal (Israel).

Laufer, Batia, in press. 'Sequence' and 'order' in the development of L2 lexis. Applied Linguistics.

Laufer, Batia, in press. The concept of "synforms" in vocabulary. Language and Education.

Laufer, Batia and Bensoussan, Marsha 1982. Meaning is in the eye of the beholder. English Teaching Forum 20, 2:10–13.

Laufer, Batia and Sim, Donald D. 1985a. Taking the easy way out: Non-use and misuse of clues in EFL reading. English Teaching Forum 23, 2:7–10, 20.

Laufer, Batia and Sim, Donald D. 1985b. Measuring and explaining the reading threshold needed for English for academic purposes texts. Foreign Language Annals 18, 5:405–411.

Lee, Hei Sook 1958. English-Korean cognates. Language Learning VIII: 57–72.

Lee, W. R. 1965. Language Teaching Games and Contests. Oxford University Press, London.

Lehrer, Adrienne 1964. Semantic cuisine. Journal of Linguistics 5:39–55.

Lehrer, Adrienne 1972. Cooking vocabularies and the culinary triangle of Levi-Strauss. Anthropological Linguistics 14, 5:155–171.

Lerea, L. and Laporta, R. 1971. Vocabulary and pronunciation acquisition among bilinguals and monolinguals. Language and Speech 14:293–300.

Levenston, E. A. 1979. Second language acquisition: Issues and problems. Inter-language Studies Bulletin 4, 2:147–160.

Levenston, E. A. 1987. Second language lexical acquisition: Issues and problems. English Teachers Journal (Israel) 35:44–48.

Levenston, E. A. and Blum, S. 1976. Aspects of lexical simplification in the speech and writing of advanced adult learners. 5th Colloque de Linguistique Appliquée de Neuchatel.

Levin, J. R. 1981. The mnemonic '80s: Keywords in the classroom. Educational Psychologist 16:65–82.

Levin, J. R. and Pressley, M. 1983. Understanding mnemonic imagery effects: A dozen obvious outcomes. In Mental Imagery and Learning, M. L. Fleming and D. E. W. Hutton (eds.), Educational Technology, NJ: 33–52.

Levin, J. R. and Pressley, M. 1985. Mnemonic vocabulary instruction: What's fact, what's fiction? In Individual Differences in Cognition, Vol. 2, R. F. Dillon (ed.), Academic Press, Orlando, FL: 145–172.

Levin, J. R. et al. 1982. Mnemonic versus non-mnemonic vocabulary learning strategies for children. American Educational Research Journal 19:121–136.

Levin, Joel R. et al. 1982. Mnemonic versus non-mnemonic vocabulary-learning strategies for children. American Educational Research Journal 19, 1:121–136.

Levin, J. R. et al. 1984. A comparison of semantic- and mnemonic-based vocabulary learning strategies. Reading Psychology 5:1–15.

Levin, J. R., Dretzke, B. J. et al. 1985. In search of the keyword method/vocabulary comprehension link. Contemporary Educational Psychology 10:220–227.

Levin, J. R., Pressley, M., McCormick, C. B. and Miller, G. E. 1979. Assessing the classroom potential of the keyword method. Journal of Educational Psychology 71: 583–594.

Lewis, Richard 1973. Winter Sleep: Reading for Adults. Longman, London.

Li Aiqun 1983. Low frequency words in scientific writing. Unpublished paper.

Lindstromberg, Seth 1987. Vocabulary learning and defining. Practical English Teaching 7, 4:43–44.

Lindstromberg, Seth 1985. Schemata for ordering the teaching and learning of vocabulary. English Language Teaching Journal 39, 4:235–243.

Litowitz, B. 1976. Learning to make definitions. Journal of Child Language 4:289–304.

Liu Na and Nation, I. S. P. 1985. Factors affecting guessing vocabulary in context. RELC Journal 16, 1:33–42.

Ljung, Magnus 1974. A Frequency Dictionary of English Morphemes. AWE/Gebers, Stockholm.

Llamzon, Teodoro 1980. Constructing multiple-choice vocabulary tests. Guidelines 3:118–121.

Long, M. N. and Nation, I. S. P. 1980. Read Thru. Longman, Singapore.

Long, Michael H. 1983. Native speaker/non-native speaker conversation and the negotiation of comprehensible input. Applied Linguistics 4, 2:126–141.

Longman 1968. Handbook to Longman Structural Readers. Longman, London.

Longman 1976. Longman Structural Readers Handbook. Longman, London 2nd ed.

Looby, Ruth 1939. Understandings children derive from their reading. Elementary English Review 16:58–62.

Lord, R. 1974. Learning vocabulary. IRAL 12, 3:239–247.

Lorge, I. and Chall, J. 1963. Estimating the size of vocabularies of children and adults: An analysis of methodological issues. Journal of Experimental Education 32, 2:147–157.

Lovell, George D. 1941. Interrelations of vocabulary skills: Commonest versus multiple meanings. Journal of Educational Psychology 32:67–72.

Ludwig, Jeannette 1984. Vocabulary acquisition as a function of word characteristics. Canadian Modern Language Review 40, 5:522–562.

Lynn, Robert W. 1973. Preparing word lists: A suggested method. RELC Journal 4, 1:25–32.

Lyons, John 1981. Language, Meaning and Context. Fontana Paperbacks, London.

Macaulay, R. K. S. 1966. Vocabulary problems for Spanish learners. English Language Teaching Journal 20, 2:131–136.

MacFarquhar, Peter D. and Richards, Jack C. 1983. On dictionaries and definitions. RELC Journal 14, 1:111–124.

MacKay, Ray 1986. Review of Rudzka, B., Channell, J., Putseys, Y. and Ostyn, P. The words you need. English Language Teaching Journal 40, 1:75–76.

Mackey, W. F. 1965. Language Teaching Analysis. Longman, London: 164–190.

Mackey, William F. and Savard, Jean-Guy 1967. The indices of coverage. IRAL 5, 2–3:71–121.

Mackin, Ronald and Carver, David 1968. A Higher Course of English Study. Oxford University Press, London.

Madden, J. F. 1980. Developing pupils' vocabulary-learning skills. Guidelines 3:111–117.

Mager, N. H. and Mager, S. K. 1982. The Morrow Book of New Words. Morrow, New York.

Magni, J. A. 1919. Vocabularies. Pedagogical Seminary 26, 3:209–233.

Magoto, Jeff 1986. CALL, task-based learning, and vocabulary learned in context: A pilot study. Ohio University Working Paper in Linguistics and Language Teaching 8:63–81.

Maiguashca, Raffaella Uslenghi 1984. Semantic fields: Towards a methodology for teaching vocabulary in the second-language classroom. Canadian Modern Language Review 40, 2:274–297.

Manzo, A. V. 1970. CAT—a game for extending vocabulary and knowledge of allusions. Journal of Reading 13:367–369.

Manzo, A. V. and Sherk, J. K. 1972. Some generalizations and strategies for guiding vocabulary learning. Journal of Reading Behavior 4, 1:78–89.

Marckwardt, Albert H. 1964. The New Webster Dictionary: A Critical Appraisal. In Applied English Linguistics, H. B. Allen (ed.). Appleton Century Crofts, New York.

Marckwardt, Albert H. 1973. The dictionary as an English teaching resource. TESOL Quarterly 7, 4:369–379.

Marks, C. B., Doctorow, M. J. and Wittrock, M. C. 1974. Word frequency and reading comprehension. Journal of Educational Research 67:259–262.

Martin, Anne V. 1976. Teaching academic vocabulary to foreign graduate students. TESOL Quarterly 10, 1:91–97.

Martin, Marilyn 1984. Advanced vocabulary teaching: The problem of synonyms. Modern Language Journal 68, 2:130–136.

Mason, Charles 1982. How much do they know? Assessing ESL vocabulary range. Unpublished paper.

Mason, J. M., Kniseley, E. and Kendall, J. 1979. Effects of polysemous words on sentence comprehension. Reading Research Quarterly 15:49–65.

Mastropieri, M. A., Scruggs, T. E. and Levin, J. R. 1985. Maximizing what exceptional children can learn: A review of research on the keyword method and related mnemonic techniques. Remedial and Special Education 6:39–45.

Mateer, Florence 1908. The vocabulary of a four year old boy. Pedagogical Seminary 15:63–74.

Maurice, Keith 1983. The fluency workshop. TESOL Newsletter 8:83.

McArthur, T. 1981. Longman Lexicon of Contemporary English. Longman, London.

McCarthy, Dorothea 1954. Language development in children. In Manual of Child Psychology. 2nd ed., L. Carmichael (ed.). Wiley, New York.

McCarthy, M. J. 1984. A new look at vocabulary in EFL. Applied Linguistics 5, 1:12–22.

McCarthy, Michael 1988. Some vocabulary patterns in conversation. In Carter and McCarthy: 181–200.

McComish, Johanne 1982. Spoken English. English Language Institute, Victoria University of Wellington.

McCormack, P. D. and Colletta, S. P. 1975. Recognition memory for items from unilingual and bilingual lists. Bulletin of the Psychonomic Society 6(2):149–151.

McCullough, Constance M. 1943. Learning to use context clues. Elementary English Review 20:140–143.

McCullough, Constance M. 1945. The recognition of context clues in reading. Elementary English Review 22, 1:1–5, 38.

McCullough, Constance M. 1958. Context aids in reading. Reading Teacher 11, 4:225–229.

McDaniel, M. A. and Masson, M. E. 1977. Long term retention: When incidental semantic processing fails. Journal of Experimental Psychology: Human Learning and Memory 3:270–281.

McDaniel, M. A., Friedman, A. and Bourne, L. E., Jr. 1978. Remembering the levels of information in words. Memory and Cognition 6:156–164.

McDaniel, M. A. and Pressley, M. 1984. Putting the keyword method in context. Journal of Educational Psychology 76:598–609.

McGivern, J. E. and Levin, J. R. 1983. The keyword method and children's vocabulary learning: An interaction with vocabulary knowledge. Contemporary Educational Psychology 8:46–54.

McKay, J. M. 1975. Review of the Oxford Advanced Learners Dictionary. TESOL Quarterly 9, 1:77–79.

McKay, Sandra 1980. Teaching the syntactic, semantic and pragmatic dimensions of verbs. TESOL Quarterly 14, 1:17–26.

McKay, Sandra L. 1980. Developing vocabulary materials with a computer corpus. RELC Journal 11, 2:77–87.

McKay, Sandra 1982. Verbs for a Specific Purpose. Prentice-Hall, Englewood Cliffs, NJ.

McKeown, M. G. 1985. The acquisition of word meaning from context by children of high and low ability. Reading Research Quarterly 20:482–496.

McKeown, M. G. and Curtis, M. E. (eds.) 1987. The Nature of Vocabulary Acquisition. Erlbaum, Hillsdale, NJ.

McKeown, M. G., Beck, I. L., Omanson, R. G. and Pople, M. T. 1985. Some effects of the nature and frequency of vocabulary instruction on the knowledge and use of words. Reading Research Quarterly 20, 5:552–535.

McKeown, Margaret G. et al. 1983. The effects of long-term vocabulary instruction on reading comprehension: A replication. Journal of Reading Behavior 15, 1:3–18.

McNeal, L. D. 1973. Recall and recognition of vocabulary word learning in college students using mnemonic and repetitive methods. Dissertation Abstracts International 33:3394A.

Meara, P. 1984. Review of teaching vocabulary by M. J. Wallace. System 12, 1:185–186.

Meara, P. and Jones, G. 1987. Tests of vocabulary size in English as a foreign language. Polyglot 8, Fiche 1.

Meara, Paul 1980. Vocabulary acquisition: A neglected aspect of language learning. Language Teaching and Linguistics: Abstracts: 221–246.

Meara, Paul 1983. Word associations in a foreign language: A report on the Birkbeck vocabulary project. Notts Linguistic Society Newsletter.

Meara, Paul 1984. The study of lexis in interlanguage. In Interlanguage, A. Davies, C. Criper and A. R. P. Howatt (eds.), Edinburgh University Press.

Meara, Paul 1984. The Digame Project. Coleslaw, to appear in volume by V. J. Cook (ed.).

Meara, Paul 1987. Vocabulary in a second language, Vol. 2. Specialised Bibliography 4.

Meara, Paul 1988. Imaging, a powerful aid. EFL Gazette, August.

Meara, Paul and Buxton, Barbara 1987. An alternative to multiple choice vocabulary tests. Language Testing 4, 2:142–151.

Meara, Paul, Coltheart, Max and Masterson, Jackie 1985. Hidden reading problems in ESL learners. TESL Canada Journal/Revue TESL du Canada 3, 1:29–36.

Meister, Gerry 1986. A survey of vocabulary recognition among provincial high school students. TESLA (Papua New Guinea) 5, 1:54–64.

Melka Teichroew, Francine J. 1982. Receptive vs. productive vocabulary: A survey. Interlanguage Studies Bulletin (Utrecht) 6, 2:5–33.

Merriam-Webster 1983. 9,000 Words. Merriam-Webster, Springfield, MA.

Messa, Carmen De Mir 1984. The handling of vocabulary in reading texts. Modern English Teacher 11, 3:15–22.

Messer, Stanley 1967. Implicit phonology in children. Journal of Verbal Learning and Verbal Behaviour 6:609–613.

Mhone, Yvonne W. 1988. "It's my word, teacher." English Teaching Forum 26, 2:48–51.

Miller, G. A. 1977. Spontaneous Apprentices. Seabury Press, New York.

Miller, G. A. 1978. Lexical meaning. In Speech and Language in the Laboratory, School and Clinic, J. F. Kavanagh and A. E. W. Strange (eds.), Massachusetts Institute of Technology, Cambridge, MA: 394–436.

Miller, G. A. 1978. Semantic relations among words. In Linguistic Theory and Psychological Reality, M. Halle, J. Bresnan and G. A. Miller (eds.), Massachusetts Institute of Technology, Cambridge, MA: 60–118.

Miller, G. A., Levin, J. R. and Pressley, M. 1980. An adaptation of the keyword method to children's learning of foreign verbs. Journal of Mental Imagery 4:57–61.

Miller, George A. 1978. The acquisition of word meaning. Child Development 49:999–1004.

Miller, George A. and Gildea, Patricia M. 1987. How children learn words. Scientific American 257, 3:86–91.

Mishima, T. 1967. An experiment comparing five modalities of conveying meaning for the teaching of foreign language vocabulary. Dissertation Abstracts 27:3030–3031A.

Moerk, E. L. 1972. Principles of dyadic interaction in language learning. Merrill-Palmer Quarterly 18:229–257.

Molina, Hubert 1971. Language games and the Mexican-American child learning English. TESOL Quarterly 5, 2:145–148.

Morgan, C. L. and Bailey, W. L. 1943. The effect of context on learning a vocabulary. Journal of Educational Psychology 34:561–565.

Morgan, C. L. and Foltz, M. C. 1944. The effect of context on learning a French vocabulary. Journal of Educational Research 38:213–216.

Morgan, C. L. and Bonham, D. N. 1944. Difficulty of vocabulary learning as affected by parts of speech. Journal of Educational Psychology 35, 5:369–377.

Morris, C. D., Bransford, J. D. and Franks, J. J. 1977. Levels of processing versus transfer appropriate processing. Journal of Verbal Learning and Verbal Behaviour 16:519–533.

Morton, John 1969. Interaction of information in word recognition. Psychological Review 76, 2:165–178.

Moulin, Andre 1984. The problem of vocabulary teaching: An answer to Robbins Burling. System 12, 2:147–149.

Mountford, Alan 1975. English in Workshop Practice. Oxford University Press, Oxford: 6–9.

Mountford, Alan 1976. The notion of simplification and its relevance to materials preparation for English for science and technology. In Teaching English for Science and Technology, Singapore University Press, Singapore.

Murphy, B. M. Z. 1987. Bad books in easy English. Modern English Teacher 14, 3:22–23.

Nacke, P. (ed.) 1974. Interaction: Reading and Practice for College-Adult Reading. National Reading Conference, Clemson, SC.

Nagy, Luqman 1985. Picture power: A technique for reviewing vocabulary. English Teaching Forum 23, 1:38–39.

Nagy, W. E. and Herman, Patricia A. 1984. Limitations of vocabulary instruction. Technical Report 326, Center for the Study of Reading, University of Illinois.

Nagy, W. E. and Herman, P. A. 1987. Breadth and depth of vocabulary knowledge: Implications for acquisition and instruction. In McKeown and Curtis: 19–35.

Nagy, W. E. and Gentner, D. In press. Semantic constraints on lexical categories.

Nagy, William E. and Anderson, Richard C. 1984. How many words are there in printed school English? Reading Research Quarterly 19, 3:304–330.

Nagy, William E., Herman, Patricia and Anderson, Richard C. 1985. Learning words from context. Reading Research Quarterly 20:233–253.

Nagy, William E., Anderson, Richard C., and Herman, P. A. 1987. Learning word meanings from context during normal reading. American Educational Research Journal 24, 2:237–270.

Nation, I. S. P. 1974. Techniques for teaching vocabulary. English Teaching Forum 12, 3:18–21.

Nation, I. S. P. 1975. Teaching vocabulary in difficult circumstances. English Language Teaching Journal 30, 1:21–24.

Nation, I. S. P. 1977. The combining arrangement: Some techniques. Modern Language Journal 61, 3:89–94. Reprinted in English Teaching Forum 17, 1 (1979) 12–16, 20.

Nation, I. S. P. 1978. Translation and the teaching of meaning: Some techniques. English Language Teaching Journal 32, 3:171–175.

Nation, I. S. P. 1978. "What is it?": A multipurpose language teaching technique. English Teaching Forum 16, 3:20–23, 32.

Nation, I. S. P. 1980. Strategies for receptive vocabulary learning. Guidelines 3:18–23.

Nation, I. S. P. 1981. Language Teaching Techniques. English Language Institute, Victoria University of Wellington, Wellington, New Zealand.

Nation, I. S. P. 1982. Beginning to learn foreign vocabulary: A review of the research. RELC Journal 13, 1:14–36.

Nation, I. S. P. 1983. Testing and teaching vocabulary. Guidelines 5, 1:12–25.

Nation, I. S. P. 1984. Understanding paragraphs. Language Learning and Communication 3, 1:61–68.

Nation, I. S. P. (ed.) 1984. Vocabulary Lists: Words, Affixes and Stems. English Language Institute, Victoria University of Wellington, Wellington, New Zealand.

Nation, I. S. P., and Coady, J. 1988. Vocabulary and reading. In Vocabulary and Language Teaching, R. Carter and M. McCarthy (eds.), Longman, London.

Nattinger, James 1988. Some current trends in vocabulary teaching. In Carter and McCarthy (1988): 62–82.

Ndomba Benda 1983. Acquiring English vocabulary and structures: Some problems and procedures. English Teaching Forum 21, 2:18–24.

Neher, H. L. 1918. Measuring the vocabulary of high school pupils. School and Society 8:355–359.

Nemko, B. 1984. Context versus isolation: Another look at beginning readers. Reading Research Quarterly 4:461–467.

Neubach, Abigail and Cohen, Andrew D. In press. Processing strategies and problems encountered in the use of dictionaries. Journal of Lexicography.

Nice, Margaret M. 1915. The development of a child's vocabulary in relation to environment. Pedagogical Seminary 22:35–64.

Nice, Margaret Morse 1926. On the size of vocabularies. American Speech 2, 1:1–7.

Niles, J. A. and Harris, L. A. (eds.) 1983. Searches for Meaning in Reading / Language Processing and Instruction. 32nd Yearbook of National Reading Conference, Rochester, NY.

Nilsen, Don L. F. 1976. Contrastive semantics in vocabulary instruction. TESOL Quarterly 10, 1:99–103.

Ninio, Anat 1983. Joint book reading as a multiple vocabulary acquisition device. Developmental Psychology 19, 3:445–451.

Nisbet, John D. 1960. Frequency counts and their uses. Educational Research 3:51–64.

Nolte, Karl F. 1937. Simplification of vocabulary and comprehension in reading. Elementary English Review 14:119–124.

Nord, J. R. 1980. Developing listening fluency before speaking: An alternative paridigm. System 8, 1:1–22.

Noss, Richard B. 1980. Teaching vocabulary through cloze dialogues. Guidelines 3:38–53.

O'Connor, J. D. 1980. Better English Pronunciation, 2nd ed., Cambridge University Press, Cambridge.

Odlin, Terence and Natalicio, Diana 1982. Some characteristics of word classification in a second language. Modern Language Journal 66, 1:34–38.

Omanson, Richard C. et al. 1984. Comprehension of texts with unfamiliar versus recently taught words: Assessment of alternative models. Journal of Educational Psychology 76, 6:1253–1268.

Onions, C. T. (ed.) 1973. The Shorter Oxford English Dictionary, 3rd ed., Oxford University Press, Oxford.

O'Rourke, J. P. 1974. Toward a Science of Vocabulary Development. Mouton, The Hague.

Orszagh, Ladislas 1969. Wanted: Better English dictionaries. English Language Teaching Journal 23, 3:216–222.

Orwell, G. 1945. Animal Farm. Longman, London.

Osgood, Charles E. 1949. The similarity paradox in human learning: A resolution. Psychological Review 56:132–143.

Ostyn, Paul and Godin, Pierre 1985. RALEX: An alternative approach to language teaching. Modern Language Journal 69, 4:346–355.

Otnes, Will 1971. Pronunciation at a glance. English Teaching Forum 9, 2:28–29.

Ott, C. Eric, Blake, Rowland S. and Butler, David C. 1976. Implications of mental elaboration for the acquisition of foreign language vocabulary. IRAL XIV/1.

Otterman, L. M. 1955. The value of teaching prefixes and word-roots. Journal of Educational Research 48:611–616.

Paikeday, T. M. 1973. Letter to the editor about Carroll et al. (1971). Research in the Teaching of English 7, 3:402–408.

Paivio, A. 1983. Strategies in language learning. In Cognitive Strategy Research: Educational Applications, M. Pressley and J. R. Levin (eds.). Springer-Verlag, New York: 189–210.

Paivio, Allan and Desrochers, Alain 1981. Mnemonic techniques in second-language learning. Journal of Educational Psychology 73, 6:780–795.

Palmberg, R. 1987. Patterns of vocabulary development in foreign language learners. Studies in Second Language Acquisition 9:202–221.

Palmberg, Rolf 1985. How much English vocabulary do Swedish-speaking primary-school pupils know before starting to learn English at school? Reports from the Research Institute of the Abo Akademi Foundation.

Palmberg, Rolf 1986. Vocabulary teaching in the foreign-language classroom. English Teaching Forum 24, 3:15–24.

Palmberg, Rolf 1987. On lexical inferencing and the young foreign-language learner. System 15, 1:69–76.

Palmberg, Rolf 1987. Five Experiments of EFL Vocabulary Learning: A Project Report. Paper delivered at AILA conference, Sydney.

Palmberg, Rolf 1987. Making Sense of Foreign Vocabulary—Evidence from a Fairytale. Faculty of Ed, Abo Akademi Foundation.

Palmberg, Rolf 1988. Computer games and foreign-language learning. English Language Teaching Journal 42, 2:247–251.

Palmberg, Rolf 1988. On lexical inferencing and language distance. Journal of Pragmatics 12:207–214.

Palmer, D. M. 1982. Information transfer for listening and reading. English Teaching Forum 20, 1:29–33.

Palmer, H. 1938. A Grammar of English Words. Longman, London.

Pany, D. and Jenkins, J. R. 1978. Learning word meanings: A comparison of instructional procedures. Learning Disability Quarterly 1:21–32.

Pany, D., Jenkins, J. R. and Schreck, J. 1982. Vocabulary instruction: Effects on word knowledge and reading comprehension. Learning Disability Quarterly 5:202–215.

Papalia, Anthony 1975. Students' learning styles in ascribing meaning to written and oral stimuli. Hispania 58:106–108.

Pelama, John R. 1914. A child's vocabulary and its development. Pedagogical Seminary 17:329–369.

Perfetti, C. A. and Lesgold, A. M. 1977. Discourse comprehension and sources of individual differences. In Cognitive Processes in Comprehension, M. Just and P. Carpenter (eds.). Erlbaum, Hillsdale, NJ: 141–183.

Perfetti, C. A. and Lesgold, A. M. 1979. Coding and comprehension in skilled reading and implications for reading instruction. In Theory and Practice of Early Reading, L. B. Resnick et al. (eds.) Erlbaum, Hillsdale, NJ 1:57–84.

Perkins, Kyle and Brutten, Sheila R. 1983. The effects of word frequency and contextual richness on ESL students' word identification abilities. Journal of Research in Reading 6, 2:119–128.

Petti, Vincent 1975. Review of the Oxford Advanced Learners Dictionary. Moderna Sprak 69, 2:169–175.

Petty, W. T., Herold, C. P. and Stoll, E. 1968. The State of Knowledge About the Teaching of Vocabulary. N.C.T.E., Champaign, IL.

Phun, Josephine 1986. Vocabulary teaching: Some principles. Guidelines 8, 1:35–41.

Pickering, Michael 1982. Context-free and context-dependent vocabulary learning: An experiment. System 10, 1:79–83.

Piczon-Llamzon, Petrona 1979. Reading the dictionary for the pronunciation of English words. Guidelines 2:49–53.

Pimsleur, P. 1967. A memory schedule. Modern Language Journal 51, 2:73–75.

Plaister, T. 1981. Teaching vocabulary, listening comprehension, and reasoning by means of analogies. Foreign Language Annals 14, 1:25–29.

Porte, Graeme 1988. Poor language learners and their strategies for dealing with new vocabulary. English Language Teaching Journal 42, 3:167–172.

Porter, Don and Williams, Eddie 1984. Review of Wallace (1982). ELT Journal 38, 1:60–61.

Praninskas, Jean 1972. American University Word List. Longman, London.

Pressley, M. and Ahmad, M. 1986. Transfer of imagery-based mnemonics by adult learners. Contemporary Educational Psychology 11:150–160.

Pressley, M. and Dennis-Rounds, J. 1980. Transfer of a mnemonic keyword strategy at two age levels. Journal of Educational Psychology 72:575–582.

Pressley, M. and Levin, J. R. 1978. Developmental constraints associated with children's use of the keyword method of foreign language vocabulary learning. Journal of Experimental Child Psychology 26:359–372.

Pressley, M., Levin, J. R. and McCormick, C. B. 1980. Young children's learning of foreign language vocabulary: A sentence variation of the keyword method. Contemporary Educational Psychology 5:22–29.

Pressley, M., Levin, J., Hall, J., Miller, G. and Berry, J. K. 1980. The keyword method and foreign word acquisition. Journal of Experimental Psychology: Human Learning and Memory 5:22–29.

Pressley, M., Levin, J., Nakamura, G., Hope, D. and Bispo, J. T. 1980. The keyword method of foreign vocabulary learning: An investigation of its generalisability. Journal of Applied Psychology 65:635–642.

Pressley, M., Samuel, J., Hershey, M., Bishop, S. and Dickinson, D. 1981. Use of mnemonic technique to teach young children foreign language vocabulary. Contemporary Educational Psychology 6:110–116.

Pressley, M., Levin, J. R. and Miller, G. E. 1981a. How does the keyword affect vocabulary comprehension and usage? Reading Research Quarterly 16:213–226.

Pressley, M., Levin, J. R. and Miller, G. E. 1981b. The keyword method and children's learning of foreign vocabulary with abstract meanings. Canadian Journal of Psychology 35:283–287.

Pressley, M., Levin, J. R. and Miller, G. E. 1982. The keyword method compared to alternative vocabulary learning strategies. Contemporary Educational Psychology 7:50–60.

Pressley, M., Levin, J., Kuiper, N., Bryant, S. and Michener, S. 1982. Mnemonic versus nonmnemonic vocabulary-learning strategies: Additional comparisons. Journal of Educational Psychology 74:693–707.

Pressley, M., Levin, J. R., Digdon, N., Bryant, S. L. and Ray, K. 1983. Does method of item presentation affect keyword method effectiveness? Journal of Educational Psychology 75:586–591.

Pressley, M., Levin, J. R., and Ghatala, E. S. 1984. Memory strategy monitoring in adults and children. Journal of Verbal Learning and Verbal Behaviour 23:270–288.

Pressley, M., Levin, J. R. and McDaniel, M. A. 1987. Remembering versus inferring what a word means: Mnemonic and contextual approaches. In McKeown and Curtis: 107–127.

Pressley, Michael, Levin, Joel R. and Delaney, H. 1982. The mnemonic keyword method. Review of Educational Research 52, 1:61–91.

Puangmali, Suraprom 1976. A study of engineering English vocabulary. RELC Journal 7, 1:40–52.

Putnam, Hilary 1975. The meaning of meaning: Language, mind and knowledge, Keith Gunderson (ed.), Minnesota Studies in the Philosophy of Science 7.

Quealy, R. J. 1969. Senior high school students' use of context aids in reading. Reading Research Quarterly 4:512–532.

Quinn, E. and Nation, I. S. P. 1974. Speed Reading. Oxford University Press, Kuala Lumpur.

Quinn, George 1968. The English Vocabulary of Some Indonesian University Entrants. IKIP Kristen Satya Watjana, Salatiga.

Raimes, Ann 1985. What unskilled ESL students do as they write: A classroom study of composing. TESOL Quarterly 19, 2:229–258.

Ramsay, James W. 1981. Vocabulary preparation for reading in the content area. In On TESOL '80, J. C. Fisher, M. A. Clarke and J. Schachter (eds.). TESOL, Washington, DC.: 214–225.

Randall, M. 1980. Word association behaviour in learners of English as a foreign language. Polygot 2, Fiche 2.

Rankin, Earl F. and Overholser, Betsy M. 1969. Reaction of intermediate grade children to contextual clues. Journal of Reading Behavior 1, 3:50–73.

Rash, J., Johnson, T. D. and Gleadow, N. 1984. Acquisition and retention of written words by kindergarten children under varying learning conditions. Reading Research Quarterly 4:452–460.

Raugh, M. R. and Atkinson, R. C. 1975. A mnemonic method for learning a second-language vocabulary. Journal of Educational Psychology 67:1–16.

Raugh, Michael R., Schupbach, R. D. and Atkinson, R. C. 1977. Teaching a large Russian language vocabulary the mnemonic keyword method. Instructional Science 6, 3:199–221.

Read, John 1988. Measuring the vocabulary knowledge of second language learners. RELC Journal 19, 2:12–25.

Repin, V. and Orlov, R. S. 1967. The use of sleep and relaxation in the study of foreign languages. Australian Journal of Psychology 19, 3:203–207.

Reznik, J. Steven and Goldsmith, Lynn 1989. A multiple form word production checklist for assessing early language. Journal of Child Language 16:91–100.

Richards, Brian 1987. Type/token ratios: What do they really tell us? Journal of Child Language 14:201–209.

Richards, I. A. 1943. Basic English and Its Uses. Kegan Paul, London.

Richards, Jack C. 1970. A psycholinguistic measure of vocabulary selection. IRAL 8, 2:87–102.

Richards, Jack C. 1974. Word lists: Problems and prospects. RELC Journal 5, 2:69–84.

Richards, Jack C. (ed.) 1974. Error Analysis. Longman, London.

Richards, Jack C. 1976. The role of vocabulary teaching. TESOL Quarterly 10, 1:77–89.

Richards, Meredith Martin 1982. Empiricism and learning to mean. In Language Development, Stan A. Kuczaj II (ed.). Erlbaum, Hillsdale, NJ. 1:365–396.

Ringbom, H. 1982. The influence of other languages on the vocabulary of a foreign language learner. In Error Analysis, Contrastive Linguistics and Interlanguage. Julius Groos Verlag, Heidelberg.

Ringbom, H. 1983. Borrowing and lexical transfer. Applied Linguistics 4:207–212.

Rinsland, Henry B. 1945. A Basic Vocabulary of Elementary School Children. Macmillan, New York.

Rinvolucri, Mario 1981. Words—how to teach them. Modern English Teacher 9, 2:19–20.

Rivero, Guillermo Alcala and Best, Margaret 1978. Strategies for solving lexical problems through discourse and context. In On TESOL '78, C. H. Blatchford and J. Schachter (eds.). TESOL, Washington DC.: 191–198.

Rivers, Wilga M. 1981. Apples of gold in pictures of silver: Where have all the words gone? Studia Linguistica 35, 1 & 2:114–129.

Rivers, Wilga M. and Temperley, Mary S. 1977. Building and maintaining an adequate vocabulary. English Teaching Forum 15, 1:2–7.

Roberts, A. Hood 1965. A Statistical Linguistic Analysis of American English. Janua Linguarum, Series Practica 8, Mouton, The Hague.

Roberts, Paul 1987. Towards a lexis syllabus. IATEL Newsletter 96:38–39.

Robinson, A. H. 1963. A study of techniques of word identification. Reading Teacher 16:238–242.

Robinson, Peter J. 1988. A Hallidayan framework for vocabulary teaching—an approach to organising the lexical content of an EFL syllabus. IRAL 26, 3:229–238.

Rodgers, T. S. 1969. On measuring vocabulary difficulty: An analysis of item variables in learning Russian-English vocabulary pairs. IRAL 7:327–343.

Rohrer, Josef 1980. Learning styles and teaching vocabulary. In Current Issues in Bilingual Education, J. E. Alatis (ed.). GURT, Washington D.C.: 280–288.

Rosch, Eleanor et al. 1976. Basic objects in natural categories. Cognitive Psychology 8:382–439.

Rosenshine, B. V. 1980. Skill hierarchies in reading comprehension. In Spiro et al.: 535–554.

Rosenweig, M. R. and McNeill, D. 1962. Inaccuracies in the semantic content of Lorge and Thorndike. American Journal of Psychology 75:316–319.

Rowe, Eugene C. and Helen 1913. The vocabulary of a child at four and six years of age. Pedagogical Seminary 20:187–208.

Royer, J. M. 1973. Memory effects for test-like-events during acquisition of foreign language vocabulary. Psychological Reports 32:195–198.

Rubin, D. C. 1976. The effectiveness of context before, after, and around a missing word. Perception and Psychophysics 19:214–216.

Rudzka, B., Channell, J., Putseys, Y. and Ostyn, P. 1981. The Words You Need. Macmillan, London.

Ruhl, C. 1975. Primary verbs. Lacus Forum I: 436–445.

Ruhl, C. 1976. Pragmatic metonymy. Lacus Forum II: 370–380.

Ruhl, C. 1977. Idioms and data. Lacus Forum III: 456–466.

Ruhl, C. 1978. Two forms of reductionism. Lacus Forum IV: 370–383.

Ruhl, C. 1978. Alleged idioms with HIT. Lacus Forum V.

Rumszewicz, Witold 1967. On contemporary dramatic and scientific English. Uniwersytet im. Adama Michkiewicza w Poznaniu Glottodidactica II: 71–83.

Russell, David H. and Fea, Henry R. 1963. Research on teaching reading. In Handbook of Research on Teaching, N. L. Gage (ed.). Rand McNally, Chicago: 883–896.

Russell, David H. and Saadeh, Ibrahim Q. 1962. Qualitative levels in children's vocabularies. Journal of Educational Psychology 53, 4:170–174.

Ryden, Einar R. 1948. Vocabulary as an index of learning in a second langauge. Journal of Educational Psychology 39.

Ryder, Randall James and Hughes, Melody 1985. The effect on text comprehension of word frequency. Journal of Educational Research 78, 5:286–291.

Rye, James 1985. Are cloze items sensitive to constraints across sentences? A review. Journal of Research in Reading (UKRA) 8, 2:94–105.

Sachs, H. J. 1943. The reading method of acquiring vocabulary. Journal of Educational Research 36:457–464.

Sadler, R. K., Hayllar, T. A. S. and Powell, C. J. 1981. Working with words. Senior Language. Macmillan, Melbourne: 79–81.

Saemen, Ruth Ann 1970. Effects of commonly known meanings on determining obscure meanings of multiple-meaning words in context. Office of Education (DHEW), Washington, DC.

Salager, F. 1984. The English of medical literature research projects. English for Specific Purposes (Oregon State University) 87:5–7.

Salager, Francoise 1983. The lexis of fundamental medical English: Classificatory framework and rhetorical function (a statistical approach). Reading in a Foreign Language 1, 1:54–64.

Salisbury, A. 1894. A child's vocabulary. Educational Review 7:289–290.

Salling, Aage 1959. What can frequency counts teach the language teacher? Contact 3:24–29.

Sandosham, Linda 1980. Using the word bank as a vocabulary building aid. Guidelines 3:54–60.

Sanford, E. C. 1891. Notes on studies of the language of children. Pedagogical Seminary 1:257–260.

Saragi, T. 1974. A Study of English Suffixes. Unpublished MA thesis, Sanata Dharma, Yogyakarta, Indonesia.

Saragi, T., Nation, I. S. P. and Meister, G. F. 1978. Vocabulary learning and reading. System 6, 2:72–78.

Sarawit, Mary 1980. Vocabulary in a communicative context: "The assembly." Guidelines 3:73–75.

Saville-Troike, Muriel 1984. What really matters in second language learning for academic achievement? TESOL Quarterly 18, 2:199–219.

Schachter, W. S. 1979. An investigation of the effects of vocabulary instruction and schemata orientation upon reading comprehension. Dissertation Abstracts International 39:A7303.

Schaefer, Carl F. 1980. Episodic memory, semantic memory, and fluency. IRAL 23, 4:321–325.

Schane, Sanford A. 1977. Rule breaking in English spelling: A study of final e. In Current Issues in Linguistic Theory 4, P. J. Hopper (ed.). John Benjamins, Amsterdam.

Schatz, E. K. and Baldwin, R. S. 1986. Context clues are unreliable predictors of word meaning. Reading Research Quarterly 21, 4:439–453.

Schleifer, Aliah 1985. Reaching out: A strategy for advanced vocabulary acquisition. English Teaching Forum 23, 2:11–15.

Scholes, Robert J. 1966. Phonotactic Grammaticality. Janua Linguarum Series Minor 50, Mouton, The Hague.

Scholfield, P. J. 1980. Explaining meaning by paraphrase: Problems and principles. Guidelines 3:24–37.

Scholfield, P. J. 1981. Writing, vocabulary errors and the dictionary. Guidelines 6:31–40.

Scholfield, P. J. 1982a. The role of bilingual dictionaries in ESL/EFL: A positive view. Guidelines 4, 1:84–98.

Scholfield, Phil 1982b. Using the English dictionary for comprehension. TESOL Quarterly 16, 2:185–194.

Schonell, F. J., Meddleton, I. G. and Shaw, B. A. 1956. A Study of the Oral Vocabulary of Adults. University of Queensland Press, Brisbane.

Schouten-van Parreren, C. 1988. Action psychology and vocabulary learning. Proceedings of the 1st International Congress on Activity Theory, Hildebrand-Nihlson and Ruckriem (eds.): 325–331.

Schreck, Richard 1983. Review essay. Language Learning 33, 2:247–258.

Seashore, Robert H. 1933. The measurement and analysis of extent of vocabulary. Psychological Bulletin 30:709–710.

Seashore, Robert H. 1948. The importance of vocabulary in learning language skills. Elementary English 25, 3:137–152.

Seashore, Robert H. 1949. Implications of the Seashore vocabulary report. Elementary English 26:407–413.

Seashore, Robert H. and Eckerson, Lois D. 1940. The measurement of individual differences in general English vocabularies. Journal of Educational Psychology 31:14–38.

Seashore, Robert H. and Morin, Robert E. 1950. Clearing the way for vocabulary development. Education Digest 16, 2:43–45.

Seegers, J. C. and Seashore, R. H. 1949. How large are children's vocabularies? A discussion. Elementary English 26, 4:181–194.

Seibert, L. C. 1927. An experiment in learning French vocabulary. Journal of Educational Psychology 18:294–309.

Seibert, L. C. 1930. An experiment on the relative efficiency of studying French vocabulary in associated pairs versus studying French vocabulary in context. Journal of Educational Psychology 21:297–314.

Seibert, L. C. 1945. A study of the practice of guessing word meanings from a context. Modern Language Journal 29:296–323.

Sen, Ann Louise 1983. Teaching vocabulary through riddles. English Teaching Forum 21, 2:12–17.

Sharma, R. S. 1985. Teaching semantic distinctions through literature. IRAL 23, 3:246–253.

Shepherd, J. F. 1974. Research on the relationship between the meanings of morphemes and the meanings of derivatives. In Nacke (ed.).

Shibles, Burleigh 1959. How many words does a first-grade child know? Elementary English 36:42–47.

Sidowski, Joseph B. et al. 1961. Prompting and confirmation variables in verbal learning. Psychological Reports 8:401–406.

Sim, D. D. and Laufer-Dvorkin, B. 1984. Vocabulary Development. Collins ELT, London.

Sim, Donald and Bensoussan, Marsha 1979. Control of contextualized function and content words as it affects EFL reading comprehension test scores. In Reading in a Second Language, Mackay et al. Newbury House, New York: 36–44.

Simensen, Aud Marit 1987. Adapted readers: How are they adapted? Reading in a Foreign Language 41.

Sims, Verner Martin 1923. The reliability and validity of four types of vocabulary tests. Journal of Educational Research 20:91–96.

Sinclair, J. (ed.) 1987. Collins Cobuild English Language Dictionary. Collins, London.

Sinclair, J. McH. and Renouf, A. 1988. A lexical syllabus for language learning. In Carter and McCarthy: 140–160.

Sloat, C. and Taylor, S. 1985. The Structure of English Words, Third Ed., Kendall Hunt, IA.

Smith, F. 1982. Understanding Reading. Holt, Rinehart & Winston, New York.

Smith, M. K. 1941. Measurement of the size of general English vocabulary through the elementary grades and high school. Genetic Psychology Monographs 24:311–345.

Spaulding, Seth 1951. Two formulas for estimating the reading difficulty of Spanish. Educational Research Bulletin 30:117–124.

Spearitt, D. 1972. Identification of subskills of reading comprehension by maximum likelihood factor analysis. Reading Research Quarterly 8:92–111.

Spiro, R. J., Bruce, B. C. and Brewer, W. F. (eds.) 1980. Theoretical Issues in Reading Comprehension. Erlbaum, Hillsdale, NJ.

Spitza, Kimett and Fischer, Susan D. 1981. Short term memory as a test of language proficiency. TESL Talk 12, 4:32–41.

Stahl, Steven 1983. Differential word knowledge and reading comprehension. Journal of Reading Behavior 15, 4:33–50.

Stahl, Steven A. and Fairbanks, Marilyn M. 1986. The effects of vocabulary instruction: A model-based meta-analysis. Review of Educational Research 56, 1:72–110.

Stahl, Steven A. and Vancil, Sandra J. 1986. Discussion is what makes semantic maps work in vocabulary instruction. Reading Teacher: 62–67.

Stalnaker, John M. and Kurath, William 1935. A comparison of two types of foreign language vocabulary test. Journal of Educational Psychology 26:435–442.

Stanovich, K. E. 1980. Toward an interactive-compensatory model of individual differences in the development of reading fluency. Reading Research Quarterly 16:32–71.

Statman, Stella 1981. The activation of semantic memory: A pedagogical technique in the EFL classroom. English Language Teaching Journal 35, 3:232–233.

Stauffer, Russell G. 1942. A study of prefixes in the Thorndike list to establish a list of prefixes that should be taught in the elementary school. Journal of Educational Research 35, 6:453–458.

Stein, Gabriele 1988. ELT Journal dictionaries, the teacher and the student. JALT Journal 11, 1:36–45.

Steinbeck, John 1949. Of Mice and Men/Cannery Row. Penguin Books, Harmondsworth.

Steinbeck, John, retold by Winter, Martin 1975. Of Mice and Men. Heinemann Educ. Books, London.

Steinberg, J. S. 1978. Context clues as aids in comprehension. English Teaching Forum 16, 2:6–9.

Sternberg, R. J. 1987. Most vocabulary is learned from context. In McKeown and Curtis: 89–105.

Sternberg, R. J. and Powell, J. S. 1983. Comprehending verbal comprehension. American Psychologist 38:878–893.

Stieglitz, Ezra L. 1983. A practical approach to vocabulary reinforcement. English Language Teaching Journal 37, 1:71–75.

Stieglitz, Ezra L. and Stieglitz, Varda S. 1981. SAVOR the word to reinforce vocabulary in the content areas. Journal of Reading 25, 1:46–51.

Stock, P. 1984. Polysemy. International Conference on Lexicography (Exeter 1983) R. R. K. Hartmann (ed.).

Stoddard, G. D. 1929. An experiment in verbal learning. Journal of Educational Psychology 20:452–457.

Stone, Clarence R. 1943. A reply to "all in favor of a low vocabulary . . . " Elementary School Journal 44:41–44.

Stratton, E. P. and Nacke, P. L. 1974. The role of vocabulary knowledge in comprehension. In Nacke: 185–192.

Strick, Gregory J. 1980. A hypothesis for semantic development in a second language. Language Learning 30, 1:155–176.

Stubbs, Michael 1986. Language development, lexical competence and nuclear vocabulary. In Language Development in the School Years, K. Durkin (ed.), Croom Helm.

Summers, Della 1988. The role of dictionaries in language learning. In Carter and McCarthy: 111–125.

Swaby, B. E. 1977. The effects of advance organizers and vocabulary introduction on the reading comprehension of sixth grade students. Dissertation Abstracts International 39:A115.

Sweeney, C. A. and Bellezza, F. S. 1982. Use of the keyword mnemonic for learning English vocabulary. Human Learning 1:155–163.

Swenson, E. and West, M. P. 1934. On the Counting of New Words in Textbooks for Teaching Foreign Languages. 1. Bulletin of the Department of Educational Research, University of Toronto.

Sykes, J. B. (ed.) 1982. The Concise Oxford Dictionary, 7th ed. Oxford University Press, Oxford.

Symonds, P. M. 1926. Size of recognition and recall vocabularies. School and Society 24:559–560.

Tate, Harry L. 1939. Two experiments in reading—vocabulary building. Modern Language Journal 23:214–218.

Taylor, C. V. 1983. Vocabulary for education in English. World Language English 2, 2:100–104.

Tennyson, R. D. and Cocchiarella, M. U. 1986. An empirically based instructional design theory for teaching concepts. Review of Educational Research 56:40–71.

Terman, Lewis M. and Childs, H. G. 1912. A tentative revision and extension of the Binet–Simon measuring scale of intelligence. Pt. 2. Journal of Educational Psychology 3:204–208.

Terrell, T. D. 1982. The natural approach to language teaching: An update. Modern Language Journal 66, 2:121–132.

Tharp, James B. 1940. The measurement of vocabulary difficulty. Modern Language Journal 24:169–178.

Thomas, Helen 1984. Developing the stylistic and lexical awareness of advanced students. English Language Teaching Journal 38, 3:187–191.

Thompson, Brian 1982. Initial Vocabularies for Reading. 'Set' research information for teachers, No. 2, Item 3(a), NZCER, Wellington, New Zealand.

Thompson, Ernest 1958. The "master word" approach to vocabulary training. Journal of Developmental Reading 2:62–66.

Thompson, Geoff 1987. Using bilingual dictionaries. English Language Teaching Journal 41, 4:282–286.

Thompson, Irene 1987. Memory in language learning. In Learner Strategies in Language Learning, A. Wendon and J. Rubin (eds.), Prentice-Hall, London: 43–54.

Thorndike, E. L. 1908. Memory for paired associates. Psychological Review 15:122–138.

Thorndike, E. L. 1914. Repetition versus recall in memorizing vocabularies. Journal of Educational Psychology 5:596–597.

Thorndike, E. L. 1924. The vocabularies of school pupils. In Contributions to Education, J. Carelton Bell. World Book Co., New York 1:69–76.

Thorndike, E. L. 1941. The Teaching of English Suffixes. Teachers College, Columbia University, New York.

Thorndike, E. L. and Lorge, I. 1944. The Teacher's Word Book of 30,000 Words. Teachers College, Columbia University, New York.

Thorndike, R. L. 1973. Reading as reasoning. Reading Research Quarterly 9:135–147.

Thorpe, Rhona 1982. My Word Book. Multilithed material: 19 pages.

Tilley, Harvey C. 1936. A technique for determining the relative difficulty of word meanings among elementary school children. Journal of Experimental Education 5, 1:61–64.

Tomaszczyk, Jerzy 1981. Issues and developments in bilingual pedagogical lexicography. Applied Linguistics 2, 3:287–296.

Tracy, F. 1893. The language of childhood. American Journal of Psychology 6, 1:107–138.

Tritch, Marla 1981. Improving vocabulary: Problems in co-occurrence and grammatical marking. English Teaching Forum 19, 2:22–27.

Tuckman, Bruce W. 1972. Conducting Educational Research. Harcourt Brace Jovanovich, New York (Units 3–4).

Tuinman, J. J. and Brady, M. E. 1974. How does vocabulary account for variance on reading comprehension tests? A preliminary instructional analysis. In Nacke: 176–184.

Turner, Sharman Jane 1986. Self-correction jigsaw pictures. Modern English Teacher 13, 4:28–30.

Twaddell, Freeman 1973. Vocabulary expansion in the TESOL classroom. TESOL Quarterly 7, 1:61–78.

Uhrbrock, Richard Stephen 1935. The vocabulary of a five-year-old. Educational Research Bulletin 14, 4:85–97.

Underhill, A. 1980. Use Your Dictionary. Oxford University Press, Oxford.

Underwood, Benton J., Ekdstrand, B. R. and Keppel, G. 1965. An analysis of intralist similarity in verbal learning with experiments on conceptual similarity. Journal of Verbal Learning and Verbal Behaviour 4:447–462.

United States Information Agency, Washington, D.C. 1964. Special English Word List used in The Voice of America's World-Wide Radio Broadcasts in Special English.

Van Daalen-Kapteijns, M. M. and Elshout-Mohr, M. 1981. The acquisition of word meanings as a cognitive learning process. Journal of Verbal Learning and Verbal Behaviour 20:386–399.

Van Parreren, C. F. and Schouten-Van Parreren, M. 1981. Contextual guessing: A trainable reader strategy. System 9, 3:235–241.

Vasey, F. T. 1919. Vocabulary of grammar grade school children. Journal of Educational Psychology 10:104–107.

Venezky, Richard L. 1970. The Structure of English Orthography. Janua Linguarum Series Minor 82, Mouton, The Hague.

Viberg, Ake 1989. A semantic field approach to vocabulary acquisition. Unpublished paper: 38 pages.

Vincent, Monica 1983. Writing non-fiction readers. In case studies in ELT, R. R. Jordon (ed.), Collins ELT, London: 170–178.

Visser, A. 1989. Learning vocabulary through underlying meanings. Unpublished M.A. thesis. Victoria University, Wellington, New Zealand.

Von Elek, Tibor 1982. Test of Swedish as a second language: An experiment in self-assessment. Work papers from the Language Teaching Research Centre, SPC, Goteborgs Universitet No. 31.

Wagner, Michael J. and Tilney, Germaine 1983. The effect of "superlearning techniques" on the vocabulary acquisition and alpha brainwave production of language learners. TESOL Quarterly 17, 1:5–17.

Wajnryb, Ruth 1987. Vocabulary—consolidation through clusters. English Teachers Journal (Israel) 35:67–70.

Walker, Laura J. 1983. Word identification strategies in reading a foreign language. Foreign Language Annals 16, 4:293–299.

Wallace, Michael 1982. Teaching Vocabulary. Heinemann, London.

Warkentein, Edgar 1982. Is this a hammer which I see before me? Teaching technical vocabulary. TESL Talk 13, 3:155–159.

Webb, W. B. 1962. The effects of prolonged learning on learning. Journal of Verbal Learning and Verbal Behaviour 1:173–182.

Wepman, Joseph M. and Haas, Wilbur 1969. A Spoken Word Count: Children. Western Psychological Services, Los Angeles.

Werner, H. and Kaplan, B. 1952. The acquisition of word meanings: A developmental study. Monographs of the Society for Research in Child Development 15.

Werner, Heinz and Kaplan, Edith 1950. Development of word meaning through verbal context: An experimental study. Journal of Psychology 29:251–257.

Wesman, A. G. and Seashore, H. G. 1949. Frequency vs. complexity of words in verbal measurement. Journal of Educational Psychology 40:395–404.

West, M. 1955. Learning to Read a Foreign Language. Longman, London 2nd ed.

West, M. 1955. English spelling. English Language Teaching 9, 4:132–136.

West, M. P., Swenson, E. et al. 1934. A critical examination of Basic English. Bulletin of the Department of Educational Research, University of Toronto, No. 2.

West, Michael 1932. New Method Readers. Longman, London std. ed.

West, Michael 1935. Definition Vocabulary. Bulletin of the Department of Educational Research, University of Toronto, No. 4.

West, Michael 1953. A General Service List of English Words. Longman, Green and Co., London.

West, Michael 1955. Catenizing (chaining words together). In West, 2nd ed: 61–68.

West, Michael 1960. Teaching English in Difficult Circumstances. Longman, London: 38–42, 95.

Whipple, Guy Montrose and Mrs. 1909. The vocabulary of a three-year-old boy with some interpretive comments. Pedagogical Seminary 16, 1:1–22.

Whitcut, J. 1979. Learning with LDOCE. Longman, London.

White, Cynthia J. 1988. The role of associational patterns and semantic networks in vocabulary development. English Teaching Forum 26, 4:9–11.

Wicklow, C. H. 1974. Review of Advanced English Vocabulary. Language Learning 24, 1:167–170.

Widmann-Sadler, Pauline 1988. Getting involved with words. Practical English Teaching, June: 17.

Widdowson, H. G. 1979. Explorations in Applied Linguistics (esp. "The authenticity of language data," "The simplification of use," "The significance of simplification"). Oxford University Press, Oxford.

Wijk, Axel 1966. Rules of Pronunciation for the English Language. Oxford University Press, London.

Wilcox, George 1979. Teaching and testing vocabulary: A method to use with advanced students. English Teaching Forum 17, 3:2–9.

Wilford, Judith 1982. Guessing Words from Context. Unpublished research paper. Victoria University of Wellington.

Wilhelm, Albert E. 1986. Building vocabulary through exercises in context. English Teaching Forum 24, 2:45.

Williams, C. B. 1970. Style and Vocabulary: Numerical Studies. Griffin, London.

Williams, E. and Porter, D. 1983. Review of the words you need. Reading in a Foreign Language 1, 1:68–71.

Williams, Harold M. 1932. Some problems of sampling in vocabulary tests. Journal of Experimental Education 1, 2:131–133.

Williams, Ray 1985. Teaching vocabulary recognition strategies in ESP reading. ESP Journal 4, 2:121–131.

Willis, Dave 1988. A lexical approach to syllabus design. EFL Gazette, August.

Wilson, David 1988. Vocabulary for business. EFL Gazette, August.

Winks, M. 1975. Simplification of Of Mice and Men by John Steinbeck. Heinemann, London.

Wittrock, M. C., Marks, Carolyn and Doctorow, M. 1975. Reading as a generative process. Journal of Educational Psychology 67, 4:484–489.

Wodinsky, M. and Nation, I. S. P. 1988. Learning from graded readers. Reading in a Foreign Language 5, 1:155–161.

Wolff, Fanne E. 1910. A boy's dictionary. Child-Study Monthly 2:141–150.

Wolfle, Lee M. and McGee, Lea M. 1979. On the determination of causal ordering between vocabulary and comprehension. Journal of Reading Behavior II, 3:273–277.

Woodeson, Elizabeth 1982. Communicative crosswords. Modern English Teacher 10, 2:29–30.

Woodward, Tessa 1984. Vocabulary review game. Modern English Teacher 11, 3:49.

Woodward, Tessa 1985. From vocabulary review to classroom dictionary. Modern English Teacher 12, 4:29.

Woodward, Tessa 1988. Vocabulary posters. Modern English Teacher 15, 3:31–32.

Woolard, S. 1988. The battering ram: Some observations on graded texts. Modern English Teacher 15, 2:19–20.

Xiaolong Li 1988. Effects of contextual cues on inferring and remembering meanings. Applied Linguistics 9, 4:402–413.

Xue Guoyi and Nation I. S. P. 1984. A university word list. Language Learning and Communication 3, 2:215–229.

Yamada, Jun et al. 1980. On the optimum age for teaching foreign vocabulary to children. IRAL 18, 3:245–247.

Yap Kim Onn 1979. Vocabulary—Building blocks of comprehension? Journal of Reading Behavior 11, 1:49–59.

Yap Kim Onn 1979. On the determination of causal ordering—Between vocabulary and comprehension—a rejoinder. Journal of Reading Behavior 11, 3:279–280.

Yarmohammadi, Lotfollah 1980. Contact analysis of English and Persian measure words for pedagogical purposes. IRAL 18, 1:1–20.

Yasui, Minoru, Consonant Patterning in English. Kenkyushu, Tokyo.

Yorkey, Richard 1974. Which dictionary is "best." English Teaching Forum 12, 4:16–33.

Yorkey, Richard 1979. Review of Longman Dictionary of Current English. TESOL Quarterly 13, 3:393–403.

Yoshida, Midori 1978. The acquisition of English vocabulary by a Japanese speaking child. In Second Language Acquisition, E. M. Hatch (ed.). Newbury House, New York: 91–100.

Zettersten, Arne 1978. A Word Frequency List Based on American English Press Reportage. Akademisk Forlav, Copenhagen.

Zimmerman, Rudiger 1987. Form-oriented and content-oriented lexical errors in L2 learners. IRAL 25, 1:55–67.

Zipf, George K. 1935. The Psycho-Biology of Language. M.I.T. Press, Cambridge Mass.

# Words from the *General Service List* Which Are Not Likely to Be Well-Known

The following lists are taken from studies by Barnard (1961) and Quinn (1968). Using substantially the same translation test, Barnard and Quinn tested the vocabulary of preuniversity students in India and Indonesia. Most of the words in the *General Service List* were tested. The words in the following lists were known by 50 percent or less of the students tested by Barnard and by less than 10 percent of the students tested by Quinn. The asterisk * indicates that no students at all in the Quinn study knew these words.

## ADJECTIVES AND ADVERBS

| | | | |
|---|---|---|---|
| almost | familiar | peculiar | steep |
| annoyed | firmly | perfect | sticky |
| *bound to | *greasy | *plain | stiff |
| cautious | *humble | promptly | strict |
| *complicated | idle | punctual | tough |
| *conscious | just | purple | *unfair |
| *convenient | | relieved | unlikely |
| *curious | *merely | rusty | vain |
| *disgusting | mildly | sacred | *violent |
| | moderate | severe | worth |
| *earnest | modest | solemn | |
| envious | noble | sore | |
| exciting | | | |
| *faint | occasionally | | |

## NOUNS

| | | | |
|---|---|---|---|
| *account | *approval | bar | beam |
| *allowance | arch | *bargain | block |
| *applause | average | barrel | blow |

233

brass
carriage
case
collar
*confession
*course
coward
damage
decision
defense
dependent
descent
despair
effort
excuse
*fancy
*fate

*figure
flavor
funeral
harvest
haste
host
instant
*joint
judgment
lack
limb
*lump
manner
mass
note
*nuisance

order
outline
pad
*passage
paste
pattern
performance
*pile
*prejudice
*rubbish
*rug
*saucer
saw
scent
*scorn
sheet
*shower

solution
spade
*spot
stage
stairs
stem
stuff
substance
*tap
temper
trunk
tune
verse
waist
weed
witness

## VERBS

adopt
afford
apologize
appear
approve
avoid
blame
boast
bribe
*charge
claim
concern
confuse
cure
deserve
*dive
*encourage
*entertain
fry
get rid of
grind

handle
heal
*hinder
intend
interfere
introduce
last
lead
lean
neglect
*offend
persuade
preach
propose
recommend
*refer
regard as
regret
remark
replace
represent

*resist
scatter
scold
*scrape
scratch
*seize
share
*spare
*spin
split
swallow
swear
swell

swing
tempt
*tend
threaten
twist
upset
*weave
whisper
wind
wipe
wrap
yield

## PREPOSITIONS AND CONJUNCTIONS

in case
*in spite of
since

# A University Word List

## A

abandon 3*
abnormal 6
absorb 5
abstract 5
academic 6
accelerate 2
access 10
accompany 6
accomplish 3
accumulate 11
accurate 5
achieve 2
acid 9
acquire 4
adapt 3
adequate 3
adhere 8
adjacent 2
adjective 6
adjust 3
administer 4
adolescent 7
advocate 5
adult 6
aesthetic 4
affect 2
affiliate 7
affluence 7
aggregate 8
aggression 8
agitate 6
aid 5
alcohol 7
align 8
allege 4
allocate 4
allude 8
ally 8

alter 4
alternative 1
ambiguity 9
amorphous 9
analogy 4
analyze 1
angular 10
annual 11
anomaly 10
anonymous 10
anthropology 10
apparatus 11
appeal 6
append 10
appendix 10
appraise 4
appreciate 3
approach 1
appropriate 3
approximate 2
arbitrary 1
area 3
aristocrat 7
arithmetic 11
arouse 6
ascribe 10
aspect 6
aspiration 10
assemble 4
assent 10
assert 2
assess 1
asset 9
assign 1
assimilate 10
assist 6
assume 1
assure 4
astronomy 7

atmosphere 4
atom 4
attach 11
attain 6
attitude 3
attribute 4
auspices 10
authorize 2
automatic 2
avail 4
averse 9
aware 2
awe 6
axis 4

## B

battery 11
benefit 6
biology 5
bomb 4
bore 8
breed 11
bubble 11
bulk 11
bureaucracy 8

## C

calendar 11
cancel 11
capable 4
capture 11
carbon 9
career 11
catalog 11
category 5
cater 8
cease 4
cell 7
challenge 11

channel 11
chapter 2
chemical 3
circuit 11
circulate 8
circumstance 3
civic 6
clarify 6
classic 3
client 5
clinic 10
code 5
coefficient 10
cogent 10
coincide 8
collapse 7
collide 6
colloquial 7
column 11
comment 6
commit 6
commodity 7
commune 3
communicate 11
compel 11
compensate 1
competence 7
complement 9
complex 1
complicate 2
comply 1
component 1
compound 5
comprehend 2
comprise 10
compulsion 10
compute 6
conceive 2
concentrate 2

*The numbers after the words group them according to frequency and range. So the words with 1 following them are in the most frequent group and have the widest range.

concentric 7
concept 1
conclude 1
condense 9
conduct 3
confer 7
configuration 7
confine 9
conflict 3
conform 6
confront 5
congress 7
conjunction 6
consent 8
consequent 2
conserve 7
consist 1
console 6
constant 1
constitute 4
construct 1
construe 9
consult 1
consume 3
contact 3
contaminate 4
contemplate 6
contend 6
context 1
contingent 6
continent 7
contract 5
contradict 4
contrary 5
contrast 2
contribute 2
controversy 6
convene 3
converge 10
converse 6
convert 2
cooperate 6
coordinate 3
corporate 7
correlate 8
correspond 3
create 2
credible 3
creditor 7
crisis 5
criterion 1
critic 3
crucial 2

crystal 7
culture 4
cumbersome 7
currency 8
cycle 6
cylinder 11

**D**

data 1
debate 11
decade 2
decimal 11
decline 6
dedicate 4
defect 11
defer 7
deficient 3
define 1
definite 1
deflect 10
degenerate 6
degrade 7
deliberate 10
democracy 7
demonstrate 2
denominator 4
denote 1
dense 4
deny 5
depress 7
deprive 8
derive 1
design 2
detect 8
detriment 8
deviate 3
devise 1
devote 2
diagram 4
diameter 11
dictate 5
diffuse 5
digest 11
dimension 1
discern 8
discourse 4
discrete 3
dispense 10
disperse 3
displace 9
dispose 3
dispute 5
dissipate 8

dissolve 7
distinct 1
distort 2
distribute 4
diverge 9
diverse 4
divine 7
doctrine 6
domestic 7
dominate 4
drain 11
drama 3
drastic 9
drug 8
duration 5
dynamic 3

**E**

economy 3
edit 5
efficient 9
elaborate 4
electron 5
element 1
elevate 10
elicit 10
eliminate 4
eloquent 10
emancipate 10
embody 4
embrace 10
emerge 10
emotion 4
emphasize 2
empirical 2
enable 11
energy 4
enhance 10
enlighten 5
enrich 10
ensure 2
entity 2
enumerate 9
environment 1
episode 10
equate 1
equidistant 10
equilibrium 2
equipment 11
equivalent 1
err 5
establish 1
estimate 3

ethics 7
evaluate 1
evaporate 9
evident 1
eventual 4
evoke 9
evolve 8
exclude 3
execute 5
exert 3
exhaust 9
expand 2
expel 5
expert 11
explicit 3
exploit 3
exponent 10
export 11
expose 2
external 2
extract 6

**F**

facilitate 10
faction 9
factor 3
fallacy 8
fare 11
fate 11
feasible 2
feature 3
federal 9
fertile 6
final 3
finance 7
finite 8
fluctuate 2
fluent 10
fluid 11
focus 2
forgo 4
formulate 1
fossil 10
found 6
fraction 7
fragment 4
fraternal 8
fraud 5
friction 7
frontier 9
frustrate 8
fuel 11
fulfill 11

function 2
fundamental 11
fund 9
fuse 7

**G**

generate 2
genuine 11
geography 3
geometry 7
germ 11
goal 4
grant 5
graph 5
gravity 5
guarantee 1

**H**

harbor 11
hero 11
hemisphere 6
heredity 4
hierarchy 6
homogeneous 5
horror 7
hostile 11
huge 11
hypothesis 1

**I**

identical 6
identify 1
ignore 1
illuminate 9
illustrate 1
image 3
impact 1
imperial 8
implement 5
implicit 1
imply 1
import 11
impose 5
impress 4
impulse 11
incentive 7
incessant 7
incident 4
incline 6
income 6
incompatible 4
inconsistent 10
incorporate 5

index 8
indicate 1
indigenous 9
individual 2
induce 4
infer 2
inferior 11
inflation 10
ingenious 10
inherent 10
inhibit 2
initial 1
injure 11
innate 9
innovation 2
insist 5
inspect 11
instance 11
instinct 6
institute 5
instruct 5
integer 9
integrate 4
intellect 3
intelligent 3
intense 2
interact 6
interlock 6
interlude 6
intermediate 7
internal 4
interpret 1
interrelate 10
intersect 5
interval 5
interview 10
intervene 4
intimacy 10
intrinsic 9
intuitive 2
invade 7
inverse 7
invest 8
investigate 4
invoke 7
involve 1
irrigate 11
isolate 2
issue 3
item 11

**J**

job 5

journal 11
judicial 4
justify 4

**K**

kindred 5

**L**

label 5
laboratory 11
labor 3
launch 8
layer 11
lecture 11
legal 6
legislate 8
legitimate 5
leisure 11
lens 8
liable 8
liberate 9
linguistic 8
litigate 4
locate 6
locomotion 8
logic 4
luxury 11

**M**

magic 8
magnetic 2
magnitude 1
major 2
maintain 3
manifest 3
manipulate 2
margin 9
material 9
maternal 10
mathematics 2
matrix 9
mature 2
maximum 3
medium 6
mental 11
metabolism 6
metaphor 8
method 1
microscope 6
migrate 7
military 4
minimum 1
minor 6

mobile 4
modify 1
moist 11
molecule 9
momentum 9
monarch 8
morphology 7
motive 3
muscle 7
myth 10

**N**

navy 7
negative 1
nerve 6
network 3
neutral 7
niche 6
norm 3
notate 3
notion 2
novel 11
nuclear 8
null 10
nutrient 7

**O**

objective 5
oblige 6
obsolete 7
obtain 2
obvious 1
occupy 3
occur 2
odd 9
odor 7
option 10
orbit 9
orientate 3
oscillate 8
outcome 10
overlap 5
oxygen 8

**P**

parenthesis 5
parliament 7
participate 6
partisan 8
passive 2
peasant 7
pendulum 8
period 2

perpendicular 4
perpetrate 5
perpetual 10
persist 4
perspective 2
pertinent 2
pervade 8
pest 11
phase 2
phenomena 2
philosophy 4
physical 3
planet 6
plead 7
plot 3
pole 3
policy 7
pollution 11
port 11
portion 2
positive 3
postulate 8
potential 1
pragmatic 7
precede 2
precipitate 7
precise 2
predict 4
preliminary 5
premise 8
preposition 3
prestige 3
presume 1
prevail 7
previous 3
prime 1
principle 2
priority 10
proceed 1
process 11
proclaim 8
procure 10
prohibit 10
project 4
propagate 6
propensity 6
proportion 4
proprietor 3
prosper 6
protest 6
province 10
provoke 8
prudence 7

psychology 4
publish 1
purport 10
pursue 1

**Q**

quote 10

**R**

radical 6
radius 5
random 1
range 1
ratio 11
rational 3
react 2
rebel 8
rectangle 7
recur 10
reform 7
refute 7
region 1
reign 6
reinforce 6
reject 4
release 4
relevance 3
reluctant 8
rely 3
remove 10
render 10
repress 10
reproduce 8
repudiate 7
require 1
research 4
reservoir 4
resident 10
residue 9
resource 11
respective 2
respond 5
restore 5
restrict 1
retain 5
retard 5
reveal 3
reverberate 9
reverse 1
revise 6
revive 7
revolt 4
revolve 11

rhythm 7
rigid 8
rigor 10
role 1
rotate 3
route 11
rudimentary 5
rural 9

**S**

saint 7
sanction 6
satellite 3
saturate 10
scalar 6
schedule 7
scheme 3
score 7
secrete 8
section 2
secure 5
seek 3
segment 2
select 2
sequence 2
series 2
sex 8
shift 2
shrink 11
sibling 7
signify 2
site 11
similar 1
simultaneous 2
skeleton 10
sketch 7
sociology 7
solar 8
sophisticated 2
source 3
spatial 8
species 2
specify 1
spectrum 7
speculate 4
sphere 4
spontaneous 4
stable 2
starve 11
stationary 9
statistic 2
status 1
stereotype 7

stimulate 5
stipulate 4
strata 6
stress 5
structure 2
style 5
subdivide 9
subjective 6
subordinate 8
subsequent 1
subside 4
subsidize 4
subtle 5
suffice 1
sum 1
summary 1
superficial 3
superimpose 4
superior 5
supplement 5
suppress 5
supreme 8
surplus 10
survey 11
suspend 9
sustain 6
switch 11
symbol 4
symptom 5
synthetic 5

**T**

tangent 6
tangible 10
tape 11
task 3
team 11
technique 1
technology 2
telescope 11
temporary 11
tense 1
tentative 4
terminology 6
territory 8
terror 7
text 4
texture 7
theft 11
theorem 4
theory 2
thermal 7
tiny 5

tire 11
tissue 7
tolerate 10
tone 6
topic 6
trace 2
tractor 11
tradition 2
traffic 11
trait 5
transact 7
transfer 5
transform 5
transition 3
transmit 2
transparent 11

transport 11
treaty 8
trend 8
triangle 10
trivial 5
tropical 11

**U**

ultimate 1
undergo 2
underlie 3
undertake 11
unduly 9
uniform 6
upsurge 4
urban 6

usage 1
utilize 8
utter 8

**V**

vague 10
valid 1
vary 1
vast 5
vein 11
velocity 9
verbal 2
verify 2
version 5
vertical 1

vibrate 9
violate 9
virtual 6
visual 3
vital 11
vocabulary 9
volt 11
volume 6
voluntary 9

**W**

withdraw 11

**X**

x-ray 7

# A Passage with Words of Various Frequency Levels Omitted

This is the passage with words outside the first 1000 base words of the *General Service List* omitted.

### Forestry

In 1978/1979 New Zealand produced 9.15 million _____ meters of _____ _____ ( _____ _____ _____ ) of which 59 per _____ was _____ (as _____ , _____ , _____ _____ , _____ , and so on). Productive _____ is expected to remain at about this level throughout most of this _____ . But based on the _____ of wood which will become _____ from existing forests and planned new plantings, production will progressively increase to 20 million _____ meters a year by the turn of the _____ .

If _____ planting rates are _____ with planting_____ _____ in each _____ and the forests _____ at the earliest opportunity, the _____ wood supplies could further increase to about 36 million _____ meters _____ in the _____ 2001–2015. The additional _____ wood supply should greatly _____ _____ _____ , even if much is used for _____ production.

Even if used in an _____ form, the increasing wood supplies will _____ a larger _____ force, an _____ roading _____ , and _____ _____ and _____ _____ . If the trees are to be _____ then certain _____ must be made. They will include _____ in:

- _____ machinery and _____ ;

- _____ _____ , and other _____ _____ for the _____ of _____ products;
- _____ and _____ roads (or rail or coastal shipping _____ where _____ );
- _____ _____ .

The _____ could be extended to include overseas shipping, and _____ and township _____ for forestry workers.

Other _____ costs will depend on the degree of _____ and the _____ of total production which is _____ . At the_____ _____ of 36 million _____ meters per _____ there would be _____ _____ to allow the _____ of a number of _____and _____ _____ costing up to $4000 million at 1978 prices (_____ upwards of another $1000 million for extra _____). Although the_____ total _____ is large over the next 35 years (possibly _____ $6000–$7000 million inclusive of _____ and _____ _____ ), the_____ _____ would probably average only 2–2.5 percent of total _____ in all _____ , though it would be higher in the years of most _____ _____ .

It may well be that the best rate of return will be on _____ _____ . But there will be pressure for further _____ to give more employment and _____ more overseas _____ .

This is the passage with words outside the *General Service List* omitted. This list contains 2000 base words.

## Forestry

In 1978/1979 New Zealand produced 9.15 million _____ meters of _____ logs (_____ _____ _____) of which 59 percent was _____ (as newsprint, _____ , sawn _____ , logs, and so on). Productive _____ is expected to remain at about this level throughout most of this _____ . But based on the _____ of wood which will become _____ from existing forests and planned new plantings, production will progressively increase to 20 million _____ meters a year by the turn of the century.

If _____ planting rates are _____ with planting _____ satisfied in each _____ and the forests milled at the earliest opportunity, the _____ wood supplies could further increase to about 36 million _____ meters _____ in the period 2001–2015. The additional _____ wood supply should greatly _____ _____ _____ , even if much is used for _____ production.

Even if used in an _____ form, the increasing wood supplies will _____ a larger _____ force, an improved roading network, and _____ _____ and _____ _____ . If the trees are to be _____ then certain _____ must be made. They will include _____ in:

- logging machinery and _____ ;
- logging trucks, and other _____ _____ for the _____ of _____ products;
- _____ and _____ roads (or rail or coastal shipping _____ where _____);
- _____ _____ .

The list could be extended to include overseas shipping, and _____ and township _____ for forestry workers.

Other _____ costs will depend on the degree of _____ and the _____ of total production which is _____ . At the_____ _____ of 36 million _____ meters per _____ there would be _____ _____to allow the _____ of a number of _____ and newsprint mills costing up to $4000 million at 1978 prices (_____ upwards of another $1000 million for extra electricity). Although the _____total expenditure is large over the next 35 years (possibly _____$6000–$7000 million inclusive of _____ and _____ _____), the _____ _____ would probably average only 2–2.5 percent of total _____ in all _____ , though it would be higher in the years of most rapid _____ .

It may well be that the best rate of return will be on _____ logs. But there will be pressure for further _____ to give more employment and earn more overseas _____ .

This is the passage with words not in the *General Service List* and the *University Word List* (Appendix 2) omitted. These two word lists give you a vocabulary of 2800 base words or between 4000 and 5000 base words plus derivatives.

### Forestry

In 1978/1979 New Zealand produced 9.15 million _____ meters of _____ logs (_____ _____ _____) of which 59 percent was exported (as newsprint, _____ , sawn _____ , logs, and so on). Productive capacity is expected to remain at about this level throughout most of this decade. But based on the volumes of wood which will become available from existing forests and planned new plantings, production will progressively increase to 20 million _____ meters a year by the turn of the century.

If current planting rates are maintained with planting targets satisfied in each region and the forests milled at the earliest opportunity, the available wood supplies could further increase to about 36 million _____ meters annually in the period 2001–2015. The additional available wood supply should greatly _____ domestic requirements, even if much is used for energy production.

Even if used in an unprocessed form, the increasing wood supplies will require a larger labor force, an improved roading network, and expanded transport and processing facilities. If the trees are to be exported then certain investments must be made. They will include investments in:

- logging machinery and equipment;

- logging trucks, and other _____ required for the transport of processed products;
- upgrading and maintaining roads (or rail or coastal shipping facilities
where appropriate);
- port facilities.

The list could be extended to include overseas shipping, and accommodation and township facilities for forestry workers.

Other capital costs will depend on the degree of processing and the proportion of total production which is processed. At the potential maximum of 36 million _____ meters per _____ there would be sufficient timber to allow the construction of a number of _____ and newsprint mills costing up to $4000 million at 1978 prices (excluding upwards of another $1000 million for extra electricity). Although the potential total expenditure is large over the next 35 years (possibly approaching $6,000–$7,000 million inclusive of _____ and transport investment), the _____ requirements would probably average only 2–2.5 percent of total investment in all _____ , though it would be higher in the years of most rapid expansion.

It may well be that the best rate of return will be on exported logs. But there will be pressure for further processing to give more employment and earn more overseas funds.

This is the original passage.

## Forestry

In 1978/1979 New Zealand produced 9.15 million cubic meters of exotic logs (predominantly *Pinus radiata*) of which 59 percent was exported (as newsprint, pulp, sawn timber, logs, and so on). Productive capacity is expected to remain at about this level throughout most of this decade. But based on the volumes of wood which will become available from existing forests and planned new plantings, production will progressively increase to 20 million cubic meters a year by the turn of the century.

If current planting rates are maintained with planting targets satisfied in each region and the forests milled at the earliest opportunity, the available wood supplies could further increase to about 36 million cubic meters annually in the period 2001–2015. The additional available wood supply should greatly exceed domestic requirements, even if much is used for energy production.

Even if used in an unprocessed form, the increasing wood supplies will require a larger labor force, an improved roading network, and expanded transport and processing facilities. If the trees are to be exported then certain investments must be made. They will include investments in:

- logging machinery and equipment;
- logging trucks, and other vehicles required for the transport of processed products;

- upgrading and maintaining roads (or rail or coastal shipping facilities where appropriate);
- port facilities.

The list could be extended to include overseas shipping, and accommodation and township facilities for forestry workers.

Other capital costs will depend on the degree of processing and the proportion of total production which is processed. At the potential maximum of 36 million cubic meters per annum there would be sufficient timber to allow the construction of a number of pulp and newsprint mills costing up to $4000 million at 1978 prices (excluding upwards of another $1000 million for extra electricity). Although the potential total expenditure is large over the next 35 years (possibly approaching $6000–$7000 million inclusive of harvesting and transport investment), the incremental requirements would probably average only 2–2.5 percent of total investment in all sectors, though it would be higher in the years of most rapid expansion.

It may well be that the best rate of return will be on exported logs. But there will be pressure for further processing to give more employment and earn more overseas funds.

# Words in Context

Use context clues to help you guess the meaning of the underlined words. Write whatever you can guess about the meaning of each word even if it is only that it has a positive or negative meaning.

### Leibniz

Leibniz was born in Leipzig, Germany. His father, a professor of moral philosophy at the University of Leipzig, died when Leibniz was six years old. The prolatic boy then gained advelt to his father's library and began reading emartically on a wide range of subjects, a habit that he maintained throughout his life. At age 15 he entered the University of Leipzig as a law student and by the age of 20 received a doctorate from the University of Altdorf. Culberously, Leibniz followed an aleand in law and international politics, serving as quelson to kings and princes.

During his numerous foreign latments, Leibniz came in contact with outstanding mathematicians and scientists who stimulated his interest in mathematics—most notably, the cheltian Christian Huygens. In mathematics Leibniz was self-taught; he learned the subject by reading papers and glises. As a result of this fragmented mathematical education, Leibniz often duplicated the results of others. This ultimately led to a raging conflict over who invented calculus, Leibniz or Newton. The argument over this question selteranded the scientific circles of England and Europe. Most scientists on the continent supported Leibniz, while those in England supported Newton. The conflict was unfortunate, and both sides lost in the end. (Anton, 1980, pp. xxi–xxii)

### Answers

precocious    access    voraciously    subsequently    a career counsel        missions    physicist        journals        engulfed

The underlined words are nonsense words. They replace all the words in the text which are not in the *General Service List* or the *University Word List*.

# To Examine the Vocabulary of a Textbook

1. a. Count the total number of words
   b. Count the number of different words

   b : a is the density index

2. At regular intervals (suitable to the book)
   a. Count the number of previously encountered words
   b. Count the new words on one page

   the set of a : b proportions shows the consistency or otherwise of the density

3. Count the number of words occurring
   one time
   two times, etc.
   Express each as a proportion of the number of different words. Examine the repetition-spacing.
4. Count the number of "loan words"
5. (Where appropriate) note separate, and especially "idiomatic" use of words—for instance, *in – in a hurry*
6. (Where appropriate) note old-fashioned words
7. Where a first-year book has been "completed" by a class, the efficiency of the textbook presentation and arrangement of the vocabulary items might, for comparison, be expressible as:

   $$\frac{\text{number of different words known (you would have to test this)}}{\text{number of different words presented}}$$

   a. The counting convention is that a regular inflection of a verb (*mends mended mending*) or of a noun (*picture picture's*) is not a different word, and an irregular inflection, or a regular inflection carrying a meaning additional to or different from the stem form, is a different word. "Structural words" are counted in the list of different words, and in the total number of words, but, unless you are curious, the number of repetitions need not be counted.

b. The best schedule for counting arranges for the state of items 1–4 to be apparent at any stage in the counting. This means, say, entry of different words in a column on the left of the schedule and vertical spaces for the pages of the textbooks:-

|       | 1   | 2 | 3 | 4 | 5  | 6 | etc. |
|-------|-----|---|---|---|----|---|------|
| a     |     |   |   |   |    |   |      |
| able  |     |   | / |   | // |   |      |
| about | //  |   |   |   |    | / |      |

Entries for items 1 and 2 may be made in colored pencil.

# Appendix 6

# Conjunction Relationships

**Table A6.1  CONJUNCTION RELATIONSHIPS**

| Relationship[a] | Markers | Meaning | Most important part |
|---|---|---|---|
| 1. Inclusion | and, furthermore, besides, also, in addition, similarly | A and B should be considered together | AB = [b] |
| 2. Alternative | or, nor, alternatively | A and B represent alternatives | AB = |
| 3. Time; arrangement | when, before, after, subsequently, while, then; first, finally, in the first place | A and B actually occurred with this time or sequence relationship; or A and B are arranged in this sequence by the writer | AB = |
| 4. Explanation | in other words, that is to say, I mean, namely | B restates or names A | AB = |
| 5. Amplification | to be more specific, thus, therefore, consists of, can be divided into | B describes A in more detail | A |
| 6. Exemplification[c] | for example, such as, thus, for instance | B is an example of A | A |
| 7. Summary/ conclusion | to sum up, in short, in a word, to put it briefly | B summarizes A | B |
| 8. Cause-effect | because, since, thus, as a result, so that, in order to, consequently | A is the cause of or reason for B | B |

**Table A6.1　CONJUNCTION RELATIONSHIPS (continued)**

| Relationship[a] | Markers | Meaning | Most important part |
|---|---|---|---|
| 9. Contrast | but, although, despite, yet, however, still, on the other hand, nevertheless | B is contrary to the expectation raised by A | B |
| 10. Exclusion | instead, rather than, on the contrary | B excludes A | B |

[a] Most of the relationships involve only two parts. However, *inclusion, alternative,* and *time and arrangement* may involve more than two.

[b] AB = means that the items in the relationship are of equal weight.

[c] The *exemplification* relationship could be included in the *amplification* class, but because it is usually clearly marked, it has been made a separate class.

# Appendix **7**

# Vocabulary Puzzles

Puzzles are teaching techniques which bring their own motivation with them. They challenge learners and focus attention on language. They can be used by learners who finish their work before others, or on a Friday afternoon!

1. This is called a word circle.

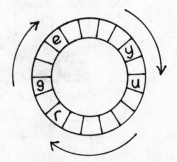

Find the words and put them in the right places in the circle. The first and the last letters of each word are already written for you.

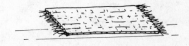

You put this _____ on the floor.

How are _____ ?

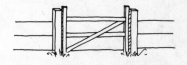

Please close the _____ .

You must do it _____ day.

The ball is _____ the table.

The clues can be pictures, sentences with the word missing, or definitions. If this is done as a class exercise, real objects, actions, etc., can be used.

2. This is called a word square.

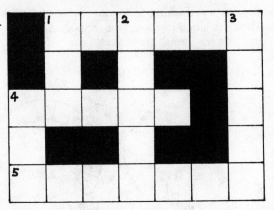

1->    Can you _____ English?

2    The boy is playing with a _____ .

3->    There are many _____s by the side of the road.

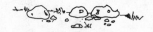

1          He _____ on the chair.

This is really a small crossword puzzle. Bigger crossword puzzles are very good for reviewing words (see Hill & Popkin, 1968). If these are too difficult for the learners, the teacher can help by giving multiple-choice answers to the clues. A dictionary from the mother tongue to English is also very helpful.

3. This is like a crossword puzzle, but the result is a sentence.

Try to find the sentence by finding the words. Each number is one letter, so the first word has seven letters. As you find each word, put the letters in the right place in the sentence. The first one is answered for you. (In this puzzle, one number is always the same letter, so 8 is always a, but one letter can have several numbers.)

7 2 8 4 12 16 6        His bag is strong. It is made from _____ .

l e a t h e r

11 18 8                People drink it.

17 13 15

1 19 8 17 5           Not afraid of anything

3 10 14 9

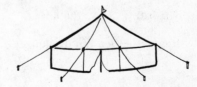

*The sentence*

What does this sentence say? It has four words.

1 2 3 4 5 6     7 8 9 10     11 12 13 14     15 16 17 18 19.

e  t         l a             h             e

To make this puzzle, choose a sentence. Give each letter a number. Then choose words that will use all the letters in the sentence.

4. This puzzle is like the word circle or word square. It is called *The last letter.*

Find the words. Each short line is one letter. The second word begins with the last letter of the first word. The third word begins with the last letter of the second word, and so on.

h _ _ _ _

_ _ _ _        This room is _____ . Everything is clean and is in the right place.

_ _ _ _ d      Three feet long

A variation of this is to let the first letters of all the words make another word.

_ _ _ _

_ _        The ball is _____ the table.

_ _ _ _      It is white. You can drink it. It comes from a cow.

_ _ _ _      You have two.

5. By following each line correctly the learner can spell the word and find its meaning. If the teacher is reviewing words, then the pictures at the end of each line are not needed.

Another way is write the words at one end of the lines, and the meanings at the other end. The learner finds the meaning of each word by following the lines.

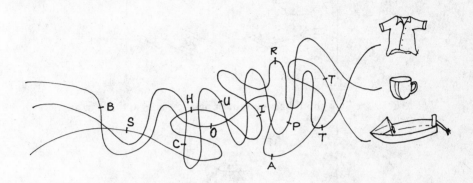

Instead of pictures, translations or definitions may be used. Then verbs, adverbs, etc., can be taught in this way.

6. The teacher gives the learners a list of words that have been cut in half. The learners must match the halves. A clue to the meaning can be given.

Join these halves together to make the names of animals.

| at  | ho  |
| --- | --- |
| du  | go  |
| bit | rab |
| ck  | rse |

7. The learners are given a group of letters of the alphabet, or a long word. They must make words using these letters.

How many words can you make using the letters in the word *airplane?*

Some possible words are: ripe, lane, pile, plan, pan,  pea.

The learners can be helped by also being given a list of the meanings of words that can be made. A dictionary is also helpful.

8. Which word does not belong in each group?

| tree | grass  | car  | vegetable |
| --- | --- | --- | --- |
| hot  | hungry | warm | cold      |

9. Learners can match pictures and words. The picture and the word are cut from the same card. The pieces are mixed and then the learners match the parts. The shape of the cut helps the learners to match correctly.

For review, the cuts should be straight or all the same so that the learners are not helped.

10. Code can be used to draw attention to words. It gets learners to look closely at the spelling while making use of meaning and grammar clues.

Some words in this poem are in code. Try to find these words. The first word has one letter, the second word has four letters, the third word has two, and so on. If you need some help, look at the bottom of the page.

| ? | )?~$ | =( | %( | (:= | ?0 | =#$ |
| %<>!$0 | | | | | | |
| I | like | to | climb | on | the | wall. |
| I | like | to | play | any | game | I |
| know, | | | | | | |
| ":= | ? | #<=$ | =( | !( | <0* | '(>~ |
| <= | <)) | | | | | |

Some help for you:

a. Four words in the first line are the same as four words in the second line.
b. The word at the end of the second line is almost the same as the word at the end of the fourth line.

11. Riddles give an insight into a type of humor and are good vocabulary extension exercises. In the following examples, the first riddle shows parts of different things that are included in one concept. Often this concept will differ
from the mother tongue. The second riddle requires the learners to differen-
tiate between homographs and homophones. The third riddle contains an
example of included homophony. The fourth riddle requires the learners to
look at a familiar object from a slightly unusual point of view. The last riddle
draws attention to similar features between seemingly unrelated objects, and
in this way shows the extended meanings of words.

Riddles have an added advantage of being reasonably easy to remember because they are short and because they are amusing and can be used with
one's friends.

Match the answers with the sentences.

a. It has legs but it cannot walk.
b. What has four legs and flies?
c. Half of it is sand, but people eat it.
d. It grows down.
e. Why is water like a horse?

Answers: a dirty horse, a beard, they both run, a sandwich, a table

# Appendix 8

# A Vocabulary Levels Test*

This vocabulary test can be used to decide where learners should be given help with vocabulary learning. The test is divided into five levels. The 2,000- and 3,000-word levels contain high-frequency words. Because each of the words at this level occurs frequently, it is worth spending class time on them. The university word level represents one type of specialized vocabulary. The 5,000-word level is on the boundary of high- and low-frequency words. The 10,000-word level contains low-frequency words.

Let us look first at how the test was made and how to use it. Then we will look at how to use the results to guide vocabulary teaching and learning.

## Making the Test

Each section of the test consists of six words and three definitions. This type of item was chosen because it was easy to make and easy to mark, provided very low chances of guessing correctly, tested a large number of words in a short time, and allowed learners to make use of whatever knowledge they had of the meaning of a word. The words in each section of the test were chosen so that they would be representative of all the words at that level. No capital-letter words—for example, the names of people, countries, or cities—were chosen. Words like *homesick* or *complexity* which were closely related to words of a higher frequency level were not chosen. Although only 18 words are matched at each level, in fact 36 words at that level are tested. This is because the distractors in the test are not meanings but words.

People who know the words at one level well can do that level very quickly because there are only a few things to read. A native speaker did the whole test in 5 minutes and got full marks. Usually a maximum of 50 minutes should be allowed for taking the test. Most people will need less than this.

The items put together in each section were not related in their meanings. For example, in an early draft of the test, *static* (which was to be matched with the definition *not moving or changing*) and *reliable* were in the same section. Because *reliable* has a slight connection with *not moving or changing*, it was replaced by another word. Thus, if people taking the test had a rough idea of the meaning of a tested word, they should have been able to match it correctly. This came

*From Nation, 1983.

through very strikingly in the results of one person during the trials of the test. This person's scores for the five sections were 12, 14, 5, 15, 6. The surprising feature of these scores is the relatively high score, 15, on the university word list level section. Most other people taking the test gained lower scores as they moved from one level to another. This person's high score on the university level occurred because his mother tongue was Spanish and he was able to use this knowledge to guess the large number of words derived from Latin at that level. This partial knowledge of the words was sufficient to allow correct guessing. Thus, someone's score on the test should not be considered as a conservative estimate. This also indicates that the test is not suitable for learners whose mother tongue is a language which has been strongly influenced by Latin. The definitions in the test use words from a higher frequency level than the tested words. The words from the 2000-word level use words in the first 1000 words of English. The words at the 3000-word level are defined by words in the *General Service List.*

## Using the Test

The instructions should not require any explanation, but people taking the test should be helped with the instructions if this is necessary.

When marking the test, give one mark for each correct matching of a word and its definition. The test can be objectively marked by matching a slip of paper containing the correct answers with the spaces provided for the learners to write their answer. On an average it takes two minutes to mark and add the score of one test. Record the scores for each of the five sections of the test. These are more useful than the total score for the test. If someone scores 12 or less out of 18 in a section of the test, then it is worth helping that learner study the vocabulary at that level. The chances of guessing are low, and learners' scores on the test can be taken as a close approximation to the proportion of words in the test that they know. A score of 12 out of 18 indicates that approximately one-third of the words at that level are not known. Thus, there will be at least 200 to 300 words worth studying at that level. Table A8.1 gives guidelines about how to help learners study the vocabulary at the various levels.

The suggestions in the table for increasing knowledge of high-frequency words are based on the idea that high-frequency words are worth individual attention and thus activities such as learning lists of words and vocabulary study using books like Barnard (1972) are appropriate. Teachers who are doubtful about getting learners to study vocabulary lists should read Nation (1982), which reviews experimental research on list learning. Direct teaching of vocabulary is also appropriate for high-frequency words. Besides learning words by direct study of vocabulary, large numbers of words can be learned by meeting them incidentally in context. Thus, extensive reading of simplified texts and extensive listening activities are an essential part of a vocabulary learning program.

Specialized vocabulary can be treated in much the same way as high-frequency vocabulary because it is frequent within a specialized area. Its frequency justifies attention to individual words as a part of a vocabulary learning program. Because many words in the University Word List are of Latin derivation, learning prefixes and roots is a useful aid to learning.

**Table A8.1    VOCABULARY LEVEL AND LEARNING**[a]

| Vocabulary level | Type of vocabulary | Learning required to increase vocabulary knowledge at each level |
|---|---|---|
| 2,000-word level | The *General Service List;* the vocabulary of simplified reading books. | 1. Learning lists of words based on the Longman Structural Readers Lists or the *General Service List*<br>2. Intensive and extensive reading of simplified reading books.<br>3. *Advanced English Vocabulary,* Workbook 1 (Barnard, 1972). |
| 3,000-word level | A basis for beginning to read unsimplified texts. | 1. Intensive reading of a variety of texts<br>2. Extensive reading of the Bridge Series |
| 5,000-word level | A wide vocabulary | 1. Training in guessing words in context<br>2. Wide general reading—novels, newspapers, university texts, etc.<br>3. Intensive reading of a variety of texts<br>4. *Advanced English Vocabulary,* Workbooks 1 and 2 |
| The university word level | The specialized vocabulary of university texts. | 1. Learning words in the University Word List<br>2. Intensive reading of university texts<br>3. *Advanced English Vocabulary,* Workbooks 2 and 3<br>4. Learning prefixes and roots |
| 10,000-word level | A large wide vocabulary | Activities similar to the 5,000-word level, combined with learning prefixes and roots. |

[a]The direct teaching of vocabulary through class teaching and individualized exercises is appropriate for most high-frequency words.

Individual low-frequency words do not deserve teaching time unless they contain useful prefixes or roots or are an example of some other regular feature that will help vocabulary learning in general. The strategy of guessing words using context clues is particularly useful and is worth spending time on in class (Clarke & Nation 1980, Honeyfield 1977a).

The basic idea behind the vocabulary test is that the statistical distribution of vocabulary should guide the teaching and learning strategies. The test samples various frequency levels and provides information about where learners need to increase their vocabulary. Teachers can then direct the learners to the appropriate vocabulary and use suitable teaching and learning strategies.

Table A8.2 shows the frequency criteria which were used in selecting the words at each frequency level.

As the table shows, the words chosen from the Thorndike and Lorge list were checked against the *General Service List* (West 1953), against the *Computa-*

**Table A8.2  FREQUENCY CRITERIA**

| Word level | Thorndike and Lorge | General Service List | Kucera and Francis |
|---|---|---|---|
| 2,000 | A | In *GSL* | — |
| 3,000 | 30–49 | Not in *GSL* | Within first 6,000 words (15→) |
| 5,000 | 14–18 | Not in *GSL* | Within first 10,000 words (8→) |
| 6,000+ | 1–13[a] | Not in *GSL* | — |
| 10,000 | 3 | Not in *GSL* | Within 10,000–16,700 word levels (4–7) |

[a]The words at this level were chosen from Campion and Elley (1971). This list was based on a count of university textbooks and assumed knowledge of the first 5,000 words of the Thorndike and Lorge list. Any words in the university list which had related words within the first 5,000 of Thorndike and Lorge were not chosen for this test.

*tional Analysis of Present-Day American English* (Kucera & Francis 1967), and against related words in the Thorndike and Lorge list. The comparison with the Kucera and Francis list was done to avoid the effect of some of the outdated material used in the Thorndike and Lorge counts. The comparison with the *General Service List* was done because many English courses, sets of reading material, and pieces of research are based on this list. It is thus useful to consider the *General Service List* when making recommendations for vocabulary learning.

## A Vocabulary Levels Test

This is a vocabulary test. You must choose the right word to go with each meaning. Write the number of that word next to its meaning. Here is an example.

1. business
2. clock            _____ part of a house
3. horse            _____ animal with four legs
4. pencil           _____ something used for writing
5. shoe
6. wall

You answer it the following way.

1. business
2. clock            ___6___ part of a house

3. horse            _3_   animal with four legs

4. pencil           _4_   something used for writing

5. shoe

6. wall

Some words are in the test to make it more difficult. You do not have to find a meaning for those words. In the example above, these words are *business, clock, shoe*.

Try to do every part of the test.

---

## The 2,000-word level

1. original

2. private          _____   complete

3. royal            _____   first

4. slow             _____   not public

5. sorry

6. total


1. apply

2. elect            _____   choose by voting

3. jump             _____   become like water

4. manufacture      _____   make

5. melt

6. threaten


1. blame

2. hide             _____   keep away from sight

3. hit              _____   have a bad effect on something

4. invite           _____   ask

5. pour

6. spoil

1. accident

2. choice    _____    having a high opinion of yourself

3. debt    _____    something you must pay

4. fortune    _____    loud, deep sound

5. pride

6. roar

1. basket

2. crop    _____    money paid regularly for doing a job

3. flesh    _____    heat

4. salary    _____    meat

5. temperature

6. thread

1. birth

2. dust    _____    being born

3. operation    _____    game

4. row    _____    winning

5. sport

6. victory

---

### The 3,000-word level

1. administration

2. angel    _____    managing business and affairs

3. front    _____    spirit who serves God

4. herd       _____    group of animals

5. mate

6. pond


1. bench

2. charity       _____    part of a country

3. fort          _____    help to the poor

4. jar            _____    long seat

5. mirror

6. province


1. coach

2. darling      _____    a thin, flat piece cut from something

3. echo        _____    person who is loved very much

4. interior     _____    sound reflected back to you

5. opera

6. slice


1. marble

2. palm       _____    inner surface of your hand

3. ridge      _____    excited feeling

4. scheme    _____    plan

5. statue

6. thrill


1. discharge

2. encounter    _____    use pictures or examples to show the meaning

3. illustrate

4. knit        _____    meet

5. prevail     \_\_\_\_\_    throw up into air

6. toss

1. annual

2. blank     \_\_\_\_\_    happening once a year

3. brilliant    \_\_\_\_\_    certain

4. concealed   \_\_\_\_\_    wild

5. definite

6. savage

---

## The 5,000-word level

1. alcohol

2. apron     \_\_\_\_\_    cloth worn in front to protect your clothes

3. lure

4. mess      \_\_\_\_\_    stage of development

5. phase     \_\_\_\_\_    state of untidiness or dirtiness

6. plank

1. circus

2. jungle     \_\_\_\_\_    speech given by a priest in a church

3. nomination   \_\_\_\_\_    seat without a back or arms

4. sermon    \_\_\_\_\_    musical instrument

5. stool

6. trumpet

1. apparatus

2. compliment   \_\_\_\_\_    set of instruments or machinery

3. revenue    \_\_\_\_\_    money received by the government

4. scrap     \_\_\_\_\_    expression of admiration

5. tile

6. ward


1. bruise

2. exile          _____   agreement using property as security

3. ledge                    for a debt

4. mortgage      _____   narrow shelf

5. shovel         _____   dark place on your body caused by
                            hitting

6. switch


1. blend

2. devise         _____   hold tightly in your arms

3. embroider      _____   plan or invent

4. hug            _____   mix

5. imply

6. paste


1. desolate

2. fragrant       _____   good for your health

3. gloomy         _____   sweet-smelling

4. profound       _____   dark or sad

5. radical

6. wholesome


## *The University Word List level*

1. affluence

2. axis           _____   introduction of a new thing

3. episode        _____   one event in a series

4. innovation     _____ wealth

5. precision

6. tissue

1. deficiency

2. magnitude     _____ swinging from side to side

3. oscillation     _____ respect

4. prestige     _____ lack

5. sanction

6. specification

1. configuration

2. discourse     _____ shape

3. hypothesis     _____ speech

4. intersection     _____ theory

5. partisan

6. propensity

1. anonymous

2. indigenous     _____ without the writer's name

3. maternal     _____ least possible amount

4. minimum     _____ native

5. nutrient

6. modification

1. elementary

2. negative     _____ of the beginning stage

3. static     _____ not moving or changing

4. random     _____ final, furthest

5. reluctant

6. ultimate

1. coincide
2. coordinate        _____  prevent people from doing something they want to do
3. expel
4. frustrate         _____  add to
5. supplement        _____  send out by force
6. transfer

---

## The 10,000-word level

1. acquiesce
2. contaminate       _____  work at something without serious intentions
3. crease
4. dabble            _____  accept without protest
5. rape              _____  make a fold on cloth or paper
6. squint

1. blaspheme
2. endorse           _____  give care and food to
3. nurture           _____  speak badly about God
4. overhaul          _____  slip or slide
5. skid
6. straggle

1. auxiliary
2. candid            _____  full of self-importance
3. dubious           _____  helping, adding support
4. morose            _____  bad-tempered
5. pompous
6. temporal

1. anterior
2. concave     \_\_\_\_\_   small and weak
3. interminable   \_\_\_\_\_   easily changing
4. puny        \_\_\_\_\_   endless
5. volatile
6. wicker

1. dregs
2. flurry     \_\_\_\_\_   worst and most useless parts of
3. hostage               anything
4. jumble     \_\_\_\_\_   natural liquid present in the mouth
5. saliva     \_\_\_\_\_   confused mixture
6. truce

1. auspices
2. casualty   \_\_\_\_\_   being away from other people
3. froth       \_\_\_\_\_   someone killed or injured
4. haunch    \_\_\_\_\_   noisy and happy celebration
5. revelry
6. seclusion

# Index

*after an entry indicates a teaching technique

273